Managing External Issues:
Theory and Practice

CONTEMPORARY STUDIES IN ECONOMIC AND FINANCIAL ANALYSIS, Volume 52

Editors: Professor Edward I. Altman and Ingo Walter, Associate Dean,
Graduate School of Business Administration, New York University

CONTEMPORARY STUDIES IN ECONOMIC AND FINANCIAL ANALYSIS

An International Series of Monographs

Series Editors: **Edward I. Altman and Ingo Walter**
Graduate School of Business Administration, New York University

Volume 1. **DYNAMICS OF FORECASTING FINANCIAL CYCLES: Theory, Technique and Implementation**
Lacy H. Hunt, II, *Fidelcor Inc. and the Fidelity Bank*

Volume 2. **COMPOSITE RESERVE ASSETS IN THE INTERNATIONAL MONETARY SYSTEM**
Jacob S. Dreyer, *Office of Monetary Research, U.S. Treasury*

Volume 3. **APPLICATION OF CLASSIFICATION TECHNIQUES IN BUSINESS, BANKING AND FINANCE**
Edward I. Altman, *Graduate School of Business Administration, New York University.* Robert B. Avery, *Graduate School of Industrial Administration, Carnegie-Mellon University,* Robert A. Eisenbeis, *Federal Deposit Insurance Corporation,* and Joseph F. Sinkey, Jr., *College of Business Administration, University of Georgia*

Volume 4. **PROBLEM AND FAILED INSTITUTIONS IN THE COMMERCIAL BANKING INDUSTRY**
Joseph F. Sinkey, Jr., *College of Business Administration, University of Georgia*

Volume 5. **A NEW LOOK AT PORTFOLIO MANAGEMENT**
David M. Ahlers, *Graduate School of Business and Public Administration, Cornell University*

Volume 6. **MULTINATIONAL ELECTRONIC COMPANIES AND NATIONAL ECONOMIC POLICIES**
Edmond Sciberras, *Science Policy Research Unit, University of Sussex*

Volume 7. **VENEZUELAN ECONOMIC DEVELOPMENT: A Politico-Economic Analysis**
Loring Allen, *University of Missouri, St. Louis*

Volume 8. **ENVIRONMENT, PLANNING AND THE MULTINATIONAL CORPORATION**
Thomas N. Gladwin, *New York University*

Volume 9. **FOREIGN DIRECT INVESTMENT, INDUSTRIALIZATION AND SOCIAL CHANGE**
Stephen J. Kobrin, *Sloan School of Management, Massachusetts Institute of Technology*

Volume 10. **IMPLICATIONS OF REGULATION ON BANK EXPANSION: A Simulation Analysis**
George S. Oldfield, Jr., *Graduate School of Business and Public Administration, Cornell University*

Volume 11. **IMPORT SUBSTITUTION, TRADE AND DEVELOPMENT**
Jaleel Ahmad, *Concordia University, Sir George Williams Campus*

Volume 12. **CORPORATE GROWTH AND COMMON STOCK RISK**
David R. Fewings, *McGill University*

Volume 13. **CAPITAL MARKET EQUILIBRIUM AND CORPORATE FINANCIAL DECISIONS**
Richard C. Stapleton, *Manchester Business and New York University,* and M.G. Subrahmanyam, *Indian Institute of Management and New York University*

Volume 14. **IMPENDING CHANGES FOR SECURITIES MARKETS: What Role for the Exchanges?**
Ernest Bloch and Robert A. Schwartz, *Graduate School of Business Administration, New York University*

Volume 15. **INDUSTRIAL INNOVATION AND INTERNATIONAL TRADING PERFORMANCE**
William B. Walker, *Science Policy Research Unit, University of Sussex*

Volume 16. **FINANCIAL POLICY, INFLATION AND ECONOMIC DEVELOPMENT: The Mexican Experience**
John K. Thompson, *Mellon Bank, N.A.*

Volume 17. **CORPORATE LIQUIDITY MANAGEMENT**
Michel Levasseur, *Centre d'Enseignement Superieur des Affaires, Jouy-en-Josas, France*

Volume 18. **STABILIZATION OF INTERNATIONAL COMMODITY MARKETS**
Paul Hallwood, *University of Aberdeen*

Volume 19. **PROBLEMS IN EUROPEAN CORPORATE FINANCE: Text and Cases**
Michel Schlosser, *Centre d'Enseignement Superieur des Affaires, Jouy-en-Josas, France*

Volume 20. **THE MULTINATIONAL ENTERPRISE: International Investment and Host-Country Impacts**
Thomas G. Parry, *School of Economics, University of New South Wales*

Volume 21. **POLICY RESPONSES TO RESOURCES DEPLETION: The Case of Mercury**
Nigel Roxburgh, *Management Studies Division, The Economist Intelligence Unit, Ltd.*

Volume 22. **THE INTERNATIONAL MONEY MARKET: An Assessment of Forecasting Techniques and Market Efficiency**
Richard M. Levich, *Graduate School of Business Administration, New York University*

Volume 23. **TRANSNATIONAL CONGLOMERATES AND THE ECONOMICS OF DEPENDENT DEVELOPMENT: A Case Study of the International Electrical Oligopoly and Brazil's Electrical Industry**
Richard Newfarmer, *University of Notre Dame*

Volume 24. **THE POLITICAL ECONOMY OF ENVIRONMENTAL PROTECTION**
Horst Siebert, *University of Mannheim*, and Ariane Berthoin Antal, *International Institute for Environment and Society, Science Center, Berlin*

Volume 25. **BIDDING AND OIL LEASES**
James B. Ramsey, *New York University*

Volume 26. **THE ECONOMICS OF EXPLORATION FOR ENERGY RESOURCES**
James B. Ramsey, *New York University*

Volume 27. **TECHNOLOGY TRANSFER TO DEVELOPING COUNTRIES: The Case of the Fertilizer Industry**
Subrata Ghatak, *University of Leicester and University of Guelph*

Volume 28. **MULTINATIONALS: Bank and Corporation Relationships**
Oliver Pastre, *Universite Paris-Nord*

Volume 29. **THE PRIMARY MARKET FOR MUNICIPAL DEBT: Bidding Rules and Cost of Long-Term Borrowing**
G.O. Bierwag, *University of Oregon*

Volume 30. **EFFICIENCY IN THE MUNICIPAL BOND MARKET: The Use of Tax Exempt Financing for "Private" Purposes**
George G. Kaufman, *Loyola University of Chicago*

Volume 31. **FOREIGN INVESTMENT AND TECHNOLOGY TRANSFER: The Tire Industry in Latin America**
Peter West, *Caracas, Venezuela*

Volume 32. **DIMENSIONS OF ENERGY ECONOMICS**
Noel D. Uri, *Catholic University of America*

Volume 33. **INDIGENIZATION AND ECONOMIC DEVELOPMENT: The Nigerian Experience**
Nicholas Balabkins, *Lehigh University*

Volume 34. **INTERNATIONAL FINANCIAL MANAGEMENT: Problems, Issues, and Experiences**
John S. Oh, *Portland State University*

Volume 35. **PURCHASING POWER PARITY AND EXCHANGE RATES: Theory, Evidence and Relevance**
Lawrence H. Officer, *Michigan State University*

Volume 36. **FINANCIAL REPORTING RULES AND CORPORATE DECISIONS: A Study of Public Policy**
Bertrand Horwitz, *State University of New York-Binghamton* and Richard Kolodny, *University of Maryland*

Volume 37. **CONSUMER EMANCIPATION AND ECONOMIC DEVELOPMENT**
Hans B. Thorelli, *Villa Serbelloni, Bellagio and Indiana University* and Gerald D. Sentell, *NIDA, Bangkok and the University of Tennessee*

Volume 38. **INSURING NUCLEAR POWER: Liability, Safety and Economic Efficiency**
William C. Wood, *Owen Graduate School of Management, Vanderbilt University*

Volume 39. **NEW DIMENSIONS IN PUBLIC UTILITY PRICING**
Noel D. Uri, *Catholic University of America*

Managing External Issues:

Theory and Practice

by GUY D.D. STANLEY
Managing Partner
Public Issues Group
John Doherty and Company,
Ottawa, and
MBA Program
University of Connecticut,
Stamford

JAI PRESS INC.

Greenwich, Connecticut *London, England*

Library of Congress Cataloging-in-Publication Data

Stanley, Guy D. D.
Managing external issues.

(Contemporary studies in economic and financial analysis ; v. 52)
Bibliography: p.
Includes index.
l. Issues management. I. Title. II. Series.
HD59.5.S7 1985 658.4′01 85–24051
ISBN 0–89232–600–X

36 Sherwood Place
Greenwich, Connecticut 06836

JAI PRESS INC.
3 Henrietta Street
London WC2E 8LU
England

ISBN NUMBER: 0–89232–600–X

Library of Congress Catalog Card Number: 85–24051

Manufactured in the United States of America

In Memoriam
G.C.D.S.
1911–1981

CONTENTS

List of Figures

Chapter I

Chapter III

Chapter IV

Chapter V

Preface and Acknowledgments

Why do some strategies work while others do not, and is there any way to know in advance which is which? This book, the result of several years consulting and teaching in the public affairs field, is an attempt to answer these questions. The book is therefore primarily akin to a work of engineering, applying concepts developed by theorists to the solution of problems in the material world. The focus is on the micro-world of issues as they affect the decision-making of individual companies and government departments. Practitioners of public affairs and students of business-government relations are the two audiences to whom these arguments are primarily addressed.

Many people gave considerable help along the road to completion of this project. Ken Hart, Conference Board of Canada, was an unfailing source of encouragement and a reservoir of knowledge. Colleagues in the University of Connecticut MBA Program, Stamford, and the Business Environment and Policy Department, Storrs, CT, provided much helpful criticism of themes and ideas and contributed much useful advice besides, especially Herb Spirer, Charles Saunders, John Thompson, Barbara Beliveau, Jeff Lenn (now at George Washington) and Freda Reitman (now at Pace). Richard Stroup, commenting on a panel presentation, in particular alerted me to some critical distinctions. I have also benefited from presentations by Steven J. Brams and Mark Kilgour, and conversations with Mark Sproule-Jones of McMaster and Steven Maser of Willamette. Much of this would have been impossible without the kind assistance of the University of Connecticut, Stamford, Library staff under Carmel O'Neill.

Useful criticism also came from MBA students, especially those in my public issues seminar, and from seasoned professionals who sat through issues management workshops, either those sponsored by New York University and the Public Relations Society of America or those given annually in Canada by Public Issues Group, John Doherty & Company, Ottawa. Perhaps the largest enabling factor, however, was the administrative and research support supplied by the University of Connecticut through John Montgomery and Selma Fischer of the Stamford MBA program. Thanks to them, I was also able to benefit from the professional expertise of Jane Scott, Rose Karosi, and Irene Petix, the staff of the SBA Word Processing Center at Storrs, and Suzan Kinslow of Stamford. On the production side, thanks are due to Gayle Jerman and her staff at JAI Press.

If the book retains any sense of the daily reality of public affairs practice, it will be mainly owing to the practical guidance that comes from one's professional mentors. My debt to so many gifted and conscientious men and women can only be acknowledged, not repaid. I will single out by name only my late father, to whose memory this book is dedicated, and David Monk. There are too many others to list. Special appreciation also to my family, for whom my preoccupation with this project meant considerable inconvenience which was nevertheless cheerfully borne.

If any errors remain, naturally the responsibility is mine alone.

Guy D. D. Stanley

Jericho
October, 1983

Part I

THEORY

Chapter I

Introduction (I): The Emergence of Issues Management

"Managing Issues," a misleading phrase suggesting some kind of corporate subversion of the democratic process, became a vogue term in the late 1970s. Typically, issues management involves public affairs executives managing issues programs and corporate planners concerned with monitoring and assessing the business environment.

Despite the division of responsibilities, issues management has a single purpose, namely to help a corporation (or other organization) function optimally with regard to society's noncommercial claims on its performance, or performance outside and beyond the basic mandate of the organization.

As such, issues management is essentially a development of the functions of public relations (as these were originally conceived). The purpose of this introduction is to show how issues management emerged in step with the increasing public criticism of the autonomous, professionally managed multidivisional business corporation.

Let us briefly examine the past to see how this evolution from public relations to issues management occurred, and how the meanings of these and related management terms have subtly been altered over time in response to changing ideas of business and society.

PUBLIC RELATIONS

Public relations originated in the 1920s as a new management skill, the "engineering of consent."[1] In this respect public relations promised to be dramatically different from "press agentry" or publicity, its historical antecedent (Figure I.1). Press agentry had a simple, easily understood function: to make news, to win "free" space for clients in the news columns at less cost than advertising, thereby achieving visibility (and to some degree a sense of third-party authentication). Press agentry was show-biz puffery applied to product promotion. It had an easy-to-measure cost-efficiency: the value of the news space at advertising rates.

Public relations, on the other hand, undertook to go beyond publicity to embrace a comprehensive approach to the molding of public opinion. Publicity desperately sought news coverage. Public relations would just as readily keep the client *out* of the news as *in*. Making news was only one of a range of techniques designed to maintain relations with the "publics" of a company or organization. Usually (but not always), public relations was directed at external publics—potential and actual customers, suppliers, investors and legislators. Public relations promised to ward off or help the company adjust to potential threats or constraints posed by misunderstandings among its most influential publics.

Public relations, in other words, had an agenda. It amounted to a comprehensive regard for all factors affecting public opinion about a

Figure I.1. Public Relations vs. Publicity

PUBLIC RELATIONS		PUBLICITY
AIM: SOCIETY'S CONSENT AND SUPPORT		AIM: PUBLIC NOTICE
METHOD: REACH "KEY" PUBLICS	VS.	METHOD: MAKE NEWS
GOALS: LONG RANGE HARD TO MEASURE		GOALS: SHORT RANGE EASY TO MEASURE

firm. Public relations retained press agentry's concern with visibility, but it added a concern about accurate perception.

Interestingly, despite its beginnings in the 1920s, public relations as "engineering of consent" only achieved widespread management acceptance and understanding after World War II. This acceptance was achieved during the same period that the giant, professionally managed corporation, composed of autonomous operating divisions, became widely recognized as having become the main engine of growth in advanced capitalist societies. This recognition was not accompanied by universal acclaim. On the contrary, the rise of "big business," to many, seemed to mark the end of consumer sovereignty, since large corporations were allegedly able to withstand the dissatisfaction of individual consumers, whose actions were necessarily fragmented. Instead, only other large organizations, unions, mass retailers and above all, government, could provide "countervailing power" to keep big business from exacting near-monopoly returns from their host communities. Public relations therefore won increasing management acceptance at a time when the public's attitude towards business—only temporarily approving after World War II—was reverting to a more critical phase.

MOUNTING CRITICISM, CHANGING VALUES

Public relations thus matured in the age marked by the appearance of such works as William H. Whyte's *The Organization Man*, C. Wright Mills' *The Power Elite*, David Riesman's *The Lonely Crowd*, Vance Packard's *Hidden Persuaders*, to name but a few critiques of business society, some of which are now recognized as classics of post-war sociology. These and other works provided systematic arguments for (1) suspecting corporations of being concentrations of inadequately controlled power, and (2) attacking important values of a business or utilitarian culture as "dehumanizing." Together with other later books (e.g., Rachel Carsons' *Silent Spring*, and Ralph Nader's *Unsafe at Any Speed*), they found ready acceptance by a more critical, more highly educated, and more affluent citizenry than that of the immediate postwar period.

To be sure, these trends in academic and popular views of business and society did not go undetected by businessmen and public relations specialists. But the classic PR approach of eliminating "misunderstandings" by "telling the company story" failed dismally to "engineer consent." Instead, the 1960s and 1970s became angry decades. Opposition to corporate policies and values rose, while confidence in business leadership sank steadily in public opinion surveys.[2]

From the late 1960s onward, legislative pressure mounted on business defining the norms of acceptable conduct, providing enforcement machinery and other devices for improving the bargaining power of individual consumers and other stakeholders in the decisions of a firm.

By the middle of the 1970s, government intrusion into business decision-making had become a way of life. "Vertical" or "industry specific" regulation had already emerged in North America either from earlier outcries against business or in response to the needs of new industries (airlines and broadcasting) or the solicitation of the industries themselves (trucking and banking). But now regulation was horizontal as well, i.e., applying to particular management functions across all industries (Figures I.2a and 2b).

Whatever your business, there was now a public servant to explain how you should sell your product (truth in advertising), how you were to describe it (labeling), under what working conditions it could be made (safety legislation), what technology was used (pollution controls), and, in some areas, what sociological criteria should govern the selection of the work force (Equal Employment Rules), or what language should be used to communicate (Official Languages Acts).[3]

Whether for good or ill, public relations people had singularly failed to "engineer consent" either for private enterprise or for market forces as the automatic allocators of resources in the critical areas of consumer protection, plant safety, protection of the natural environment, safeguarding the rights of minorities, or, in Canada, for example, protecting francophone culture.[4]

WHY PR FAILED

Why did public relations fail? Like all occurrences in history, this one is "overdetermined," i.e., has more than one cause. Yet some of the failure is traceable to the actual day-to-day practice of public relations and its almost exclusive concern with "telling the company story" whether anyone wanted to hear it or not.

This focus grew naturally from public relations' roots in publicity. It was unlikely to be checked by most early practitioners who were mainly ex-newspapermen. Consequently, the management function of public relations emphasized a product (i.e., information) rather than the decision-making process that gave rise to the need for the product in the first place.

During the post-war angry decades, when modern industrial society was undergoing a change of many basic values, public relations needed to have a powerful voice at staff level as well as the creative freedom and resources to function as a line department. But this opening to corporate decision-making was rarely offered to public relations people. Instead, PR became almost exclusively a line function, which in turn

Figure I.2a. Regulation in Canada

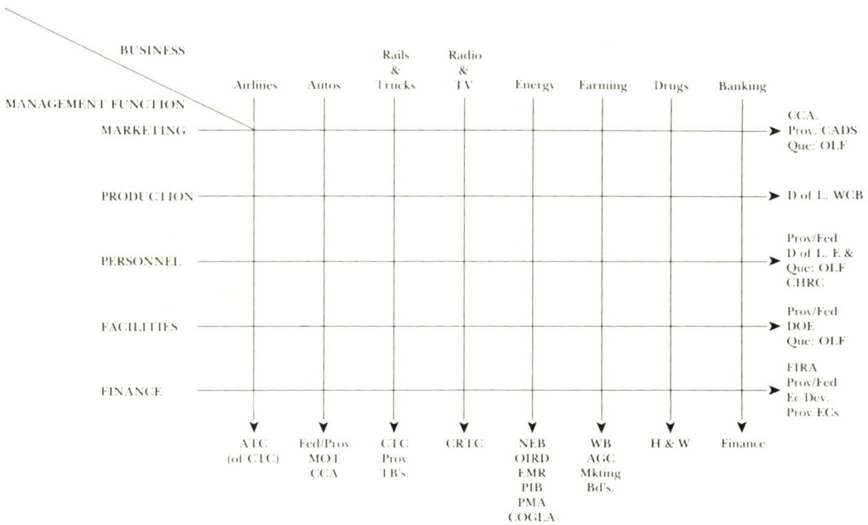

Glossary: Figure I.2a

AC	= Agriculture Canada
ATC	= Air Transport Commission (of Canadian Transport Commission)
CADs	= Consumer Advisory Departments (Provisional)
CCA	= Consumer and Corporate Affairs
CHRC	= Canadian Human Rights Commission
COGLA	= Canadian Oil and Gas Lands Administration
CRTC	= Canadian Radio and Television Commission
DOE	= Department of the Environment
DofL	= Department of Labor
E&I	= Employment and Immigration
EMR	= Energy, Mines and Resources
FIRA	= Foreign Investment Review Agency
H&W	= Health and Welfare
MOT	= Ministry of Transport
NEB	= National Energy Board
OIRD	= Office of Industrial and Regional Development
OFL	= Office de la Langue Francaise
PIB	= Petroleum Incentives Bureau
PMA	= Petroleum Monitoring Agency
WB	= Wheat Board
WCB	= Workman's Compensation Board

Figure I.2b

CAB	= Civil Aeronautics Board
FCC	= Federal Communications Commission
FDA	= Food and Drug Administration
FERC	= Federal Energy Regulatory Commission
ICC	= Interstate Commerce Commission

Figure I.2b. Regulation in the United States[3]

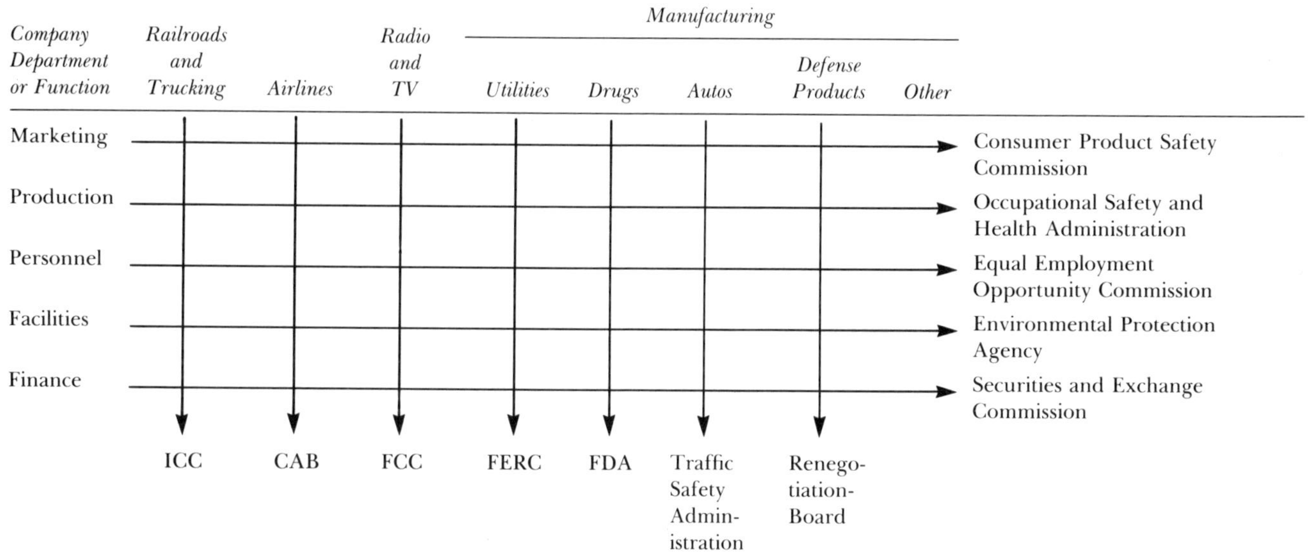

Glossary: Same as Figure I.2a.

further corroborated a public perception of PR as hype, fakery, underhanded manipulation, something somebody does to you rather than for you. As a profession, it lost during this period most of the credibility it had earned during the 1930s and 1940s.

PR DISINTEGRATES

The effect of these trends on public relations as a management function was devastating. Its previously comprehensive concern with public opinion literally disintegrated: government relations became the concern of "public affairs." Other public relations officers retreated into publicity in support of marketing and sales or investor relations. Politicians who before World War II had begun to rely on "public relations experts" increasingly turned to "political consultants," packagers whose strategies of message design and resource allocation drew heavily from market research and direct mail. By the early 1980s, landmark public relations firms in New York had been swallowed up by advertising agencies.

ISSUES MANAGEMENT

Yet the same period that witnessed the collapse of confidence in PR as a senior management concern, also saw a new awareness on the part of senior management that public issues pose a major hazard to business. CEOs now devote some 50 percent of their time (estimates differ) to coping with problems that used to be exclusive province of PR—winning approval from potential allies and veto groups. Strategic planning has increasingly become standard practice among large and even medium-sized firms, and scanning the social and political environment has become an integral part of the planning process.

An important result of these changes has been the upgrading of the role of public affairs in corporate decision-making, specifically to handle issues. More often than in the past, public affairs V.P.s are expected to add inputs about changing public perceptions and values to the mix of strategic and operational planning variables. Executives concerned with external relations are now empowered to listen to the public as well as to speak to the public and to point out implications for the company of what the public is now saying. This is a major corrective for some of the causes of PR failure during the last 20 years.

In addition, specific knowledge of the political and of social science methodologies are increasingly common requirements for a corporate issues management or public affairs team. Knowing how to assess and influence the political process, and how to set and achieve desirable

Figure I.3. Corporate Management Reorientation

MANAGEMENT POST-REGULATION		MANAGEMENT PRE-REGULATION
STAFF-LINE AUTHORITY CLOSER		LINE DOMINATES STAFF
LINE ASSESSED FOR PROFIT + COMPLIANCE	VS.	LINE ASSESSED FOR PROFIT
CEO RARELY DELEGATES ISSUES RESPONSIBILITY		CEO USUALLY DELEGATES ISSUES RESPONSIBILITY
STRATEGIC PLANNING SOCIO-POLITICAL SCANNING		STRATEGIC PLANNING RARE LITTLE SOCIO-POLITICAL SCANNING

objectives within that process, have become essential capabilities for managing successfully in today's environment.

In this connection, many industry associations and some companies have identified a new skill: that of issues analyst, who keeps his/her company or industry apprised of emerging and current issues, their likely business impacts, and how to influence or change proposals coming before legislators. As mentioned below, Atlantic Richfield Co.'s GAMIS is an extensively developed, computer assisted issues monitoring and analysis system with the issues analyst as its pivot.[5]

Ironically, the newly-discovered challenge of public affairs issues supplies to public relations what it lacked in its earlier stages of development: a senior management position, enhanced power in relation to operating divisions, and an opportunity to shape company strategy as well as to execute programs (Figure I.4). Company officers concerned with external affairs now have an improved staff position and, at the same time, perform a line function that commands top management attention. The challenge of issues actually returns PR to its originally conceived position at center stage but which in the past was enjoyed only by a handful of outstanding consultants.

How many companies are systematically addressing external issues in this way? In the case of U.S.-based companies, the answer seems to

Figure I.4. Issues Management vs. Public Relations

ISSUES MANAGEMENT		PUBLIC RELATIONS
AIM: SOCIETY'S CONSENT AND SUPPORT		AIM: SOCIETY'S CONSENT AND SUPPORT
METHOD: MONITORS, ADDRESSES & MOBILIZES COMPANY AS WELL AS "KEY PUBLICS"	VS.	METHOD: ADDRESSES "KEY PUBLICS"
GOALS: COMBINES SHORT AND LONG RANGE USES MEASURABLE INDICATORS		GOALS: LONG RANGE HARD TO MEASURE
MANAGEMENT: PROCESS-ORIENTED		MANAGEMENT: PRODUCT-ORIENTED

depend on the extent of their international involvement. Companies whose overseas operations account for 25 percent or more of total sales are significantly more likely to conduct systematic environmental reviews, annually or more often, than are companies with less international exposure. Almost all companies conduct some sort of political assessment in connection with investment decisions.[6]

Conversations with executives of leading Canadian companies (as well as direct experience) indicate that the percentage of large Canadian firms engaging in continuous political assessment—from quarterly to a year forward—is close to 100 percent. Perhaps surprisingly, crown corporations seem less developed in this area than their private sector counterparts.

THE NEW FUNCTION

Looking backward, therefore, we can see that "issues management" has grown logically from earlier attempts by management to improve public acceptance of a "business society." What is new is the expressly "interactive" relationship now developing in which business explicitly tries to anticipate changing values and political claims and to adjust or fight—or some combination of the two—as conditions appear to warrant. Yet why is "issues management" more effective than public relations?

Since its roots lie in Public Relations, which is generally regarded more as a craft than a management science, there has been little attempt to articulate for issues managers fundamental theories to explain why some approaches work and others do not, or to relate specific cases to that theory. This is the purpose of the pages that follow. It is to be hoped that the arguments presented below will show (1) that issues management can be explained, like other management functions, in primarily economic terms, (2) that mastery of basic concepts provides a framework for learning issues management not only as a craft but also as a branch of management science (i.e. in the sense of Wissenschaft or systematically organized knowledge), and (3) that the tasks, skills and concepts of issues managers are analogous to those of managers in other disciplines.

NOTES

1. See, for a brief discussion of these points, H. H. Liebhafsky, *American Government and Business*, John Wiley, 1971, pp. 79 ff.

2. For an eight-point analysis of contemporary criticism of business, see Archie B. Carroll, *Business & Society*, Managing Corporate Social Performance, Little Brown, 1981, pp. 18 ff.

3. For an argument that this amounts to a revolution, see Murray L. Weidenbaum, *Business, Government, and the Public*, Prentice-Hall, 1977, *passim*; Barry M. Mitnick, *The Political Economy of Regulation*, Columbia, 1980, provides the most comprehensive discussion of regulations. Figure I.2b is from Weidenbaum, op. cit., p. 14.

4. See, "Business Credibility: The Critical Factors," Conference Board Report No. 701; "Managing Corporate External Relations: Changing Perspective and Responses," Conference Board Report No. 679.

5. For a summary of the state of the art, see Carroll, op. cit., Part IV, and the following Conference Board Reports: This Business of Issues, No. 758; Guidelines for Managing Corporate Issues Programs, No. 795; and Assessing the Political Environment, No. 794. For Gamis, see p. 196.

6. Conference Board Report No. 794; John F. Mahon, "Public Affairs Structures and Activities in Large American Companies," *Academy of Management Proceedings*, 1982, pp. 336-370.

Chapter II

Introduction (II): Why Theory?

The purpose of this work is to improve management decision-making about public affairs problems. What is the role of theory in such an enterprise?

Practitioners will often argue that public affairs issues are usually extremely detailed and their outcomes apparently decided by such an interplay of specific circumstances that generalization is impossible. Yet without generalization, how can there be any meaningful theory?

The reply is that the purpose of theory is to make public affairs issues intelligible at a level quite different from that of apparently decisive particular occurrences. Granted that a mishandling of a specific trivial episode (e.g., President Reagan's unintended gaffe in not meeting the delegates of a national businesswomen's organization) can have decisive consequences. Napoleon believed that details decided everything. But a better question is, how has a situation arrived at such a flashpoint that the mere mishandling of a trivial detail can spell disaster?

Moreover, there are—especially in retrospect—trends or patterns of business-government behavior, such as the surge of quality-of-life regulation in the 1960s and 70s, that cannot be explained solely in terms of specifics, e.g., how a certain government official was treated at such and such a time, etc., or whether such and such a company was caught trying to smear the reputation of such and such a consumer advocate.

Theory is indispensable for rising above this level of particularities.

The purpose of theory for public affairs issues management is the same as theory in all other branches of management—to explain the past and predict future development of the phenomena with which it is concerned. The theories presented here are designed to do that for business-government relations.

These theories accomplish this aim by providing those concerned about such questions with a framework upon which to hang their judgments. The theories array the key variables which, when fleshed out by research and details specific to an issue, will show the likely interactions, predict the decisive turning points, indicate the most probable outcomes and above all, suggest optimal strategies.

RATIONAL DECISION-MAKING

The theories discussed here are based on the work of economists and political scientists concerned with so-called rational decision-making. The point of departure is an assumption that individuals are rationally maximizing, i.e., they choose actions designed to maximize the subjectively determined utility available to them. This is important to remember for what follows throughout these arguments, so let us put a box around it to help us remember:

> *Point of Departure*: individuals are rationally maximizing, i.e., seek to maximize the utility or satisfaction available to them.

Although this assumption predicts everyone will try to maximize his/her satisfaction, it most emphatically does not mean everyone will choose the same course of action all the time. On the contrary, since everyone's calculation of utility is subjective, individual choices are as likely to be conflicting as cooperative, depending on personal taste and values.

In this way we are expanding a paradigm or complex model of human behavior widely used in management to include public affairs activities. In so doing we are applying a paradigm that is under increasing attack especially in the area of economics for which it was primarily designed. Whether the theory works any better here is for the reader to judge. The justification for using these ideas in the context is twofold: (1) Economics is concerned with problems of rational choice among alternative uses of scarce resources, which is the same problem management faces in general. Use of this paradigm will thus bring public affairs into consistency with other management disciplines. (2) Despite the current difficulties with economics (and these are mainly at the macro, not micro, level where we will be operating) there is no other coherent theory that can fulfill this function with the same explanatory and predictive power. Our endeavor may therefore seem tantamount to searching for lost quarters under streetlamps at night because the visibility is zero elsewhere. But our ultimate argument is that the results justify the effort, i.e., we will in fact find a lot of quarters here.

Now this assumption of rationally maximizing behavior may have absolutely no foundation in clinical psychology, history, anthropology, sociology or any other of the sciences devoted to an observation of mankind. The assumption is not meant to be a psychology. (Indeed, at a certain level it is either a tautology or a contradiction; the case of altruism, whereby altruists are altruists because it suits them best.)[1] The only defense for beginning with this assumption is that it provides us with a useful understanding of (1) how issues develop, and (2) what outcomes are most likely. It is effective because it works.

STANDARD OF JUDGMENT

Moreover, our point of departure also provides us with a yardstick or standard of judgment against which to evaluate decision-making. For instance, how much regulation of business is appropriate? If everyone interacts on the basis of self interest, are the outcomes to everyone's benefit? In fact, as we shall see, the outcomes are not infrequently worse for all. One useful consequence of our point of departure is that such questions can be asked and answered.

It can also be argued that a great many basic questions have nothing whatever to do with rationally maximizing behavior. Belief in God (Pascal's wager aside), the cleansing power of revolution, questions of patriotism, heroic actions in the midst of hopeless situations, are probably all irrelevant to the sort of rationality implied by our point of departure. But then we are not trying to explain every aspect of human behavior, or even every aspect of political behavior. We are only concerned with the relatively narrow territory of business-government relations, and in that context, our perspective is an operational one.

Our purpose is to understand issues from the standpoint of means or techniques. Are there any general principles useful to students of the public policy process? How is consent achieved in democratic society? How can companies concerned with winning consent or improving the fit between company policies and public demands improve performance and gain greater mastery of the issues-resolving process? These are questions we will try to answer.

Our search is for universal principles and models applicable to business-government relations in parliamentary and presidential democracies. We want to derive operational tools that will quickly and accurately tell us what to expect from the issues process and how to get the most from it. We want to know what to expect from tomorrow's issues as well as today's. Our concern for yesterday's issues is only as great as the number of useful insights they can shed on the present and future. Our objective, in other words, is future oriented techniques of high utility for business executives.

USEFUL TOOLS FOR AFFECTING OUTCOMES

It is to be hoped this will seem sensible enough to practical decision-makers. But there are a number of items of concern primarily to professional theorists that will be absent from our discussion of theory. Our goals are not a comprehensive account of rational choice theory or of public policy-making. On the contrary, we want only useful tools for affecting outcomes. For that, explanations that identify and help us understand the essential points in the process are needed, and anything more is superfluous. In this work, the sole aim of theory is to illuminate and improve practice. Questions of theoretical interest only will therefore be missing from the discussion.

Also, a great deal of rational choice or public choice theory is concerned with voting behavior and elections. Since our chief concern, business-government relations, is rarely directly concerned with this, the area is neglected in our theoretical discussions and case studies. The case studies, too, are handled somewhat differently here than in the typical case book.

It is an axiom among case presenters that no suggestions be given of any "right answers." The value of the case lies in giving students the opportunity of experiencing the tensions of decision-making in a way that approximates reality as closely as possible. Guessing "what teacher wants" therefore undermines the exercise, as does the assumption that what actually happened was necessarily the "right" answer. The cases here adhere to this general view, but violate the method of presentation. For these cases are intended not only to fulfil the traditional objectives of case work, but also to use cases as examples to show the actual working out in reality of the processes discussed in the section on theory. In this sense, the cases are also designed to calibrate the theories with reality.

ETHICAL ISSUES

What about so-called ethical issues? Are these to be neglected? If not, how are ethical issues made to square with the assumptions of "rational" behavior in the sense of maximizing behavior? This is a serious question and one that requires increasing attention, given the growing importance of business "ethics" courses in many MBA programs. As a "management problem," ethics involves a study of corporate ethical values, implicit as well as explicit, and ways in which to ensure that pressures for management achievement results in performance that is consistent with ethical values. This is by no means unimportant to the survival or even the prosperity of a business. But it clearly is most helpful in interactions of two kinds: either (a) in which ethics are crystal clear, or (b) where a balance of rights and obligations can be defined by technical specialists without seriously challenging an existing social consensus (even if it is only to let the experts decide) about where the public interest lies.

For issues where reasonable people can disagree—especially if they can disagree vehemently—about where the public interest lies, ethical studies as normally conceived can provide little operational guidance without involving problems of strategic choice. In such instances, if ethics are used as merely a matter of duplicating private values in a large organization, they may conflict with public values and in consequence land that organization in considerable difficulties.

However, the advice, "When in Rome do as the Romans do," is no better than "follow your conscience." Should one's operations in South Africa respect Apartheid laws? What should policy be concerning the Arab boycott of Jewish firms and its suppliers? Questionable payments condoned in some societies but not in the United States pose a problem for some U.S. based multinationals.

On a purely ethical level, the response is straightforward: if something is offensive ethically, don't do it. But can that injunction provide sufficient guidance for a business given different ethical standards among people, without appearing to reward the less morally sensitive at the expense of the more? This raises the question, "What is meant by 'harm'?" Does it include, for instance, illegal activity per se? What if the matter is ethically amiguous? Common law allows us to choose the lesser evil, but perceptions of this will vary. A less risky rule may be the 60 Minute Test or the New York Times Test: i.e., how will it play on page one, or if Mike Wallace comes to call? But this is to base decisions on assessments of probable consequences, not on an a priori rule.

There is no getting around it. Once past the ringing simplicities of "do no harm," one is in the murkier waters of strategic choice, and the concepts and techniques considered here will dominate. Still, the matter of issues has one ethically straightforward element: if the public interest is clear, there is no issue. One adjusts policy to serve the public interest. There will only be issues when the public interest is at stake, but is also unclear.

The consideration of ethical questions and business has thus led us to the definition of issues that will be used throughout these discussions. Issues involving companies and governments should be considered as matters of public dispute in which the public interest is unclear. Let us "box" that as a definition:

> *Definition*: "Issues are matters of public dispute in which the public interest is unclear."

Now it might be argued that many issues actually involve private interests or special interests masquerading as the public interest in order to get something from the public purse (a tax expenditure, i.e., direct transfer payment, or tax abatement, which in any case costs something to the national treasury). Property, for instance, may command a hidden subsidy (through allowing the deduction of mortgage interest) that might be said unduly to favor property owners; labor may command special privileges (e.g., the right to organize in restraint of trade); particular forms of business (e.g., soft drink bottlers) may be exempted from general antitrust rules applicable to all businesses.

In this logic, the "public interest" is the result of competing private pressures and interests, ratified and made legitimate as "the public interest" by the "public policy process."[2] This may be so. But it does not materially affect the definition of issues. Indeed, the argument highlights the importance of the definition: to raise the question of which issues are private and which public is also to debate where the public interest lies.

This is not to deny the importance of questioning whether some governments are more or less friendly to certain private interests than other governments. It is rather to treat the distinction between public and private interest as less valuable operationally than from a theoretical standpoint. Operationally considered, there is no insight lost if one holds that it is in the process of resolving a dispute that the public interest is defined and clarified. If this political defining is done in such a way as to offend large and powerful voter segments, then the government will fall and a new one, more prepared, say, to take account of regional tolerance or inputs, would be formed or elected.

Our definition of issues, therefore, tells us that if there is a dispute, it will be resolved in public interest terms, although certain private interests may prevail over others. This reality, as much as concern about "government interference" in the market place, makes "issues" a vital concern for all businessmen.

Can we then summarize the principal advantages to practitioners of using the theories and concepts discussed here?

1. These theories will provide greater intelligibility than an *ad hoc* approach, and thus will help practitioners devise more effective strategies more quickly.
2. These concepts and techniques will enable practitioners to achieve greater accuracy in the management of public affairs, comparable to that of more traditional disciplines such as finance, marketing and operations.
3. These concepts will enable practitioners to defend their strategic recommendations with more eloquence and force in a language the rest of management will understand.

Finally, in closing the introduction, a word about mathematics. In order to keep the analysis rigorous, recourse will be had from time to time to mathematical reasoning and notation together with verbal explanations. The economy of mathematical notation and the logical discipline it enforces will, it is hoped, purge our arguments of unintended ambiguities and increase precision and universality.[3] For those with concern about their mathematical background, a list of mathematical symbols and their meanings is included at the end of this work.

Summary of ideas and terms

Managing issues
public relations
press agentry
engineering consent
reactions to big business
telling the company story
vertical regulation
horizontal regulation
disintegration of PR
corporate changes in response to regulation
role of theory
rationally maximizing behavior
paradigms
countervailing power
case method
ethical issues

ethical decision rules
60 Minutes, New York Times Test
public issues (definition)
public interest

NOTES

1. See, for a discussion, Gary S. Becker, *The Economic Approach to Human Behavior*, (1976) University of Chicago Press, esp. Chapter 13/2, "An Economic Model of Altruism," pp. 284-9.
2. An excellent survey of theories about regulatory origins is contained in Barry M. Mitnick, *The Political Economy of Regulation*, Columbia, 1980, pp. 80-241, and of "Public Interest," pp 242-280.
3. cf. "The chief use of pure mathematics in economic questions seems to be in helping a person write down quickly, shortly and exactly, some of his thoughts for his own use; and to make sure that he has enough, and only enough, premises for his conclusions (i.e., that his equations are neither more nor less in number than his unknowns)." Alfred Marshall, *Principles of Economics*, preface to the first edition.

Chapter III

A General Issue

What are public issues and how should companies anticipate, adjust, fight or otherwise respond to them? In this chapter we shall work towards developing an understanding of public issues as phenomena susceptible to rational coping activity, i.e., setting and attaining goals and objectives such that the result is a net benefit to the firm.

Let us begin by considering the general case in which (a) the public interest is in dispute, and (b) the dispute is conducted democratically, i.e., in the rough and tumble of open debate and political hurly-burly of a robust representative democracy. To make our models work dynamically, we should also recall our point of departure, and apply the assumption that all groups and individuals engage in "maximizing" behavior. Altruists there may be, but as James Madison put it, "If men were angels, there would be no need for governments." By applying maximizing assumptions we ensure that all sides are on their mettle.

We can think of any general issue in several different ways. First, let us consider a labor-management dispute, or the problem of striking a bargain between buyer and seller. Note, each side has, firstly, a common interest, clear to each, in reaching an advantageous solution and, secondly, a difference of opinion about what the outcome should be. "More" for one side will be "less" for the other, but the question of gain or loss must be set against the interest in reaching a solution. Obviously, the stronger party may not "compel" a bargain that imposes a "loss" on the other that is greater than the willingness or need of the weaker party to conclude a deal. Instead, the negotiations will break off. We can illustrate these points by means of the following diagram, known as an "Edgeworth Box" after the eminent 19th century economist, F.Y. Edgeworth.

Figure III.1 An Edgeworth Box[a]

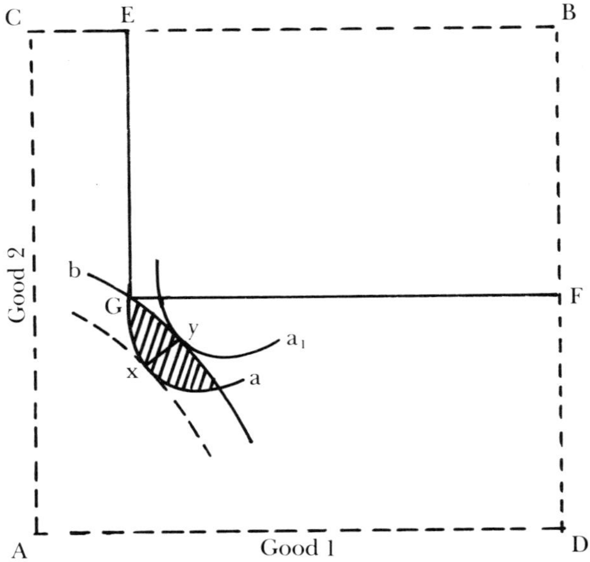

[a] The box shows preferences of A and B for different distributions of goods 1 and 2, assumed to be in fixed supply at any point in the box. For example, at G, B has BE of good 1 and BF of good 2, A has CE and DF, respectively, of each. Agreement is possible anywhere on the "contract line" xy linking points at which preference curves are tangent. Note, too, that any point within the shaded elipse is preferable to any point outside it (or there would be no inducement to exchange).

The general commonality of interest is expressed by the dimensions of the box: buyer and seller are both pursuing what they hope will be a profitable transaction; both will benefit from the transaction, or else it will not take place. At a low price (i.e., free), the buyer is prepared to take a very high quantity, but the seller offers virtually nothing. At the other extreme, a high selling price coaxes a large offering into the market, but the buyer is not interested. Instead, discussion centers around the midpoints of the two sets of supply/demand or preference curves, and the points at which they touch. These tangential points form a line of common interest, or "contract line." Logically, assuming equal power and skill on each side, we would expect the curves to be in equilibrium at the midpoint of the contract line where an agreement could be concluded, but this is not essential. All that is strictly necessary for a deal to be concluded is that the benefits of agreement equal or exceed the "costs" of not agreeing. Unions will therefore on occasion accept "rollbacks," given a poor labor market and promises of greater gains in future agreements in better years.

The above example is clearly a dispute, but is it an *issue*? That kind of discussion or bargaining goes on throughout the business world, throughout the business day, as myriad private sellers and buyers come to terms with each other. What is missing from this analysis is the public interest. Merely by constructing the box and positioning the contract line, we have assumed away questions that take a dispute out of the purely private to make it a public issue.

True, we could consider one side "society" and the other an interest group, firm or individual. But this procedure assumes the role of government before we have had a chance to examine it, thus obscuring some of the most interesting operational questions about issues.

Some of those questions are (a) how my bargaining strategy affects that of my opponents, (b) whether all costs and benefits are contained in the transaction, or whether there are third party benefits or costs external to it, and (c) what kind of good or service is being discussed, and whether the parties involved enjoy exclusive use or whether the good or service in question exhibits what economists call "jointness of supply" or "jointness of consumption," i.e., whether the good or service is public or private. This leads us to our next definition:

> *Public goods*: These are goods exhibiting jointness of supply, or jointness of consumption, in that the number of consumers does not effect the consumption of the good by other consumers. My consumption of a public good does not deny my portion to other consumers (jointness of supply). Nor is there any way to deny the benefits of a pure public good to consumers whether they pay for it or not (jointness of consumption). Examples: national defense, clean air, clean water, law and order, etc. Rationally, therefore, citizens will seek to maximize output of public goods while minimizing their own individual payment, i.e., "free riding" wherever possible.

A second, more illuminating way of approaching issues in general that allows us to explore these and other complexities is the following. Imagine the same two opposed interests in the same situation, choosing between two bargaining strategies, say "Difficult" (D) or "Compromise"

(C). Using a simple matrix, we can compare the two strategies and display the outcomes that would result from different combinations of play. This is a game of decision-making under conditions of uncertainty, i.e., neither player can be certain of the other players' strategy, and is a basic condition in the conduct of public affairs.

Figure III.2 below sets out the choices and outcomes, displayed as a matrix. Either player can play one of two strategies, "C" (Compromise) or "D" (Difficult). The quadrants show the results. Two "C's" in the top left, Player B's "C" vs. Player A's "D" in the top right, vice versa in the bottom left, and the result of both players' "D" strategies in the bottom right.

This matrix tells us quite a lot about public issues, the role of government, and incidentally, why public issues are subtly different from private bargains.

Note, first, that only one quadrant, the top left, generates compromise, the outcome following from a choice of compromise strategy by each player. Note, too, that if player A or B chooses Compromise, and his opponent chooses Difficult, then the opponent "wins." In other words,

Figure III.2 Strategy Matrix

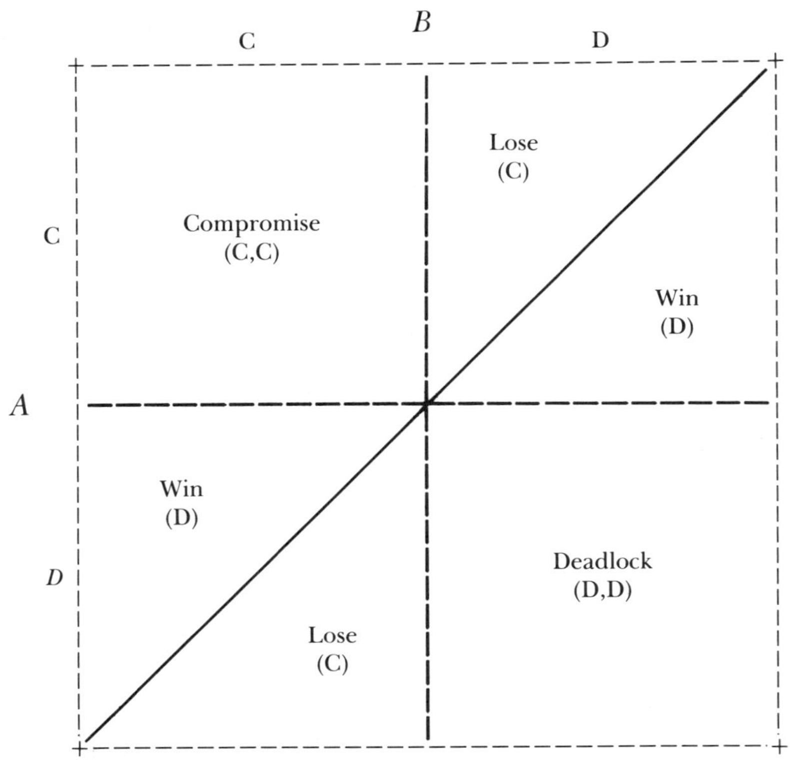

although "Compromise" may theoretically be a satisfactory outcome, the player choosing Compromise will almost certainly be defeated by the player choosing Difficult.

Remember, neither player knows in advance what the other will choose. Even if the two players discuss strategy beforehand, either could be bluffing, lying or otherwise trying to deceive his opponent into yielding an advantage. Assuming rational, i.e., maximizing, behavior and equal power and skill on both sides, the outcome actually reached will therefore be that displayed in the lower right hand quadrant, i.e., Deadlock, the intersection of two Difficult strategies. In other words, the two players may *never* make a deal, or if they do, one will have to defeat, i.e., prevail over, the other.

Yet what if Compromise were to yield more total benefits to the community than Deadlock? If players A and B ranked the outcomes as Win, Compromise, Deadlock, Lose, then the game will be played by bitter, bitter rivals, with the outcome being Deadlock, the second worst result possible.

We have here a so-called "sub-optimal" distribution or market failure situation. A dispute conducted by purely private interactions fails to generate optimal benefits, i.e., to serve, protect or uphold the public interest. Under these conditions, there is a case for government involvement to ensure an allocation of outcomes that will protect the community interest and at the same time improve the outcome of the private transaction. In the examples under consideration, public policy could use binding arbitration or some form of legislation to enhance the bargaining power of one side or another to ensure that the conditions leading to Deadlock are reduced or eliminated.

Policy could also encourage trust and confidence between the parties to the dispute by limiting the range of conflict (and thus the price of defeat) and by improving the information available to both parties. True, over time both parties might themselves establish a relationship of trust such that compromise was attainable. But, assuming maximizing behavior, the absence of absolute certainty and the possibility of manifold gains from deceit, would render such a process risky and time-consuming. Government intervention on behalf of the community (or indeed on behalf of either player) would carry with it the added gains of speed and certainty (Justice delayed is justice denied!). In our example, in other words, government can smooth and improve the efficiency of market forces.

In so doing, government also preserves the incentives inherent in the private pursuit of individual gain. Indeed, it improves their efficiency by making gains more realizable in practice (through Compromise) than would otherwise be the case (in which Deadlock would be likely to occur).

Yet the extent or degree of government involvement will depend upon the particulars of each case and the values of the community about what constitutes just, reasonable, equitable, etc.

It needs to be said that this is an extremely restrictive set of conditions. For not only is the community made better off, but the gains realized by the private parties to the dispute would be an improvement over what they could actually achieve on their own. From the standpoint of our operational concerns, we can distill three basic principles from the foregoing:

(1) The justification for government intervention (given our maximizing assumptions) *can only be the creation of net public benefits*, otherwise the incentives of the system will be reduced.

(2) The issue, once it becomes public, therefore, will be how much private interests (in terms of hope for an outright win) should be sacrificed for the public interest. (Note, in our example, although everyone was left better off, private interests had to give up hope of a clear victory to accept a less profitable, but realizable, compromise.)

(3) Public values and the process by which they are brought to bear on issues will determine the range of possible outcomes.

Note, also from our last example, the importance of expectations. In the absence of government, each side expects the other to do its worst. With government intervention a certainty, rational strategy would concern itself primarily with how to get government support and deny it to an adversary. The relationship between A and B is important, as well. Without willingness to reach a positive sum compromise, either player could be expected to veto any deal proposed by the other. If each aims to inflict loss on the other, the prospects of a compromise settlement are virtually nil unless the government is prepared or able to use force. The limits of consent would have been reached. The community optimum will remain definable, but in practice unobtainable.

Yet remarkably, in most cases the community will be better off if private disputants are left free to reach accommodation on their own. Consider a dispute between a rancher who lets cattle in his charge run over land occupied by a farmer. Either could seek to impose a solution on the other through force of arms, or government could rule in favor of one or the other and compel a solution in which the interests of one was upheld at the sacrifice of the other. However, in a liberal society, government instead creates the conditions for a mutually satisfactory bargain, i.e., enforceable property rights, in which the rancher can pay rent and compensate the farmer, or either can buy out the other. As stated in the third condition above, public values will determine which set of solutions is chosen: range war, dictatorship and coercion by one interest in favor of another, or mutually satisfactory private bargains in the context of enforceable rights.

Whatever solution is chosen, the government will likely portray the outcome in terms of net public benefit. This may mean several things: (1) that the total of utilities produced is higher than would otherwise have been the case; (2) that the public goods produced equal or exceed any private benefits sacrificed, (3) the honor of the state and its revolutionary traditions have been upheld, etc.

Note, however, the property rights solution actually provides a roughly measurable optimum mix of public and private goods:

- *Public Goods*: Preservation of peace and a legitimate method of resolution of private disputes;
- *Private goods*: exchange of rights and compensation.[1]

EXTERNAL COSTS

The general problem we have been discussing can be illustrated with more specific relation to business-government relations with the aid of a model showing "External Costs," i.e., costs passed onto the community as a result of a transaction.[2] Consider the activities of firm A, a nationally-known widget maker.

Figure III.3. Firm A

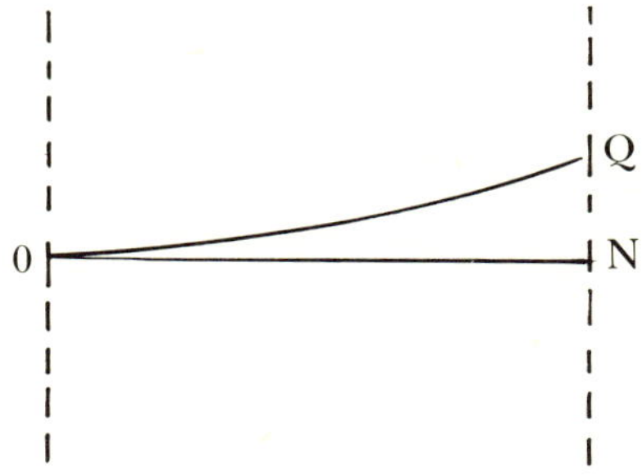

But let us now look at how these widgets are produced. For it appears that the company employs a process that emits fumes into the atmosphere. This alters our diagram of the business to show the disbenefits as well as the benefits of its operation.

Figure III.4. External Costs

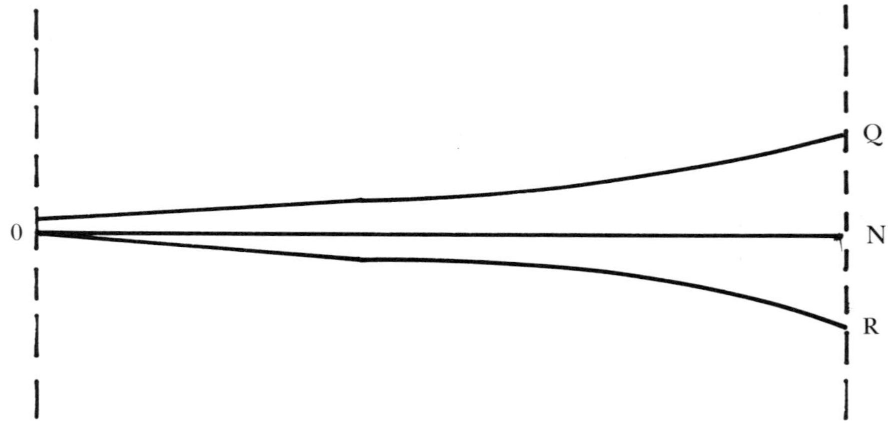

The diagram[3] now shows that as the output of the firm rises to 0 Q, the disbenefits of the society grow to ONR.

This comes about because the firm is able to pass some of its costs of operating onto the community as a whole—by lowering the "quality of community life" with its emissions.

Economists call such costs external costs, because they are external to the transactions between buyer and seller. In a perfect market, all costs are captured in the selling price. In the real, imperfect world, there is a third party to every transaction—namely, society—and it absorbs some of the costs of production, mainly as public disbenefits, i.e., the converse of public goods—disbenefits collected by no one in particular, but by everyone in general.

Of course, once again, there is an important question of values. For what one person might regard as an external cost may not be so regarded by another. Factories belching smoke, symbols of industrial squalor to us, were in grandfather's day, symbols of prosperity.

Perhaps the most important point about externalities is that there is no incentive for the firm to stop passing those costs along to the community. On the contrary, the more successfully the firm does this, the more profitable it will become.

But, since there are no easily distinguished individual victims, and damage has rather been suffered by the community as a whole, *only the community as a whole can force the firm to stop passing the costs along*. Indeed, government action to do so qualifies under our definition as a public good.

True, in theory a system of property rights could cope with this problem and different uses of air be allocated according to a system of compensations and market exchange. In practice, however, (a) no one has a right to inflict harm on others at any price (which is what pollution does), and (b) the costs of enforcement by individual court actions would likely outweigh any individual benefits. A single standard, enforced by a central government that safeguards rights of due process, provides in comparison a least cost protection of community rights. At the same time, this solution makes clean air (as officially defined) a public good, yet one that is largely obtained at private expense.

In this situation, then, given the requisite public values, government intervention—in the form of a tax or fine on the company's private benefits to compensate the community, or mandated costly technology, or an outright ban—is inevitable.

The limits of tax will not likely be the full cost of disbenefits, however, but rather as much of the costs as can be collected without so adding to the operating costs of the firm that it must move elsewhere or go out of business. An "exit" by the firm would result in more external costs: unemployment, loss of tax base, dislocations, etc. In practice, the community will likely have to absorb some external costs—unless the alternative locations are limited (as with a resource company) and alternative production schedules are out of the question (during market upswings when full production is necessary to preserve or expand market share). Offsetting this grim reality, it is to be remembered that citizens have a "quit" option too—one easily measurable by the rise in housing prices in relation to distance from production plant. As with all issues, reconciling individual and collective optima is the central dilemma. The community optimum would raise the costs or restrict the output of the firm to the point at which compensation equals the disbenefits of restricted operations. For a hated firm, this might mean it would be driven out of business. An otherwise well-regarded firm with strong community support would pay a lesser price.

EXTERNAL BENEFITS

The main function of this work is to help company officers cope with public issues and it therefore focuses on the kinds of arguments and problems most frequently encountered in business-government relations. However, it is also important for the sake of completeness to look at some external benefits problems as well, for these provide the major justification for government rather than private actions. Moreover, given the current competitive weakness of much of North American private industry, these arguments may well come to dominate business-government relations in the remainder of this decade in terms of "industrial policy" i.e., public policy aids to painful economic transitions.

Like external costs, external benefits are those captured as the result of private transactions. Often they are of community benefit, of which the classic example is the "lighthouse problem." Imagine a treacherous shoal on a body of water frequented by international shipping. Despite many wrecks each year, the loss to individual companies is less than the costs of erecting a lighthouse that would prevent those wrecks from occurring. Moreover, the shippers of a country off whose shores the wrecks occur are reluctant to combine to erect the lighthouse jointly because (a) costs would still outweigh benefits, and (b) foreign competitors would enjoy the benefits without paying and thus "ride free." Thus, although there is a need, we have a market failure situation. Without government intervention, the lighthouse will not get built (that is, under maximizing conditions; philanthropy is another solution).

There are two solutions to this problem: (1) The government of a country can establish a national harbors board that taxes national shipping companies to get the lighthouse built and maintained. The justification: benefits to the community as a whole exceed the benefits to the shippers (e.g., cheaper insurance rates, greater reliability of shipping, greater attractiveness of the area as a port, etc.). In this case, external benefits include those to the community (who may nevertheless pay higher shipping rates when using their own national "bottoms") and the international shippers who "ride free." Or (2) Erect an international shipping authority which arranges the building of lighthouses world wide, financed on some equitable basis (e.g., contributions to a common fund in proportion to export tonnage, etc.). In this case there would be no free riders, and benefits would be captured by countries and cities enjoying safe shipping traffic.

Clearly, however, only a public authority could set up the conditions necessary for an optimal solution of the problem. This arises from the non-divisibility of the product, i.e., the lighthouse. Any single shipper would be sacrificing to build the lighthouse, and a coalition of country X's shippers would pass on benefits to its competitors. Then there is the problem of expectations. Only government involvement would provide sufficient assurances that the program would stick.

Incidentally, the use of satellite technology, which provides user exclusivity through computer access codes, etc., could establish conditions for a third solution, namely a license fee for use of a private (or national) satellite.

Externalities issues, therefore, arise from market imperfection and, given the requisite climate of opinion, virtually require government intervention in the form of remedies that produce higher operating costs. The situation described by the models—both positive and negative externalities—are those in which the efficiently pursued selfish interests of the firm add to its own welfare, but lower the general welfare of the community: Adam Smith's invisible hand, upside down. Government intervention in such cases corresponds to the definition of a public good.[4]

Also, essential to a full understanding of these situations is an awareness of the role of public values and changes in public values. What was once perfectly acceptable may suddenly become unacceptable, owing to changing public perceptions. New scientific knowledge can trigger such changes, for example, with discoveries of new health hazards. Equally, if public perception fails to keep pace with new scientific developments (as in the startling increase in the capabilities of analytical chemists) the world may suddenly appear to be more dangerous than it really is—with attendant public suspicions. Similarly, popular attitudes to government deficits have moved from relative approval to disapproval after a decade of protracted inflation—but may reverse again if unemployment exceeds nine percent for long periods.

Similarly, changes in scale can alter public tolerance. One plant emitting noxious substances into a lake may escape public clamor. But if a great many plants do the same, with attendant noticeable effects, public clamor is virtually certain. As economists have long observed, more can often mean worse. More tourists mean more crowded beaches, more cars mean more traffic and thus less convenience. Such matters become issues if anticipated advantages become increasingly slender or disappear altogether. As society's material well-being increases, individuals nevertheless feel progressively gypped—with attendant pressure on government to "Do Something."

Whole industries can and have been affected by such situations. Consider the automobile: At first an amusing novelty, then a convenience and a status symbol, it became one of the first victims of expanded affluence. As cars choked highways, gulped fuel, polluted cities and jammed traffic courts and accident wards as a consequence of their abundance, the likelihood of government regulations inevitably increased. From the mid-1960s onwards, the car was hit with safety and environmental rules and after 1973 by public demands for more fuel efficiency. U.S. auto makers, reluctant to accept the change in public values, continued to leave it to offshore producers to fill the fastest growing segment of the car market, the segment reflecting America's changing values.

Failure to anticipate changing social values, or even to realize such changes have occurred, can leave even the most progressive industry leaders stranded in such a situation. Suddenly it seems to corporate decision makers that goals long cherished and held sacrosanct are under attack without reason. Alternatively, companies may be emboldened to hang on disastrously through periods of increasing public clamor, hoping for the day that public values change again. Finally, the question of positive externalities can emerge when protective subsidies and other government aid to special economic sectors is under consideration.

The argument hitherto shows, however, that the dynamics of an Externality problem are knowable in advance (and therefore that better solutions than stubborn resistance in negative or positive cases are possible).

SUMMARY

Our discussion so far has sought to show why public issues are inevitably disputes about the public interest or community optimum. We have also argued that (1) issues derive from real or apparent market failures in the perception of which community or social values have a decisive impact,[5] and (2) that government becomes involved as the sole agent empowered to articulate and defend community interests and values threatened by market failures. In a general way, we have also shown that there are limits to government intervention, set by the need to preserve economic freedom and democratic practices. The next section will look at the public policy process and argue that *reconciliation of competing interests requires position taking should be strategic, and that persuasion, by itself, is insufficient to induce a settlement..*

WHY ISSUES DEMAND STRATEGIES

In our initial discussion of issues we showed that the existence of government was necessary to produce net community benefits, and that the central political dilemma is that of inducing individuals—citizens or politicians—to forego or limit anticipated private gain on behalf of actually realizeable gains to themselves and to the general welfare. In this section, we shall argue that persuasion is not enough, and that strategic position taking is also required if the necessary inducements are to be generated.

Just what is involved in foregoing private gain for the public good can be illustrated diagrammatically, returning to our contest between two fair-minded, rational (i.e., advantage maximizing) players. As before, both players, A and B, will want to win, but will be prepared to compromise if a satisfactory arrangement can be found. On the other hand, neither player will sacrifice interests he considers vital; accordingly, each will prefer deadlock to defeat. This time, we shall score these four outcome preferences: Win = 4 units of satisfaction, Compromise = 3, Deadlock = 2, and Defeat = 1. Schematic and abstract though it is (some people prefer winning over losing considerably more than 4 to 1) the diagram will illustrate the point under discussion. As before, the strategic choice is between "Compromise" and "Difficult," i.e., C and D. As before, the matrix shows the outcomes when players choose different solutions, "C, C" (top left) = 3, 3 or 3 points to each, "C" for A and "D" for B (top right) = 1 for A and 4 for B (we have a winner), vice versa

Figure III.5. Strategy Matrix

		Player B	
		C	D
Player A	C	3,3	1,4
	D	4,1	2,2

in the lower left quadrant, and for "D, D" (bottom right), a Deadlock outcome.

As in the earliest example, the tendency of this dynamic is to let fear of the worst outcome, namely defeat, force each to take a tough, uncompromising "hawkish" approach. The players' strategies will be such that the outcome will be neither victory nor compromise, but Deadlock. Yet considering the players as a community, the best total outcome would be achieved by two compromise strategies, leading to compromise (top left cell).

Notice, too, that moving to the compromise/compromise cell requires each player to give up a unit of satisfaction that would be acquired in hypothetical victory. The sacrifice of a theoretical but unobtainable individual maximum is not lost but rather enjoyed by the community as a public good, and distributed to members as inducements to move from Deadlock to Compromise.

This emphasizes a point made earlier, namely the importance of expectations. As long as players cling to the hope of victory, they will be unwilling to substitute one unit of satisfaction derived from compromise for two units of anticipated satisfaction from victory. Only when players abandon hope of victory (or the costs of continued Deadlock begin to equal a unit of satisfaction) will compromise become possible.

As economists have long explained, optimum outputs are achieved when satisfaction over a range of factors cannot be bettered by further substitution of one factor for another. In this example, Deadlock is always preferable to defeat; compromise cannot be achieved unless players are convinced that the cherished *hope* of victory is *in fact worth less* than compromise or persisting in Deadlock as a means to that end. Then compromise becomes a reasonable substitute and since compromise is achievable, players will move off Deadlock. However, each player must also be convinced that as he moves from "Difficult" to "Compromise," his opponent will not seize advantage of this to press home to victory. An outside mediator is probably required to ensure this does not occur.

Where does the additional reward to the community come from? It derives from the fact that compromise, the second best outcome, is achievable by the whole community (i.e., the two players) whereas victory is not. Compromise in this example is thus identical with the definition of a public good. It also follows from the analysis of the two players' interactions that government could conveniently produce the safeguards that would make compromise achievable.

Optimum outcomes thus demand government intervention to enable competitors to move towards compromise, and in so doing government provides a public good. So much, however, was discussed in an earlier example. *What is not yet clear, but will be shown in the next example, is that the compromise outcome can only emerge from strategic play, i.e., that in order for government to achieve its goal of making private bargains fit the public interest, it must take positions with a view to producing or "engineering" the outcomes desired.*

To return to the basic problem of externalities, once the existence of external costs and the need for public intervention is established, then finding the optimal points is comparatively simple. Individual welfare is optimized when marginal benefits equal marginal costs. Public intervention must control harmful activity at least down to that point.

Figure III.6 illustrates the situation.

At a tax level of zero, firm I operates activity X_I at a level OA deriving net marginal gain (M_I) of zero and total gain OAE. In so doing the firm inflicts harm on group J. If J were in charge, the activity would stop. But firm I runs it up to point A where its marginal gains stop (and its total net gain is therefore highest). J's total loss is OAF, with marginal loss (M_J) equal to AF. Note, however, that even at zero, the net marginal gain to Firm I is OE.

Both I and J can improve their outcomes by cooperation, by moving activity X_I back to where marginal gains offset marginal losses (i.e., to OB, where BC equals BD).

However, identifying this optimum does not help us achieve it. On

Figure III.6. Compensation Issue

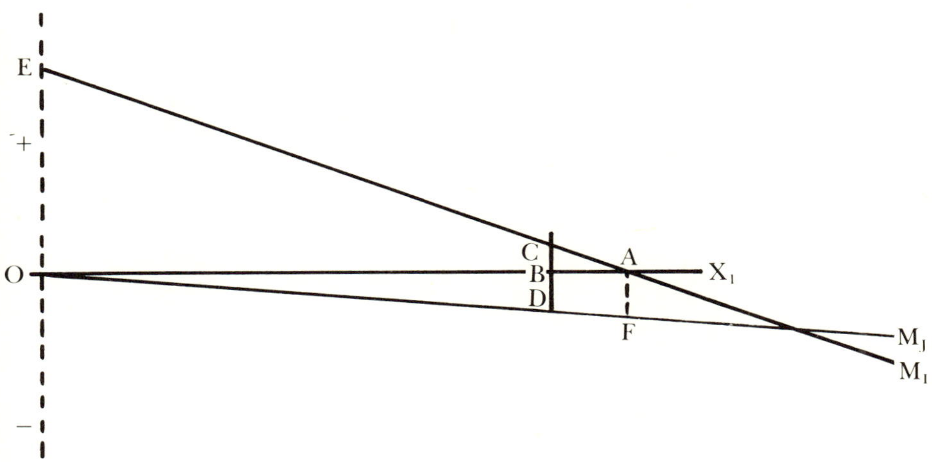

the contrary, it establishes a controversy between Firm I and Group J about how to move from OA to OB. If Firm I is the one carrying out the activity (and in the absence of other considerations) Firm I will want compensation at least equal to ABC (the net loss from the cutback). If Group J has its way, it will want OBD as payment for tolerating the move from zero, the group's favored position, to OB.

Now the cutback to OB will confer ABDF new relief on Group J, so it could compensate OA and still have ABDF – ABC left over. Similarly, Firm I could pay Group J its desired amount and still have OBCE–OBD left over. Also, if Firm I and Group J are of approximately equal power and influence, a compromise somewhere between the two compensations (OBD and ABC) is another possibility.

It is important to note, however, that the compensation will be extremely difficult to arrange. If Firm I controls the activity, it will lack any real inducement to cut back, especially since the longer it can delay agreement, the better off the firm is. Similarly, if Group J controls the activity, it will have little inducement to compromise as it will suffer no disbenefits by delaying, and this lack of harm is a certainty, whereas the degree of disbenefit and subsequent compensation will remain less than wholly certain until they have occurred.

There is also the question of managing compensation when the damage caused is greater than the company can afford to pay. While private negotiation in the context of enforceable property rights may be able to solve the first set of external costs, in the aforementioned example, the shortfall in compensation between the damage done and the amount the company can pay is a deadweight loss suffered either by Firm I or Group J. Should this loss be spread more uniformly throughout the community or not? Issues like job loss from company pullouts, or toxic dumping, involve considerations of this kind.

How could a non-dictatorial public authority produce a satisfactory outcome? To limit our considerations to the first instance only, let us assume a vote on the issue with decision according to the majority rule. The options are the compromises. Firm I prefers ABC; Group J Prefers OBD. A public arbitrator might prefer a joint payment that splits the difference (OBD–ABC/2), an option that would rank second for I and

Firm I	*Group J*	*Arbitrator*
ABC	OBD	OBD–ABC/2′
OBD–ABC/2	OBD–ABC/2	ABC or OBD
–OBD	–ABC	

J, i.e., after their first preference, but ahead of the option preferred by each other. The table below set out the preference schedules.

Notice that first ballot majorities are possible for: (a) ABC over OBD; (b) OBD–ABC/2 over OBD or ABC; and (c) OBD over ABC, depending on the agenda, and the extent to which the arbitrator used his pivotal power to block alternatives to his "split the difference" first preference. The arbitrator can vote with Firm I to defeat J and with J to defeat I, in each case getting promises of support for OBD–ABC/2.[7] Final offer arbitration, in which the arbitrator accepts (rejects) the final offer closest to (further from) his ideal solution, is another strategy for inducing compromise.

If this example establishes that governments can only enforce compromise options by strategic behavior, it also establishes the same for a firm. Companies must either (a) choose community optima themselves, (b) successfully show government it is in its interest to "vote" the issue their way.

Only by inducing government to agree that the firm's preference should be government's preference, too, can the company avoid having either an unwelcome compromise or, worse, its adversary's preferences, imposed upon it. Recalling our assumptions of maximizing behavior should convert our altruistic example into a more realistic auction between I and J with government offering to confer victory upon the highest bidder.[8] While we may balk at cash payments to serving politicians, we regard payoffs in political benefits as money legitimately spent.

In our wider example—where compensation required exceeds the company's ability to pay—then the community would join in any political settlement of the question, with those who would have to pay an additional tax likely resisting the blandishments of those to whom that tax money would go in the form of compensation. The outcome will be affected by such other considerations as whether the costs and benefits are diffused over a large number of government supporters and others or concentrated upon a readily identifiable group. These concerns are discussed in more detail below. Historically, governments tend either to pass on benefits to concentrated, readily identifiable groups, while diffusing costs over a much larger, generally less concerned, aggregation of voters, or to pass on widely diffused benefits, and concentrate costs on narrow, politically vulnerable industrial or other sectors.

The implications for corporations and their advocates are serious. Our arguments indicate that merely putting the company case will as a general rule be far from sufficient. In handling issues, policy and persuasion must combine to enable the company to "play" strategically. In some cases, persuasion will be enough; in others, positioning. But in general, both must be considered with a view to what the other stakeholders in the issue are likely to do. This explains why "issues management," which coordinates policy and persuasion, is better than "PR," which came to concentrate heavily on persuasion alone.

The challenge issues pose for corporate management is precisely the strategic challenge we have been discussing: designing optimum strategies to protect and enhance company welfare in the context of changing public values and new demands on business.

NOTES

1. Ronald Coase, "The Problem of Social Cost," *Journal of Law and Economics* 3 (October, 1960) pp. 1-44; Harold Demsetz, "The Exchange and Enforcement of Property Rights," *Journal of Law and Economics* 7 (October, 1964) pp. 11-26.

2. See Kenneth A. Shepsle and Barry R. Weingast, "Political Solutions to Market Problems," *Working Paper No. 74*, Center for the Study of American Business, Washington University, St. Louis, MO, June, 1982, who point out that this sort of market failure serves now as the standard justification of public intervention.

An interesting variation that explains industry drives for self-regulation, is the Commons Model. See: Garret Hardin, "The Tragedy of the Commons," *Science Magazine*, 162 (December 13, 1978), pp. 1243-8; "Freedom vs. Regulation in a Commons Model;" J. Ronald Fox, *Managing Business-Government Relations*, 1982, Irwin, pp. 44-50; Thomas C. Schelling, *Micromotives and Macrobehavior*, 1978, Norton, pp. 110-115.

3. After Schelling, *Micromotives and Macrobehavior*, p. 111.

4. Conceivably, situations could arise in which the net external benefits of a project, say a rail link between a mine and a smelter, exactly equalled the external costs, say, to farmers whose fields ran alongside the tracks. Assume, too, that compensation from the railroad at full value would force it out of business, thus denying the community the external benefits of the mine/smelter operation. In other words, private bargaining between the railroad and the farmers would be too expensive to occur. In a case like this, the community would face the choice or issue of how much it was prepared to sacrifice for "progress" and who would absorb the costs. One solution would be to deny compensation for harm done by the railroad to farmers, who would then take the land alongside the tracks out of production; another approach would be establish a fund from the receipts of the rail segment to compensate the farmers for lost production. In the first case, we might expect the new industrial (mine/smelter) to grow more quickly, providing additional gains which the farmers might enjoy in the form of more urban employment opportunities and higher crop prices. In the second approach, we might see farmers planting right up to the tracks in order to maximize compensation, with resulting financial burdens on the new industrial complex that would reduce its growth rate and thus the external benefits it would confer on the community. Coase, op. cit.

5. Values includes ideologies as well as outcome preferences in specific issues.

6. See Maurice Preston, *Public Goods and the Public Sector*, 1982, Macmillan Studies in Economics, pp. 28ff, Macmillan.

7. Note on Legislatures, below, deals with Committee and voting in more detail. Economists and others will recognize "Arrow's Paradox," initially set out in Kenneth Arrow, *Social Choice and Individual Values*, 1951, New York, John Wiley, and subsequently a major theme of debate for specialists in public choice.

8. This is a variant of the "Find the Dollar" problem (if three men find a dollar, how do they divide it? Equitably, or do two combine against one?) See "Critical Mass" and discussion of "Iron Triangles" for public affairs applications, below.

Chapter IV

An Analytical Model of Government

We are now at a critical point in our understanding of the issues process. So far, our examination of issues has shown the need for a public authority to ensure community optimum outcomes, to establish conditions for the collection of external costs and the capture of benefits. And our analysis has also shown the need for private parties to issues to create inducements for support from public authorities.

Now we must examine more closely the operation of the public authority, especially how a rationally maximizing, democratically-elected government will determine its actions. For example, how do public values actually affect the operations of government? What is the relationship between the costs of government policy, the benefits of those policies, and public support or involvement in the determination of those policies? Do "horizontal" and "vertical" regulations emerge from the same sorts of considerations? What can groups or individuals wishing to influence government do to maximize their effectiveness, and why are those techniques more effective than others? In short, what factors account for government behavior? That is the subject of this section which draws heavily on the work of University of Toronto economist Albert Breton.[1]

But before we leap into government operations, we must introduce a number of new ideas, elaborating upon what we have said previously (see box for an overview of the basic business-government relationship).

BARONS, CASTLES, SHEIKS, AND OASES: HOW MUCH TAX?

Example 1. Barons and Castles: Baron LaChantage owns a great castle and has just returned from a military expedition with his men in which they have laid waste the surrounding countryside and extracted great wealth in the form of produce from the peasants. But now his next expedition must wait until the peasants repair the damage or else he must range further afield. A crusade? That would leave his castle defenseless against his potentially marauding neighbours. Yet between raids his retainers grow restless. How to keep them satisfied with a regular income? IDEA! Instead of laying waste the surrounding area, why not offer the peasants protection in return for a portion of their produce, i.e., why not levy a tax?

What is the maximum tax Baron LaChantage can exact? Enough to discourage a population increase but not so much as to cause a decrease in the productive population, or else there will be a drop in net taxable output.

Example 2. Sheiks and Oases: Sheik Al Abuck holds an oasis that straddles the rich desert caravan route from the East. What a temptation to pounce like a tiger upon the opulent flanks of every caravan as it approaches and devour its booty. "But exalted Lord," counseled the wise and beautiful Jasmine, his favorite wife, "won't that discourage caravans from coming towards the oasis? Why not offer them protection for a fee?"

How should Sheik Al Abuck arrange his fee scale? At the most, he can take any amount that can be passed on to the customers of the caravan plus an additional amount that would lower caravan profits to the level of travelling the next cheapest route. Of course the existence of another sheik with a competitive oasis would put downward pressure on the fee unless the two sheiks form an alliance to capture maximum rents from all caravans. They can then tax up to the fair market return on the capital required to equip a caravan and cover its other costs, remembering the attractiveness of the caravan route as an investment has been enhanced by the virtually risk-free desert passage.

Important Note: The security provided above is a private good (service) given for a fee to an exclusive user. It does not become a public good until it is provided on a non-exclusive basis to the public as a whole as a matter of right or entitlement by law or custom. But do the limits of tax power change similarly? In Example 1, the limit was the productive power of the economy, in Example 2, the alternative uses of capital outside the reach of the public authority. On the other hand, if the Baron's men actually *do* provide security, then there may be additional output which could be taxed in such a way as to leave either or both sides better off and no one worse off. As for the sheik, his protection would make the caravan route more attractive, i.e., attract more caravans of greater value providing even more gains. His fee scale could in this case be set so as to leave no one worse off, and one or both parties better off. In both instances, therefore, government activities could yield a net gain to the community. The optimal tax level for both Baron and Sheik would ensure that the good received by the taxpayers equalled the tax levied, and that alternative uses of community resources would provide no greater satisfaction to taxpayers. But would taxpayers "reveal" their true preferences to an absolute ruler? Even in a democracy, how can government know how much of any public good to deliver, given few elections and many issues? Can voting reconcile all the competing pressures from individual taxpayers? These are the kinds of problems governments must resolve. How they do it is the subject of this chapter.

New Definitions

1. The Rational Voter. Why vote, except for considerations of civic duty? Unless your vote affects the outcome critically and the issue is of direct significance to you, you might very well feel the costs of voting (time spent learning about the candidates and the issues, getting to the polls, etc.) outweigh any discernible benefits. This would be particularly true if you were indifferent between the candidates. Of course voting is only one form of political participation, but the same considerations apply to other forms as well. Joining an action group, supporting a party or issue organization, watching the news and answering public opinion poll questionnaires are also ways of participating in politics and each has its costs as well as its satisfactions. The rational, that is maximizing, voter will restrict his/her political participation to cases in which the benefits to him or her equal or outweigh costs. The rational voter's comparison of costs and benefits can be expressed formally in terms of the following equation:

$$R = p.b + c - d$$

where R = the expected utility from participation, b = the expected utility from the candidate or policy preferred, p = the probable influence of the rational voter's participation plus c, his/her private satisfaction from participation minus d, his/her private costs.

The implication of this calculation is that participation is directly related to the sense of personal welfare involved. With satisfactory information, participation will therefore rise among groups fearing the loss of public or private benefits or an increase in the costs of government programs. Similarly, participation should increase among potential beneficiaries of public policies, given a constant level of participation costs and government credibility. Equally, a sudden lowering of participation costs can stimulate a dramatic surge in participation.

2. Expected Utility. The rational voter's calculations are based on expected utilities, i.e., the costs and benefits are weighted by an estimate of probability the utilities will be realized. For private benefits of vote casting, the probability is certain. For benefits derived from affecting the collective outcome, the probability is relatively slight. Remember, too, these are utilities, i.e., subjective calculations of benefit. Money returns are thus only part of the question. How much we want benefits, how much difference our participation will make to realizing the benefits, and the credibility of the promises affect the voter's calculations, too.

3. Tax Price/Tax Expenditure. Governments tax. The tax on an individual taxpayer is the price (to him or her) of government activity, even though as we have seen in our definition of public goods, the amount paid may be more or less than the benefits received. Whether a government changes a person's tax up or down, that change is the tax price paid by the taxpayer for the program. Tax price thus affects income, and citizens' ability to meet the costs of political participation. When government foregoes a tax in order to induce taxpayers to spend money in a politically desirable way (e.g., create a job by hiring women) the government is in effect spending tax money it might otherwise have collected. That tax abatement, therefore, is a tax expenditure. Direct transfers—grants and subsidies—are also called tax expenditures.

4. Median Income Voter. The median income voter is the taxpayer whose income level stands at the midpoint of national income levels so that the distance between his/her income and that of the top and bottom wage earners is even. In a progressive tax regime, the public goods received by the median income voter should equal the tax paid. Those below should receive an excess of public goods over taxes; those above, an excess of tax over public services.

5. Supply and Demand for Public Goods. Remember that public goods are characterized by jointness of supply and consumption. Supply does not change regardless of the number of consumers, and public goods cannot be withheld from those who do not pay, or who pay less than the benefits they receive (so called free riders). Therefore the supply of public goods looks very different from the supply of private goods when set against demand, as the diagrams below indicate.

Figure IV.1. Supply and Demand for Public Goods and Private Goods

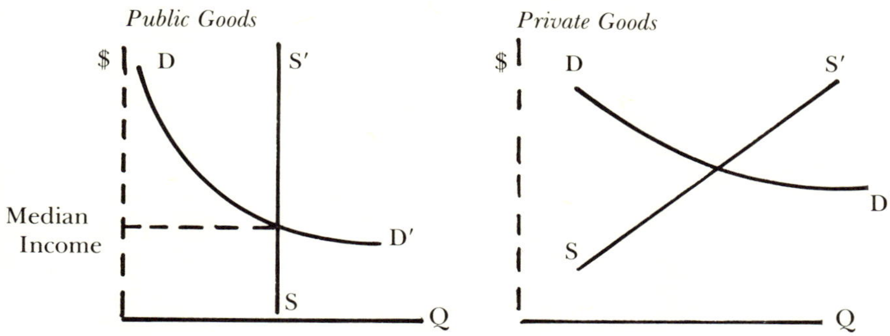

Supply in both cases is shown by the curve SS′, demand by DD′. Note that the supply of private goods varies with price, while for public goods only demand is price elastic. Note, too, that the intersection of supply and demand curves in private goods provides an optimal solution, at least under conditions of pure competition, while for public goods the optimum supply demand level is set by the income of median income voter.

We are now ready to consider government operations.

GOVERNMENT IN GENERAL

Supply Side

Let us begin by examining the factors affecting the supply of public goods. It should be emphasized that, as our comparison of public and private goods shows, public goods are supplied without direct payment by the customers. Reimbursement comes either before or after "sale" in the form of taxes which are related to political as well as economic considerations. In other words, there is no "point of sale" for public goods and no price mechanism to tell public sector decision-makers how much of what goods should be supplied to whom. From this point of view, public goods are generated by a very imperfect market process themselves as much as they are responses to market failures and imperfections. We can sum up these considerations by saying that the supply of public goods is determined by the political process. But how does that process work? We have already shown that there must be a climate of public values broadly supporting government measures. But we can go further than that. "I agree, but I don't know whether the government will," President Kennedy reportedly once told a petitioner. His remark (ironically echoing that of Russian Czar Alexander I, "Not I, but 10,000 clerks rule Russia") illustrates something we all know to be true about government, namely that beside politicians, it also includes departments and civil servants—the Crown, the State, or the Executive Branch—all supported by public funds ultimately coming from the taxpayer. Politicians, government departments and those who work in them are the agents who decide on the quantity of public goods to be supplied and who are to be the principal beneficiaries. In specific measurable terms, therefore, the supply of public goods is related to the resources commanded by each department or ministry or more generally, "the executive branch."

From the point of view of how government actually works, the supply of public goods is equivalent to the tax expenditures of each program or department. Thus we can analyze the factors governing tax expenditure to see how public goods are, in fact, supplied.

Empirical research confirms everyday experience to show that in practice the resources departments control this year are related to the amount they controlled last year. Usually this year's resource allocation is greater, but not always. How much greater or less depends upon the priorities government political judgment assigns to it.

As a general rule, therefore, we may describe the factors affecting public goods supplied by government and government departments in terms of tax expenditures this year, which in turn are a function of last year's expenditures and current government priorities. In so doing let us use mathematical notation to ensure we keep all the important variables squarely before us at all times. We also know from experience as well as research that bureaucracies expand and occasionally, though more rarely, recede. This arises from the fact that successful government programs generate independent support: the beneficiaries want to continue to benefit, and the bureaucrats, whose seniority is measured in terms of control of the three M's (men, money, material) want promotions. (Increasingly, however, we are also witnessing in North America a situation in which bureaucrats are having to fight each other for larger shares of a less rapidly swelling public purse.)

Government Resources: Key Factors[2]
Tax Expenditure Equation

$$E_t = kE_{t-1} + e^* \qquad (1)$$

where E_t = the tax expenditure of the department or ministry for the current year;
k = the political priority assigned to the ministry or department;
E_{t-1} = the tax expenditure in the previous budget period;
e^* = a random constant with an expected value of zero; indicating no guarantee that this year will be an improvement over last year.

> In words, tax expenditure equals the political priority times last period's expenditure plus a random constant, probably zero.

This equation highlights the components that can and cannot be influenced in a process that is the daily bread of political life: programs and budgets. Upon inspection, the thrust of history (or alternatively, the grip of the past's dead hand upon the living) can be readily appreciated. *Only "k," the government's priority, can arrest or control the department's growth.* E_{t-1} is old news, what happened *last* year. What factors, therefore, will affect "k," i.e., the political priority assigned to the ministry or department?

Leaving aside for a moment the details of any particular policy, the factors within government that affect the priority assigned a policy will include the bargaining power of officials vis-à-vis politicians. Officials can be convinced or the need for a certain program (for example, the reequipment of the armed forces) but that will not guarantee the accomplishment of that task, nor that if reequipment is begun, that it will be of a degree or quality to satisfy what may be called "technocratic demand." It is easy to overrate the power of officials in the short run. Although over time departments usually get what they want, in politics it is the short run that counts.

Thus it is the politician—his proclivity to strike out on his own or his disinclination to do so—that determines how much the bureaucrat receives. If the politician is strongly supported by the voters, or as a lame duck has nothing to lose, he may be more inclined to indulge his pet projects.

Bureaucratic Power

Again using mathematical notation, if $N_p < N_r$ (N_p, public support, is less than required for reelection, N_r), the politicians will insist on careful research and elaborate market testing to make sure the policy desired by bureaucrats commands overwhelming political support. In these circumstances, too, bureaucratic power will be checked.

Somewhat paradoxically, only when government enjoys just about exactly the support it needs to retain power and not much more, does the bureaucrat maximize power. For only when $N_p = N_r$ will politicians (a) feel constrained against introducing potentially damaging pet projects, and (b) feel confident in fighting for wholly necessary but not uncontroversial measures. In practice, of course, governments and political leaders will strive for a mix of policies designed to maximize N_p, and government officials will seek to cloak every program with a patina of public support, the better to "sell" to their political masters. We can therefore expand our supply equation to include B_t, the relative bargaining power to officials.

$$E_t = k(B_t)E_{t-1} + e^* \tag{2}$$

In words, tax expenditure = government priority (affected by bureaucratic bargaining power) times last period's expenditure, plus a random constant, probably zero.

Note, too, that bureaucratic bargaining power can be enhanced or diminished by skillful outside intervention at the political level, with rival departments or with the officials themselves to increase or lower credibility, to suggest practical solutions to program problems and better alternatives.

Demand Side

A further determinant of output is the demand for government policies. So far we have shown that these are related to needs and public values, as perceived by bureaucrats and politicians. Now, considering government priorities specifically, we can describe the crucial values with greater precision. Public values may be disposed toward certain policies. But remember the rational voter. If the costs of public participation are such as to exclude significant portions of the community from exerting political influence, policy will not reflect those values. Instead, it will reflect the narrower range of interests of the participants.

In democracy, governments faced with unpopularity ($N_p < N_r$) will seek to lower participation costs of potential supporters. They may do this by making information more readily available, consulting voters directly, through opinion surveys, and addressing groups of potential voters hitherto bypassed or ignored. They will, in other words, try to mobilize support and increase participation, especially participation of those who are believed to be supporters. Direct mail, television ads and the talents of media consultants are intended to achieve the most politically favorable mix of participation costs, i.e., helpful to friends, more difficult for foes.

Tax Price, Income, Political Costs

The details of policy are, of course, also important. How much extra will it cost? Is there a "tax price"—i.e., will it raise taxes, or confer net benefits, and if so, to whom? As shown in the diagram at the beginning of this section, other factors being equal, my readiness to accept new taxes will be a function of my disposable income. (This must be qualified by the realization that because governments supply public goods which in theory benefit everyone equally, those who are most productive can always expect a net outflow of private resources to government; thus, upper income groups may generally resent all tax expenditures). There is thus a limit to the amount of public goods government can supply. When the "cost to the citizen" exceeds "costs of political participation," there will be a surge of opposition. Using mathematical notation, we can summarize this part of the discussion as follows:[3]

$$D = f(Q,I,P) \tag{3}$$

where

D = demand for policy
Q = its tax price
I = personal income
P = costs of participation

> Or, in other words, *demand for policy is a function of tax price, personal income, and the costs of political participation.*

Note, that in terms of variables that can be influenced, *only the costs of participation can be affected by those outside government,* whereas government can also set the tax price.[4] The question of personal income is largely a matter of history, for which, however, government is widely blamed or credited.

Supply and Demand

Is there a "market clearing" equation of supply and demand for government policy? On the basis of what we have said about political participation costs and tax prices, we may surmise that the most successful governments will try to manage programs and priorities such that N_p stays slightly ahead of N_r to provide a margin of safety at election time; to do this, those governments must ensure that the tax price of its program does not create inducements for its opponents to increase the political participation of their supporters. However, this is an imperfect process, as elections are held infrequently, they are contests among oligopolistic suppliers (i.e., political parties), and the buyers or voters are forced to choose among clusters of programs that inevitably include programs some supporters would rather not see. In addition, information will be in imperfect supply.

Political Discount Rate

Imperfect as the process is, it requires judgment on the part of governments, whose main criterion is retaining power at elections. Another way of saying this is that political leaders are "present value oriented" with respect to election day, rather than to the immediate present. They will "discount" policies immediately or shortly after election at perhaps a lower rate than the voters, aiming to achieve identical discount rates as the next election approaches. Governments, in short, will risk unpopularity and impose their own priorities early after election, adjusting their priorities to maximize voter support as election day approaches. Government success will depend upon the collective memory of voters aided by the effectiveness of (or lack of) opposition criticism.

The community discount rate expresses the willingness of a majority in the community to forego private benefits in return for its policy preferences. A higher discount rate for certain policies by the community than by the government indicates a stronger preference for those policies by the community. Figure IV.2 illustrates these points.

As time passes between t_1 and t_2, the difference between the politicians' discount rate and that of the community (voters) moves towards zero. Public memory and opposition criticism can retard that movement and preserve the gap between politicians and the community. When totally ineffective, opposition forces would be unable to preserve a gap. (Thus, mathematically, community memory and opposition criticism can be assigned a

Figure IV.2. Political Discount Rate

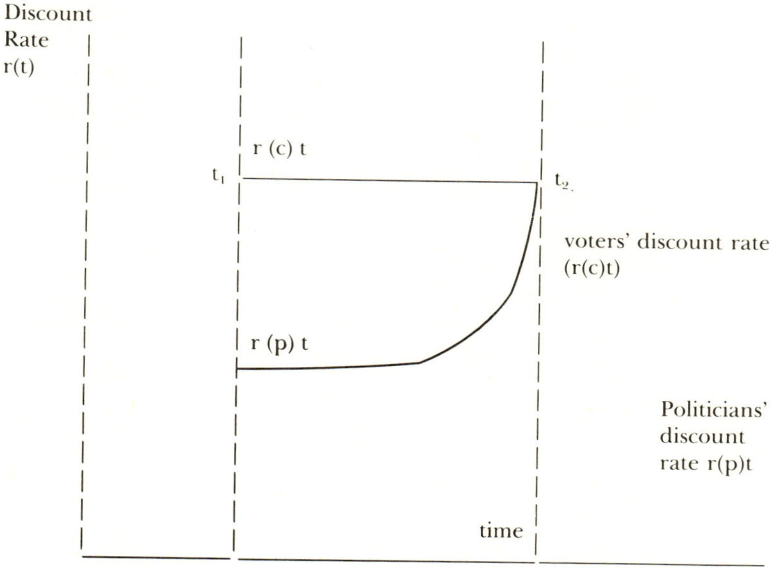

value between 0 and 1.) Again, using mathematical notation for the sake of economy, we can summarize this discussion as follows:

$$h = \int_{t_1}^{t_2} pt(ct)\,[r(c)t - r(p)t]\,dt \qquad (4)$$

where $h =$ public hostility to policy
$pt(ct) =$ public memory (fanned by opposition criticism)
$r(c)t - r(p)t =$ the difference between community values and government values
$dt =$ the passage of time between t_1 and t_2

> *In words, hostility to government policy is, over time, determined by the difference between the value placed on policy by government and by the community, fanned by public memory and opposition criticism.*

In terms of what can be influenced by those inside and outside government, this equation indicates a relatively even match when contesting public support between elections.

Government Output

Let us now try to put together the various parts of the discussion about the variables determining the output of public goods.

Supply of public goods, we saw in Eq. (2), depended on government priority, in turn affected by the relative bargaining power of politicians and bureaucrats, bureaucrats doing best when $N_p = N_r$.

$$E_t = k(B_t)\ E_{t-1}\ te^* \qquad (2)$$

By Eq. (3), however, k values were also determined by demand for public goods, which is a function of tax price, income and cost of political participation and so called "h" values (or hostility) described in Eq. (4). These k values modified the historical factors of last year's budget. So now we can write the "compleat" policy output equation:

$$E_t = k(B_t, hf(Q,I,P))\ E_{t-1} + e^* \qquad (5)$$

In words:

> Policy output (or tax expenditure) = priority
> (determined by relative bargaining power of officials), minus political hostility, plus or minus popular demand (a function of tax price, income, and costs of participation) times last year's output.

In terms of what can be influenced by those outside government this equation tells us:

a. *official bargaining power can be enhanced or undermined by access* (or denial of access) *to reliable technical information;*
b. *political hostility can be enhanced by support to opposition parties and information that keeps public memory alive, and by delaying outcomes* (extending time $t_1 - t_2$);
c. *popular demand can be modified by increasing or decreasing the costs of political participation, a function of information and organization: e.g., Political Action Committees lower participation costs for members.*

Government, on the other hand, can determine (a) relative bargaining power of officials; (b) tax price; and (c) costs of political participation and the weight to be given last year's command of resources. The will to exercise that power will depend upon factors government can influence but not control: "h" values and income—areas where those outside government can compete with those inside government.

More simply, one can say that government output is determined by the balance between bureaucratic factors (B_t and Q), public opinion factors (h, P), and past performance (I, E_{t-1} + e*). Of these, clearly public opinion is the likely arena of contest—both in terms of rousing or dampening public hostility and changing costs of political participation.

Finally, it is interesting to note that the chain of reasoning the output equation depicts on the government side reflects the chain of reasoning already discussed under the heading, "Rational Voter," in expanded form. According to the rational voter equation, R = p.b + c − d, the decision to participate in politics reflects p.b, the individual's estimate of his likely effect on the outcome times his satisfaction from the policy of his choice. But consider p.b: the evaluation of policy benefit derives from personal knowledge influenced by opinion leaders, which is a restatement of pt(ct) in the "h" value equation. The dissatisfaction measured in the "h" value equation includes the community preferred discount rate, that is the personal discount rate the majority of the community would like to see applied to its policy preferences, compared to the weighting actually applied by the government. This difference affects both the collective and private benefits from political participation.

Written in integrated form over time, the rational voter calculation is:

$$R = \int_{t1}^{t2} pb + c - d \cdot dt,$$

an echo of the "h" values required to bring out the rational voter in opposition to government policies. Note, too, that the policy demand function in the government output equation, f(Q,I,P) is similarly an expansion of the private benefits calculation of the rational voter equation (c − d).

The difference between the two equations is that the rational voter calculation contains an estimate of personal effectiveness, which in turn affects the willingness of citizens to act on their political preferences. The constraints on government priority setting are, in contrast, past actions (E_{t-1}) and a permanent bureaucracy prepared to insist upon its own preferences (B_t).

Comparing the government policy output equation and the rational voter equation, we can therefore conclude that the government maximizes very much as do other rational actors in the political system. These points are touched upon again under Critical Mass, below. We should not be surprised by these observations, as they are perfectly consistent with our assumptions that issue outcomes are decided by the interplay of rational action on all sides.

REVIEW

This chapter moved beyond the general issue examples of earlier sections to examine in some detail the factors affecting government output, i.e., the supply and demand for public goods. Basing our arguments upon the work of University of Toronto economist Albert Breton, we found we were able to express supply and demand pressures and market clearing results in four equations:

1. *Supply of public goods.*

$$E_t = k(B_t)\,E_{t-1} + e^*$$

with B_t maximized when $N_p = N_r$

i.e., tax expenditure = priorities (k) affected by officials' bargaining power, last period's tax expenditure, plus a random constant with an expected value of zero.

2. *Demand for public goods.*

$$D = f(Q,I,P)$$

where demand is a function of tax price, personal income, and costs of political participation.

3. *Clearing Discount Rate* (applied to demand by government when setting priorities).

$$h = \int_{t1}^{t2} rt(ct)\,[r(c)t - r(p)t]\,dt$$

where public hostility between elections is a product of community memory, opposition criticism, and the difference between community and politician's priorities.

So that we can write a "compleat" policy output equation:

4. *Government Output.*

$$E_t = k[B_t, hf(Q,I,P)\,]\,E_{t-1} + e^*$$

i.e., output = priorities [determined by official bargaining power, hostility, and public demand (a function of tax price, income and political participation costs] × last period's output.

In non-mathematical terms, government output is determined by bureaucratic factors (B_t, Q), public opinion factors (h, P), and past performance (I, E_{t-1} + e*). Of these, bureaucratic bargaining power (B_t) and public opinion factors (h, P) are the only areas where outside influence can normally be exerted.

Practical Implications

The practical implications of this theorizing underpin the importance of issues management. For the theory shows the primordial importance of organization and participation costs in determining political outcomes. The lower the participation costs to your supporters, the greater the range of projects they will be interested in and the easier it will be to meet P (participation costs) to offset Q (tax price). A sudden drop in the cost of P can have a devastatingly important effect on N_p (government support) and hence on the bargaining power of officials and, thus, on policy. Of course the reverse is also true and this can be important for business-government questions that combine technical complexity and political unattractiveness.

Interestingly, these relationships can also be used to explain analytically a relationship between program costs and benefits and the type of politics that produced that program, as first described by Professor James Q. Wilson of Harvard.[5] Basing his analysis on the distribution of program costs and benefits, professor Wilson accounts for program outputs in terms of national majorities, client politics (i.e., industry lobbies), entrepreneurial politics (i.e., popular advocates like Ralph Nader) and interest group politics (e.g., union or management lobbies). The following matrix sets out his case:

Figure IV.3. Issue Typology

		Benefits	
		Widely Distributed	Concentrated
Costs	Widely Distributed	Majoritarian Politics (1)	Client Politics (2)
	Concentrated	Entrepreneurial Politics (3)	Interest Group Politics (4)

The explanation is this:

Quadrant 1. *Costs and Benefits Widely Distributed.* These issues are settled by a successful national appeal and the construction of a nationwide majority, e.g., national health insurance programs (U.K., Canada).

Quadrant 2. *Costs Widely Distributed, Benefits Concentrated.* These issues are settled by "client" politics, with the result usually in the form of vertical or industry specific regulation, (e.g., trucking, CAB airline rules, etc.) more or less favoring industry at the expense of its customers or the taxpayers.

Quadrant 3. *Costs Concentrated, Benefits Widely Distributed.* These issues are settled through the actions of political entrepreneurs, who see opportunities to pillory an industry and push government to distribute benefits to a vast aggregate grouping (e.g., auto safety legislation).

Quadrant 4. *Costs and Benefits Concentrated.* These issues are settled by means of deals between interest groups, (e.g., labor and management, Taft-Hartley, Bank Regulations, etc.).

From our own analysis, we can see that where this schema holds true, it is because of the relationship between income, the costs of political participation and the tax price (costs or benefits) of the program itself, i.e., our demand function (f(Q,I,P)). Even costs and benefits that are widely distributed (Quadrant 1) must leave tax-payers sufficiently able to meet the costs of participation such that their approval of the program in question can override any vested interest or veto group opposed to the program. Otherwise, despite the distribution of costs and benefits, the program would not be enacted. Quadrant 2 outcomes reflect the relative organizational power of the "clients" for whom the benefits are more attractive than the costs to non-clients are onerous—or again, groups would emerge to block the bills at the embryo stage. Airline deregulation is an example of how a client politics relationship was broken up through the gradual awakening of airline passengers to the costs of regulation following waves of successful airline fare increases after the oil price shocks of the 1970s. As for Quadrant 3 politics, the activities of political entrepreneurs, in our analysis, are essentially to spot quickly where political costs act as a barrier to widespread popular access to public benefits, and move to lower those costs dramatically. The interest group politics of Quadrant 4 again reflect the fact that the matters discussed between interest groups do not have enough impact outside the interests themselves to overcome barriers to political participation put up by rational citizens.

Another aspect revealed by our consideration of tax prices and participation costs is the way specific issues can move from one quadrant to another as the balance changes between cost/benefits of the program on the one hand and political participation costs on the other. Thus, railroad regulation began in the 1880s as a Quadrant 1 or 2 issue, with shippers benefitting primarily and costs borne by the railroads, then shifted to a Quadrant 4 issue. The case of airline regulation by the CAB is the reverse.

Thus beneath the neat formulae of political typologies lies the dynamic interplay of the cost calculations of the rational voter. It explains why governments can coerce resources from some taxpayers (the costs thus imposed are less than the costs of resistance), how political entrepreneurs succeed (they create opportunities for imposing additional costs on narrow political bases, such as an industry, simply by lowering the public's political costs to match anticipated benefits) and equally, why the bargaining power of officials may be sufficiently strong to stand pat or urge new approaches if a government is otherwise confident of its political strength.

In actual practice, of course, most economic legislation embodies a complex allocation of costs and benefits designed to satisfy a patchwork of supporting constituencies and erect barriers to the opposition of others. The section below discusses government choices from the standpoint of the relationship of tax prices to political participation costs.

Choice of Policy Instrument[6]

From what has been said so far, it should be clear that questions of "technical efficiency" or "least cost" methods of achieving an aim will be only one of the criteria political leaders apply when selecting from an array of policy instruments. Their chief concerns will be political costs, not economic ones.

Optimality

A general systematic statement of optimality can be developed for policy instrument choice given that the choice will be subject to political constraints. Except under unusual circumstances, a politician will be unlikely to choose methods of achieving a policy goal that could cost him his hold on power. Using notation already introduced, we may therefore state as the major constraint on government output that:

$$N_p - N_r \geq 0$$

(It will be remembered that B_t, bureaucratic bargaining power, is maximized at $N_p = N_r$, and reduced for all other conditions. Thus, the statement we will derive will assume that B_t is at a maximum, although in practice it may well be less.)

Remember also that the popular response to government policy is essentially a function of tax price, income and the costs of political participation, i.e., f(Q,I,P). Of these I, income, is outside government control; but Q and P, the tax price and costs of political participation, can be manipulated by government and, in the case of P, also by issue group organizers. Now, if $N_p - N_r \geq 0$, the tax price of government programs must be less than or equal to costs of organizing additional opposition. Optimization of policy instrument choice, therefore, is mainly a question of choosing which instruments will maximize rewards for government without making political opposition worrisome, i.e., for all policies such that

$$Q \leq P \qquad (\text{when } N_p - N_r = 0).$$

In a theoretical two-person community ruled by unanimity, there is little more to say about optimization. The choice of policy instrument will impose tax prices such that $Q - P \leq 0$, or else the other community member would feel induced to veto the measure. This is a condition of Pareto optimality (i.e., that no one can be made worse off), and it allows general adjustments to adversity (i.e., downturns in community productivity options and trade) if neither community member is made worse off than the other. Instead, given maximizing behavior, both would become impoverished at the same rate (or else no decision would be possible).

An N–Person Community

The problem of optimizing policy instrument choice becomes more interesting in communities of three or more persons where approval by a majority is necessary, again producing results corresponding to Wilson's schema discussed above.[7] In such cases, our constraint could operate in several different ways. First, it might operate up to the point—and not beyond—that a majority formed: in other words, tax prices could exceed the costs of political participation for a minority, provided majority support was certain. Thus, as is often the case in newly-elected parliamentary governments, unwelcome measures can be imposed on a hapless and recently-defeated minority, despite their vehement protests. Second, the constraint could operate such that the government would use persuasion to reduce political participation costs for supporters of its policy choice while simultaneously raising it for opponents. Finally, a third possibility for the operation of our constraint is that, given general community indifference, narrow interests, which were well organized and with therefore significantly lower (incremental) political participation costs than unorganized opposition to a particular measure, could compel a government uncertain of its majority to impose tax prices on the general community. Those tax prices would remain below the community participation threshold, but would confer new benefits on the interest group (whose P costs are lower than those of the rest of the community). The optimizing condition that explains all three cases is again, $Q \leq P$.

Figure IV.4 on page 58 sets out the relationship between Q and P. Note that the ratio Q/P is the marginal tax price to the government for the public goods supplied.

This allows us to come to a general conclusion[8], namely, that in a community of 1 . . . J persons, governments will optimize their offerings of public goods if the sum of the tax prices for 1 . . . K programs corresponds to the (incremental) political participation costs of the groups representing a winning majority at any time: i.e.,

$$\Sigma\, Q_1 \ldots k = \frac{\Sigma P_1 \ldots j}{2} + P_i$$

In words, the sum of the tax prices = the sum of the costs of political participation for a community majority (when N_p - N_r = 0).

Figure IV.4. Marginal Tax Price

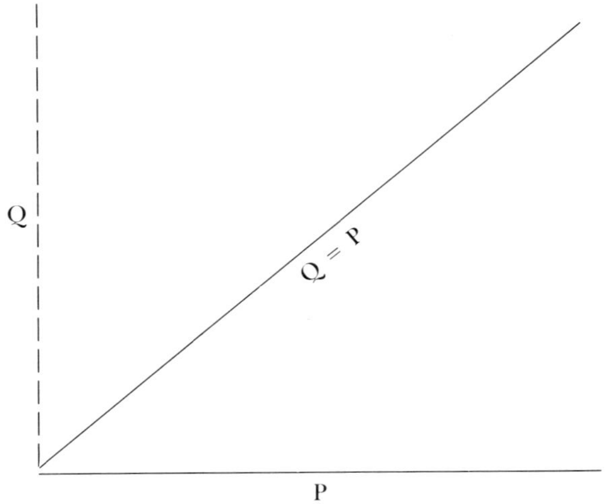

Note the pivotal role played by *i*, the *i*th taxpayer, in forming majorities. This critical "kingmaker" position can add a premium to the value of *i*'s support, especially when it can convert a potential loss into a victory. In practice, however, repeated "play" will tend to cancel out the potential differences, and make any such premiums hard to realize. Thus, for example, the Business Roundtable, the National Association of Manufacturers, the American Petroleum Association, and several prominent chief executive officers, supported tax increases contained in the 1982 tax bill, even at some cost, because in repeated play their organizations might have to ask favors themselves. Political discounting, in other words, tends to keep $Q_{i \ldots k}$ uniform over the range of the majority's "P". However, a desire to hold key constituencies will open government to their special demands, or tempt governments to offer them special benefits as part of wider, national programs[9]

This conclusion underlines everything we have so far said about the need to play the political game effectively. For net public benefits will tend to flow towards (or be shaped in the interest of) those best organized and informed, i.e., *towards* those for whom the costs of political action on any particular issues are lowest, *and away from* those for whom political protest appears too troublesome and expensive.

Summary of Terms and Concepts

rational voter
participation calculus

expected utility
tax price/tax expenditure
median income voter
supply and demand for public goods
two equations determining the supply of public goods
an equation determining demand for public goods
political discounting as a market clearing mechanism
relative bargaining power of officials
policy output equation
Wilson's issue typology
choosing the policy instrument
extra power of king makers and key constituencies

NOTES

1. Particularly, *The Economic Theory of Representative Government*, Aldine Publishing Company, Chicago, 1974.
2. Those with no patience for mathematical notation will find the points explained in words below the formulae. Note that the main discussion centers on last year's tax expenditure (E_{t-1}) and the political priority attached 'k' to the spending agency this year.
3. For simplicity, this discussion assumes equality between average and marginal tax prices. In practice, however, it is changes of tax prices at the margin that stimulates or stifles public participation.
4. This is particularly true when governments control legislatures as in Westminster-style Parliamentary democracies. It is less true where governments do not, as in minority Parliaments or U.S.-style congressional governments.
5. James Q. Wilson, *The Politics of Regulation*, Basic Books, 1980, especially chapter 10; also J. Ronald Fox, *Managing Business-Government Relations*, Irwin, 1982, pp. 146-7.
6. M. J. Trebilcock, Douglas C. Hartle, J. Robert S. Prichard, Donald N. Dewees, *The Choice of Governing Instrument*, Economic Council of Canada, 1982.
7. In this section, we relax our assumption of equality between marginal and average tax prices, to consider change at margin or *i*th tax payer.
8. Note that this discussion has ignored "h" factors relating to the political discount rate. Adding "h" considerations only reinforces what has been said, however, since "h" is essentially a judgment measure of the effectiveness of government and opposition on a given issue.
9. See Richard I. Kirkland, Jr., "Taxing the Business Lobby's Loyalty," *Fortune*, October 18, 1982, p.144.

APPENDIX:
NOTE ON LEGISLATURES

So important are committees to the resolution of public affairs problems that their behavior, as explained by political scientists and economists, merits special examination from the operational standpoint of the public affairs practitioner.

A frequent source of frustration for public affairs counsel is the often inexplicable response of committees to good, fully researched and well-delivered presentations. The boxed example illustrates the basic problem: why outcomes can bear little apparent resemblance to inputs.

Example: Committee Behavior

You are concerned with a legislative committee on banking that is holding hearings to consider important and complex regulations governing admission of foreign banks into financial areas that hitherto have been exclusively reserved for domestic banks.

You favor and have urged Option A as the best outcome for your firm and the defeat of Option E as the worst case. Polling the committee members prior to the voting, you learn that because of the complexity of the issue, there is no dominant consensus. The pattern of committee members' individual orders of preference looks like the table below:

	Committee Members' Preferences				
Members	*1*	2	*3*	*4*	*5*
O	a	b	c	d	e
P	b	c	d	e	a
T	c	d	e	a	b
I	d	e	a	b	c
O	e	a	b	c	d
N					
S					

Member 1, for example, prefers Option "a" above all others. Member 2, on the other hand, finds it the least attractive of all. Member 5 prefers Option "e" before all others. Members 3 and 4 both prefer "a" to "b", but also rank "e" and "a" in the schedule of preferences.

At first glance, you may feel that at least Option e is out of the running. After all, there are majorities for "a" over "b", "b" over "c", "c" over "d", and "d" over "e". *But upon further inspection, you can also see, there is a majority for "e" over "a"!*[1]

Consider the following scenario: (1) The government brings forward a proposal based on Option "a". (2) Member 5 proposes Option "e" as an amendment. (3) "e" carries over "a", and the bill as amended ultimately becomes law. You have been hit by what political scientists call "intransitive majorities."

Examples of this inconsistency, or circularity (because of the circular voting involved) as this type of voting is called, have occurred in legislatures as different as the U.S. Congress and the Dutch Parliament.[2] They can occur in any committee where details of legislation are examined without affecting the principle of the legislation under discussion.

The aim of the example is to demonstrate that committee majorities can be inconsistent.

A Simple Strategy

Forewarned is forearmed. At the very least, you must work to ensure that "e" cannot defeat "a". Persuading Members 2 and 3 to prefer "a" over "e" might cause total preferences to change sufficiently that "e" would be defeated and thus the amendment would never be introduced.

It may be argued that real committee decisions are not taken that way — i.e., on the basis of commonly ranked preferences; instead, members pick one or two alternatives which they will support and are indifferent towards the rest.

Perhaps surprisingly this procedure does not induce consistency in our example, but it does create additional problems. As the diagram shows, there are no clear majorities, but there are two-person coalitions for each of the five alternatives if second choices are included.

Members	1 and 5	1 and 2	2 and 3	3 and 4	4 and 5
Choices	a	b	c	d	e

Not only is the "transitivity" problem still unresolved, but now there is a new one. Majorities must now be created, requiring inducements sufficient to be stable over three members. Given our assumptions of maximizing behavior, such stability will be nearly impossible—the higher price that hold-outs can command (as the "makers" of majorities) and will "dominate" inducements to form stable pairs. This will be true unless the special circumstances of the issues (e.g., an outside force or, more usually, party discipline or a force such as Critical Mass) creates a stampede to form majorities around a singly uncontestably superior (in terms of political rewards) alternative.

How then do committees form majorities? If majorities are present to begin with (e.g., through party discipline), agenda manipulation can suffice. But, if not, then bargaining occurs. Members offer pivotal assistance on some issues in return for assistance in the construction of majorities on other issues — in a word, logrolling.

SOME USEFUL CONCEPTS

Role of the Chairman

From the examples already discussed, it will be apparent that the role of the chairman in framing and presenting proposals to the committee can be crucial. This "agenda-setting" power can enable a subtle and energetic committee chairman to produce majorities that otherwise might not occur. This can be accomplished by splitting a set of options for discussion into subsets to facilitate committee choice.

Consider, for example, a measure containing three options (A,B,C) for decision among a committee of three members. Their preference rankings are as follows:

	Options
Chairman prefers	A to B to C
Member 2 prefers	B to C to A
Member 3 prefers	C to A to B

As in our earlier example, this is a clear voting cycle, i.e., that majorities exist for A over B, B over C and C over A. The unique outcome will therefore depend on voting rules and the chairman's agenda-setting power.

Committees usually decide such questions in one of three ways:

a. *Successive Procedure*: the first poll is taken between A and the rest, and if A is rejected, then a second poll is taken between B and C.
b. *Plurality Procedure:* a single poll is taken between A, B and C. The outcome with the most votes wins. The Chairman's vote can be tie making (which is a vote to reject) or breaking, but he cannot vote twice.
c. *Amendment Procedure:* a first poll is taken between two alternatives. The second poll is taken between the winner and the third item, which must itself be approved subsequently.

Assume that each committee member votes "sincerely," i.e., votes for his true preference. Then under the *successive procedure*, A will be rejected in the first poll and B selected in the second. Why? Supporters of A as a first choice are outnumbered by supporters of the rest. On the second poll, supporters of B over C outnumber those for C over A. The chairman can suggest the vote be taken on the options in turn and cast his tie-breaking vote for B on round two. But given our rule of sincere voting only, the best the chairman can hope for is his second choice.

Under *the plurality procedure*, each member (including the chairman) will vote his preference A, B, C. The chairman's vote effectively makes the outcome a tie (thus rejection of all choices), or he can again confer victory on his second choice.

Under the amendment procedure, however, we encounter a paradox in that the chairman can have his last choice imposed upon him even under conditions of sincere voting. Consider the following scenarios:

Scenario 1:

(a) Chairman introduces choice AB vs. C, winning Member 2's support.
(b) Chairman now calls question A vs. B, winning 3's support for A over B.

Outcome: A over B over C

This can be displayed diagrammatically as a "tree":

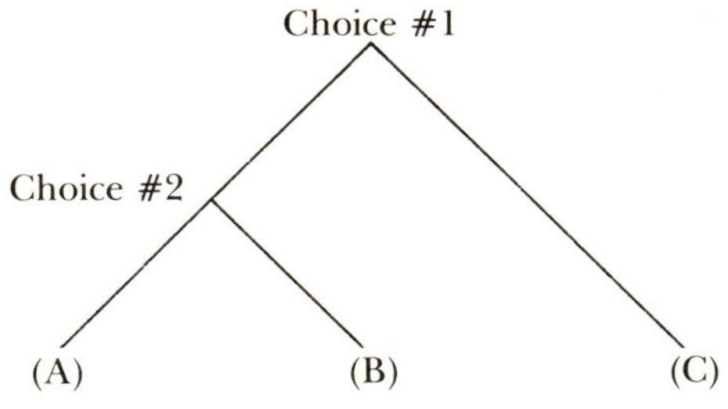

But, consider the following variation.

Scenario 2:

(a) Chairman introduces AB vs. C.
(b) Member 2 suggests an amendment, "Let A and C be interchanged It carries, as member 3 also supports C over A.

(c) On question, CB vs. A, CB carries, as Members 2 and 3 prefer C to A.
(d) On question C vs. B, B carries, as Chairman and Member 2 prefer B over C.

outcome: B over C

As a diagram:

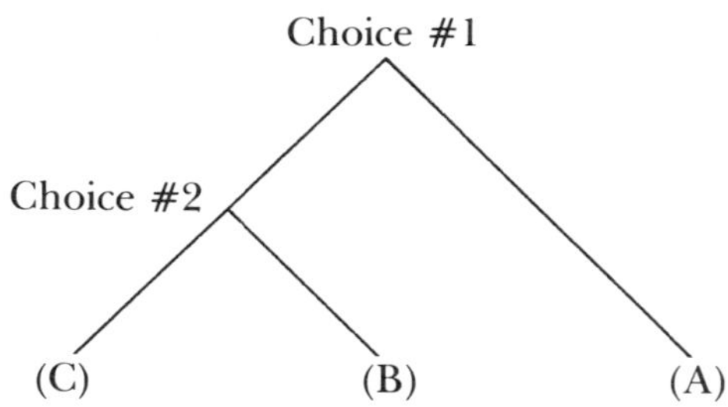

And now, the following:

Scenario 3

(a) Chairman introduces AB vs. C.
(b) Member 3 calls for an amendment, "Let B and C be interchanged," which carries with support of Member 2.
(c) On question AC vs. B, Member 3 and Chair pass AC.
(d) On question A vs. C, Members 3 and 2 defeat A.

Outcome: C prevails

The result, Chair has his last preference imposed upon him. (This is known in some quarters as "The Chairman's Paradox.") Again, as a "tree":

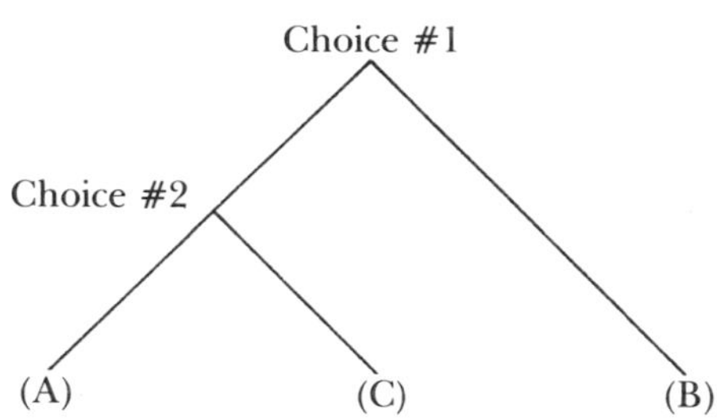

Given the "Amendment Procedure," what guidance emerges from this discussion for the presentation of resolutions to committees? The crucial question is how to partition the choices. Optimally, *the partition should be*

so placed that the choice offered comes at the point of indifference between sets of those voters whose support is desirable. The choice should enable voters to choose between one subset and another such that the least desirable member in one subset is as desirable as any member of the other subset. In our example, Chairman's choice AB vs. C set up conflicts with the other members whose first and second choices straddled the alternatives presented. Given our requirements of sincere voting, however, the chair had little alternative. Chair's best defense was to undertake negotiations prior to voting in order to forestall amendments.

Resource Allocation

Now let us develop a set of concepts that optimize the allocation of scarce "lobbying" resources designed to head off the potential difficulties posed by inconsistent majorities. These concepts, useful in themselves, can also be used as checks or bench marks against which to test actual strategies and programs. Using worked examples is probably the most effective way to introduce these methods.

Consider: A shareholder's meeting is faced with a resolution condemning investment in South Africa (although the company's investment policy does not further apartheid and benefits the company's employees—of all races).

You have limited resources at your command. The problem: How to "spend" them most effectively (a) to defeat the resolution, and (b) to pass it.

There are four blocs of shareholders, with 5, 5, 3 and 2 million shares respectively. It takes 8 million votes (a simple majority) to pass the motion.

Proportionately, how much time should you spend with each bloc (assuming each block wants advice before making up its mind)? Intuitively, you might divide the time according to the votes held by each bloc: 5/15, 5/15, 3/15, and 2/15. In fact, this would be less than efficient. Instead, ask yourself a key question: which voters are pivotal? Which are not? Look first for voters who by themselves make up a majority: These are Dictators. Second, look for voters who can never be pivotal: as in bridge, these are Dummies.

Are there any Dictators or Dummies in our example? No Dictators. But the "2 million vote" bloc can never be pivotal—i.e., transform a minority into a majority (or Lose to Win).

Thus, out of the four blocks, there are only three effective groups. 5 million, 5 million, and 3 million. Each can make a majority in combination with one of the others.

There are, therefore, two possible winning strategies: (1) Divide time

50/50 between each of the 5 million bloc representatives. Notice, however, that you must convince each of them—i.e., achieve 100 percent effectiveness—to win; (2) Divide time 1/3, 1/3, 1/3 among the 5, 5, and 3 million vote groups. Note that 67 percent effectiveness is enough to win (you only need to convince any two).

Try the example with a two-thirds majority rule: you need 10 million votes to win.

Any Dummies? No. Even the 2 million bloc counts in this case.

Any Dictators? Not exactly. To defeat the motion (i.e., deny it a two-thirds majority) any 5 plus the 3 million groups are pivotal, and will carry the day.

Strategies to Pass (or win 10 million votes):

(a) Divide time between the two fives.
Effectiveness required = 100%.
(b) Divide time among the four voters equally.
Effectiveness required = 75%.

Strategies to defeat the resolution (i.e., deny it a 2/3 majority):

(a) Divide time between the two blocks of five million voters.
Required effectiveness = 100%
(b) Divide time among the 5, 5, and 3 million blocs respectively.
Required effectiveness = 67%.

N.B. The two-thirds rule (a) requires supporters to court one extra group, (b) demands only slightly more effectiveness, to pass the resolution than to defeat it.

Probabilities

So far, our calculations have assumed equal probability of support from the different voting blocs. For the sake of additional realism, let us now relax that condition and, considering the three pivotal blocs as A, B and C respectively (A and B with 5 million votes and C with 2 million) assign subjective probabilities of voting in our favor as .8, .5 and .5 respectively. How should our resources of time best be spent to deny a two-thirds majority?

Attacking this requires a knowledge of some common sense probability rules governing relations between independent events.[4]

AXIOM 1: *The probability of two independent events both occurring at the same time is the product of their individual probabilities* (p.A x p.B)

AXIOM 2: *For two independent events, the probability of either occurring is the sum of their individual probabilities minus the probability of their occurring together* (pA + pB − (pA.pB))

The voting results we want are independent events.

Strategy 1. A + B (i.e., A and B voting together in favor) = two independent events occurring together or .8 × .5 = .4

Strategy 2. A or B (i.e., support of either A or B) = either of two independent events, that is .8 + .5 − (.8 × .5) = .9
But to win, these must occur together with independent event C. The chances of this: .9 × .5 = 45%.

Strategy 2 therefore involves less risk for the same 100 percent payoff.

How should resources be allocated? Consider as the cost of achieving our result, the "cost" or difference between our probable events and certainty, i.e., (1-p). Thus, for A or B, the cost of converting 90 percent into 100 percent is 10 percent. Therefore devote at least 10 percent of our time to ensuring either A or B. But support from C is only 50 percent certain, although 100 percent necessary. Therefore, devote up to 90 percent of resources to getting C's support.

Exercise:
A bill favoring unionization is about to pass the state legislature. Democrats have 79 votes, Republicans 78 votes, Independents 3 votes. A simple majority, 81 votes, is enough to pass the measure. Analyze how you would divide your resources (a) to defeat the bill, (b) to pass it. (Each party votes as a bloc!) Also, would you go public or prefer to lobby behind the scenes? Why?

Solution:
Any dictators? No, but n.b. Independent's potential veto power if the two big parties stay split. Any dummies? No.
The lineup as a table:

	R	D	I	Majority
The votes	78	79	3	81

Options (assuming equal probability of support)	*Required Effectiveness*
1. Allocate time between D and R for 157 votes	100 %
2. Allocate time between R and I for 81 votes	100 %
3. Allocate time between D and I for 82 votes	100 %
4. Allocate time between R, D, and I for 81 votes	67 %
5. (to defeat only) Rely on I's veto power and R/D mutual opposition.	

Do these choices change if probability of D and R collaboration is 50% respectively? (n.b., collaboration is a simultaneously occurring independent event, i.e., (pA × pB) = (.5 × .5) = 25%.)

What about going public? To defeat the bill, working with the Independents while going public to mobilize support (see "critical mass" model below) against the proposed law might well prove more effective than relying on the committee route. Both major parties would prefer to have the votes and financial support of organized labor *unless the general public mobilized to add some cost to that support.* This is especially true, given the probabilities of collaboration. To pass the bill, on the other hand, unless the state's public is noteworthy for its support of organized labor, Option 4, trying for agreement between the two major parties, would likely be most effective, given the resources labor can offer at election time.

An additional technique merits discussion: the introduction of new alternatives to create cyclicity. This is particularly applicable to minority government situations in parliament or the United States, where the executive does not have automatic control of the legislative branch.

Using Cyclicity

Assume that the Independents are opposed to the check-off measure and would like to defeat it, but the Republicans and Democrats are committed to the idea in principle, although their specific plans are diametrically opposed. The situation can be visualized as set out in the diagram below.

Republicans prefer a modest check-off, being unwilling to gainsay the principle but even less willing to reward traditional Democrats with a new source of funds with which to garner political influence. For just the opposite reasons, Democratic preferences for the measure rise with the rate of allowable check-off. Another way of writing these choice is R = A over B over C; D = C over B over A. How can Independents defeat the measure using strategic or insincere voting to generate the outcome they want?

Consider the following scenarios based on alternative Administration presentations of the bill.

Figure A.1. Republican and Democrat Positions on Union Check Off Legislation

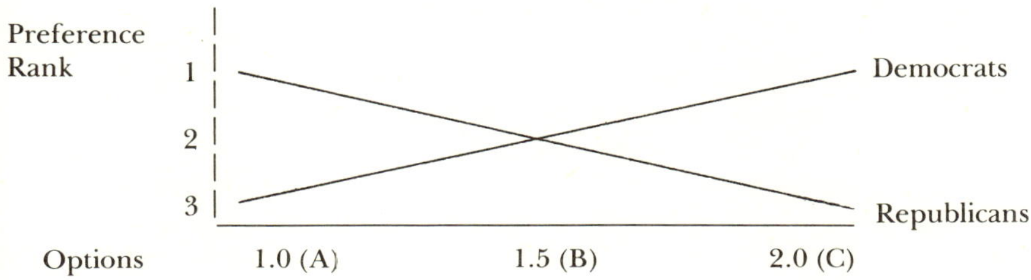

Scenario 1:

Under this scenario, the administration presses for Option C (i.e., 2 percent). In practice, therefore, they present legislators with a choice (B, C) vs. (A).

Outcome: I votes with Republicans to defeat BC and then with Democrats to defeat A.

Scenario 2:

Arguably, the administration might improve its support by partitioning its initial bill or resolution differently, i.e., as a vote for B. The immediate danger for I is coalition of R + D. I therefore responds by moving as an amendment the adoption of an intermediate percentage AB or BC (i.e., between 1 and 1.5 or 1.5 and 2 percent). If this succeeds in attracting support from either R or D, then at the next vote on the resolution as amended, I can switch to defeat this alternative.

The Independents thus have considerable strategic power under conditions of majority rule. If they can maintain the division between the Republicans and Democrats, they will be pivotal (i.e., determine the outcomes) in every choice put to the vote. When the issue is to them one of high salience despite relative public indifference, this voting power will translate into bargaining power that would help them write legislation.

But what if everyone was "voting strategically," which is in practice the usual case? Then we are back to logrolling—trading votes now for votes in the future.

VOTING AND COALITION BUILDING: SOME GENERAL POINTS

Our analysis of committee behavior has shown that the power of a committee member depends not only upon the number of votes he controls (where for instance share ownership is a factor) but also upon the ability of that member to combine *pivotally* with other members: that is, to transform losing coalitions into winners.

Therefore, *the voting power of a committee member is the ratio of the number of alignments in which he/she is pivotal, to the total number of alignments.*

This definition of voting power allows us to compute the power balance among the members of a committee in the absence of other knowledge,. Since a member will be pivotal if he/she is the last to join the minimum winning coalition, a member's power is equivalent to the number of ways this can occur, divided by the total number of alignments possible.

Now, the total number of alignments is n!, for a committee of n members (n! is known as factorial n, and represents the product of integers n × n - 1 × n - 2 . . . 1).

For example, in a four-person committee, the total number of possible alignments is 4 × 3 × 2 × 1 = 24. If 3 votes are required for a majority, Member C can be pivotal in coalition with {a,b}, {b,a}, {d,a}, {d,b}, {a,d} and {b,d}: i.e., six out of 24 possibilities, or 1/4 or one chance in four. The same is true for each other committee member.

Now let us consider a four-member committee with votes of 5, 5, 3 and 2 respectively. The majority required to pass a measure is therefore 8 votes.

By inspection, we can easily determine that the member with two votes can never be pivotal. Note, too, that there are no dictators, or singleton majorities, and that the total number of possible alignments is 4! (i.e. 4 × 3 × 2 × 1 = 24), the total number of ways any four objects can be arranged.

Now, by inspection, we can see that Member one, with five votes, can be pivotal in two coalitions of two persons (of Members two and three) and pivotal in two coalitions of three members (of Members two and four, and Members three and four). Note that the two person coalitions only allow one way in which Member one can be pivotal, but the three person coalitions can each form two ways before Member one joins. Summing these in relation to the total number of permutations gives the following results:

For the two-person coalitions: 2(1/24) = 2/24
For the three-person groups: 2(2/24) = 4/24

Remembering our probability axioms (discussed earlier in this chapter) the probability of any of these coalitions forming is the product of the probabilities of the two categories, that is 8/24, or 1/3. Similar results can be derived for the other pivotal members of the committee, with the result {1/3, 1/3, 1/3,0}.

This result tells us that despite the committee members' different voting strengths, we should divide our lobby resources equally among the first three members, as each one stands an equal chance of being pivotal. Moreover, in any tradeoffs resulting from the coalition forming process, we would expect the political spoils to fall to committee members in proportion to their coalition-forming strength rather than their numerical voting strength: in this political market, the committee member controlling 3 votes is worth just as much as the 5-vote member.

Of course, this theoretical result should be modified in the light of practical information about personal ideologies, old feuds and loyalties that would constrain the coalition building process.

For those who prefer formulas, there is a general expression for the probability of any coalition forming for which a member is pivotal:

$$Pn_s = (s - 1)!\,(n - s)!/\,n!$$

where n is the number of committee members and s the number of coalition members.

The voting power of any member is therefore the sum of Pn_s for all such coalitions.

The formula simply states what we have already seen to be true, that the probability of coalitions forming in which a particular member is pivotal is the product of two independent events occurring simultaneously: other members entering coalitions without the particular member, and other members aligning themselves with the non-s group. There are (s-1)! ways the first can happen, (n-s)! ways the second can occur. The product of the two divided by the total number of possible alignments gives the probability of the outstanding member's "pivotality."[5]

SUMMARY AND CONCLUSION

Understanding committee behavior is or should be vital for public affairs practitioners. The discussion in the chapter concerns methods of allocating time among committee members. It also investigates some interesting paradoxes of committee behavior: in particular, the fact that committees can produce majorities that conflict with each other (e.g., options "a" over "b", "b" over "c", and "c" over "a").

Economists and political scientists find this phenomenon worrisome.

For the public affairs practitioner, understanding its workings can help snatch victory from defeat.

Practical Requirements

Besides an ability to put forward the company case convincingly, public affairs practitioners active in legislative work should also possess:

1. an intimate knowledge of the political and legislative process;
2. an intimate knowledge of alliance and coalitions, formal and informal, that develop on a committee;
3. an ability to work with politicians and their staffs to help them meet their goals while meeting those of the practitioner.

As the examples in this section show, exact, detailed knowledge of the committee process is a precondition of repeated success. Yet achieving that knowledge and using it effectively is nothing less than the full exercise of citizenship.

Summary of Terms and Concepts

Preference ranking
Intransitive majority
Role of the chairman
Successive procedure
Plurality procedure
Amendment procedure
Voting trees
Partitioning sets
Chairman's paradox
Dictators and dummies
Probabilities of independent events
Using cyclicity

NOTES

1. As economists would say, "Committee preferences are "intransitive"; that is, "a" preferred to "x" preferred to "e" does *not* exclude a preference for "e" over "a".
2. See W. H. Riker and P. C. Ordeshook, *An Introduction to Political Theory*, 1973, Englewood Cliffs, N.J., p. 49, n. 15; R. Farquharson, *Theory of Voting*, 1969, New Haven, pp. 52-3; J. C. Blydenburgh, "The Closed Rule and the Paradox of Voting,"*Journal of Politics*, No. 1, 1971, pp. 57-71; Hans van den Doel, *Democracy and Welfare Economics*, 1979, Cambridge, pp. 82-4.
3. See R. Farquharson, *Theory of Voting*, 1969, Yale; Richard G. Niemi, "An Exegesis of Farquharson's Theory of Voting," *Public Choice* Vol. 40, no. 3, 1983, p. 293.

4. Proofs of the theorems can be found in any book of finite mathematics. An excellent introduction is Marvin L. Bittinger and J. Conrad Crown, *Finite Mathematics, A Modelling Approach*, 1977, Addison-Wesley, esp. chapter 7. The logic behind them can easily be grasped intuitively, however. Consider a coin. Adding another coin doubles the number of coins but quadruples the number of possible outcomes. What was previously a 50% proposition (e.g., heads on each independently) now becomes as 25% proposition. Chances of a head or tail is of course 100% as before, but which? Only a joint turnup of the unwanted alternative (e.g., two tails when we want a head) would rule out a win—a 25% chance as we have just seen, making a "win" 75% certain.

5. For further reading in the literature on coalitions: Bittinger and Crown, pp. 364-370; John G. Kemeny et al., *Introduction to Finite Mathematics*, Prentice-Hall, 1961, pp. 74-78, 108-113; Sven Groennings et al., eds., *The Study of Coalition Behavior*, Holt, Rinehart and Winston, 1970; L.S. Shapley and M. Shubik, "A Method For Evaluating the Distribution of Power in a Committee System," *American Political Science Review*, 48 (September, 1954), pp. 787-792; William Riker, *The Theory of Political Coalitions*, Yale University Press, 1962; Howard Raiffa, *The Art and Science of Negotiation*, Harvard, 1982, chap. 17.

Chapter V

Issue Models

The analysis up to now has shown issues to revolve around the question of inducing private sacrifices in the interests of net public good. The role of public values has been shown to be crucial, as well as the role of rational expectations. Also, we have argued, strategic behavior (as opposed to merely articulating one's individual preference) is an inescapable part of the resolution process.

But what strategies ought to be followed? Clearly, the stakes or costs of solution have a bearing on this. Business impact—as measured in terms of effect on cash flow, asset value, profitability, and vital business strategy—must be a part of any issue analysis. But these will be virtually unique from company to company, even within a given sector. While they permit ranking of critical issues (see Anticipation of Issues, below) normal business data give little indication of how to oppose outcomes or how to engage in the issues process so as to achieve the optimum outcome for the company. Nor do historical reviews of the origins, and the past or new information on present involvements in issues—although helpful for a full appreciation of the forces at work—shed much light on what to do next and then what to do after that. Business and historical analyses did not, for example, help the automobile industry adapt to changing public demands, did not help Firestone cope effectively with the attacks on its 500 line of radial tires, did not help Nestlé deal effectively with the campaign attacking its promotion of infant formula in Third World countries.

Those crucial strategic decisions can profit from a framework against which to plot the likely outcomes of issues. Issue decision-making will be enhanced by a capability of seeing how the whole course of the issues will develop, what the likely results will be at each stage and what, if any, interventions are likely to be effective or counterproductive. To be sure, instinct and experience are excellent guides. But a framework that (a) tests assumptions at each stage, (b) points out the the information necessary for accurate decision-making, (c) highlights the best mix of policy and persuasion at every point, and (d) underlines the next steps to be taken, would at once be a powerful guide to correct action and a useful tool for demonstrating to other management officers the need to make the right moves, which may seem ahead of their time and as yet unwarranted or unnecessary.

The models that will perform these tasks, drawn from marginalist school of international conflict and public choice economics, are straightforward and rest on two self-evident assumptions about issues: *first, issues concern people, usually the stakeholders in the decision, and second, the outcomes will be determined by the interactions of those stakeholders, including governments.* Analytic models of stakeholder interactions in a private sector-public sector environment will meet our basic needs if the models can tell us where we have been, where we are, and where we are going. If the models are relatively direct and easy to apply, they will have the utility required for assistance in decision-making. They will answer the basic strategic questions of when to resist, when to adjust, and when or how to combine both strategies for optimum results.

The models that follow are models of stakeholder interaction in typical issue situations. They show how each situation typically arises, how it unfolds, where the optima lie and, most important, what factors best help determine outcomes.

MODEL NO. 1: EXTERNALITY PROBLEMS

The first "interactive pattern" to be discussed is one we have already met in summary form: Externalities, which we have seen, set up the primary justification for government intervention in the marketplace. The model describes the pattern of interactions that follow the emergence of a demand or claim by the public that cannot be met in timely fashion by market forces. These issues, in other words, arise from suddenly perceived market failures. The efficient pursuit of individual welfare lowers society's welfare as so-called external costs are passed on to society, on whose behalf the government intervenes as a collector. There is no alternative to government intervention once this pattern of interactions becomes firmly established.

The key to its emergence and its unfolding is public values: changes in what the public views as acceptable. As one commentator remarked after Watergate, the shift in the 1960s to a permissive morality in private life was matched by a shift in the 1970s to a new puritanism in public life. Imperceptible changes in individual levels of tolerance can become dramatic changes in a national mood.

Virtually every business-government collision begins with a real or alleged externalities situation. A political change may bring into power a leader who articulates a long-held grievance against, say anti-union companies. New scientific knowledge may implicate a product, a business, or a whole industry. A change in scale of operations may actually cause an externality that before was too small to notice. Environmental problems, worker safety problems, even human rights problems, begin as externality type issues and follow the pattern of interactions predicted: emergence of the issue, debate over costs and benefits to discourage activity and to compensate alleged victims, resolved by government intervention and the imposition of new norms. Typical company responses follow the pattern of (a) denial that an externality problem exists; (b) drawing attention to the heavy price to be paid in the form of trade-offs for change; and then (c) grudging acceptance of government-imposed norms, often with bitterness and legacies of mistrust all around.

These responses are not equally sound, however. Denial in this context amounts to telling the public that the company knows better than they what causes harm. Yet what matters, insofar as influencing outcomes is concerned, is that the members of the public already believe themselves to have been harmed. The public may have elected a leader expressly to redress that harm. The time to influence public opinion about externals is while that opinion is forming, especially among the most powerful stakeholders in an externality issue, including government. Recall what has been said about government behavior, especially the key variables affecting public opinion: the tax price, and the costs of political participation. It is during the emergence of an externality situation that the arguments over trade-offs can be brought out. Public opinion surveys can help companies test which arguments would be most effective ("Would you still believe A if you learned B?"). Communications and the use of political action committees can lower the political participation costs of allies, such that the emergence of the mood is delayed. Most effective of all, however, is corrective action to nip the problem and win credit for enlightened management.

Once it becomes clear that the situation is established, political interest will already have been aroused and government intervention will be inevitable. Optimally, it should be at your timing rather than theirs, so go to them and work out a program in cooperation with them—influencing first "technocratic demand" and strengthening the bargaining power of officials. Change technology where practicable, otherwise begin to cut back on the offending center and show that without transition assistance, externalities will have to be passed on to the community (fewer jobs, smaller tax base, attendant dislocations), and take public positions with a view to attracting allies needed for the bargaining process that typically marks the final stages of the situation (see Model 3, bargaining).

Figure V.1 illustrates the development of an externality situation and the points of strategic decision it contains.

Phase I

0 to A Establishment of activity x as legitimate using standard PR techniques:

Phase II

A to B Emergence of an Externality situation. The issue to the Corporation is cost of adjustment. By Point B, Activity x has arguably netted the company EDCA benefits, while costing the community ABC disbenefits. A solution requiring full compensation would therefore leave the company at most OEA returns.

Note, too, that as the issue progresses, company returns = (DC x time) – costs (BC x time). That is, costs of prolonging the conflict = DC – BC (time).

If DC > BC, the net is positive, whereas if DC < BC, the net is negative. *Optimally, therefore, the more damaging the problem, the sooner it should be*

Figure V.1. Externalities Issues

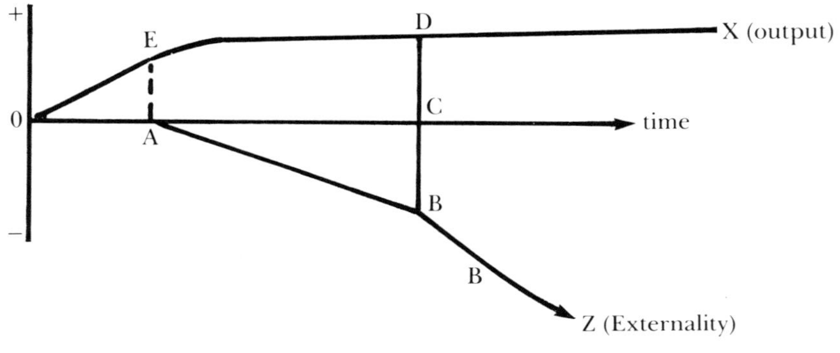

stopped. Otherwise a deadlock will arise which the company cannot possibly win, yet will be increasingly unable to end for fear of the penalty it faces.

These considerations also suggest that different types of plants and businesses will have different "best" strategies. *New Plant,* just coming on stream, still capturing rising marginal revenues, *will have to move as quickly as possible* to achieve a settlement at minimum cost. Otherwise gains will be significantly eroded by the negative effects of continued production.

Older plants, especially those producing non-differentiated industrial products whose marginal revenues are constant and which have already netted the company substantial returns above payback *may be able to afford a more resistant,* less accommodating stance.[1]

Older plants making consumer products and subject to popular action, such as boycotts or even widespread hesitation to buy, should also seek to limit damage by means of a speedy settlement. Companies, too, are subject to some of the same factors governing behavior in the public sector: if the "tax price" of clean up or continuing adverse policies (loss or additional costs to voters) begins to equal or exceed the costs of political participation, then the company can expect suddenly to be the object of political attack. Naturally, emotional factors as well as economic ones will enter into this, as will public expectations.

If stakeholders are adversely affected by company policy or even expect at some future time to be adversely affected, they will discount accordingly. As we have seen with government, not only the trade-offs between tax price, income and participation costs enter into consideration, but also the so-called "h" values, or public hostility. Heavily affecting the public's decision to protest will be the business equivalent of memory plus opposition criticism, namely good will or reputation. Companies with reputations for neglecting the public interest will thus face significantly high probabilities of encountering public protests. In the interests of achieving less expensive settlements, they should move quickly in externalities situations to reach outcomes they can live with, rather than struggle over time for abstract "best" solutions.

In such situations tactical emphasis should be on stimulating technocratic demand (i.e., working with knowledgeable officials) rather than public persuasion. *Only in the phase before the issue fully arises is public persuasion likely to play a significant role* (by delaying issue emergence). Once the issue situation emerges, the key factors for the company will be: (1) established reputation, (2) age/service of a plant or product; and (3) type of industry.

Public persuasion can play an important secondary role, however, by creating opportunities for maximum influence with government technocrats and keeping public temperatures low enough for a rational outcome to emerge. Doing otherwise could stimulate adverse expectations that would lead to consumer boycotts or other public action.

MODELS NO. 2 AND 2A: COLLECTIVE ACTION: LOBBIES AND CRITICAL MASS

If "externalities" situations demonstrate the importance of policy over persuasion, the collective action of people in lobbies and even more so in what we have called Critical Mass, demonstrates the reverse, the importance of persuasion over policy. These are models of interactions to which all champions of the power of public advocacy, including "legislative support systems" consciously or unconsciously defer. Both models describe phenomena whereby a small group of advocates or critics manage by a combination of skill and zeal to mobilize impressive support from other stakeholders in an issue. Under "lobbying," the most usual outcome is the existence of a permanent lobby, i.e., an industry group or association with which an issue is resolved in a bargaining mode (bargaining is treated separately below). Another variation is that a group of stakeholders which may hitherto have been discounted enters, as a result of their collective action, into the calculations of decision-makers. Here again, however, the issue will be settled ultimately by bargaining, albeit with the new group of stakeholders included. Our first collective action model thus describes successful grass roots lobbying.

Critical mass, on the other hand, our second model, describes an explosive variation of collective action whereby the mobilization of grass roots stakeholders achieves such striking results in such a short time that the stakeholders are able to impose their terms on a settlement precluding any bargaining beyond the adjustment of its targets to a new political reality. Although both phenomena are mentioned in political science, public affairs and historical literature, they tend to be confused with each other. Here both will be elucidated and the important distinctions made.[2]

Collective Action: Lobbying

How do powerful action groups form? Traditional theories emphasize the common interests of participants and the ideologies that bind them together. But common interests and values, while necessary, are not sufficient to explain the difference in effectiveness and longevity among such groups, for example the AFL-CIO, the American Medical Association and, more recently, the emergence of the so-called "environmental lobby." For each of these groups (or clusters of groups in the case of the environmentalists) to be successful, they had to overcome basic structural problems or barriers to effectiveness in the conduct of lobbying. Our analysis so far has provided the tools to discuss these structural problems, but we have up to now not drawn attention to them. In doing so, we will be drawing heavily upon the work of Mancur Olson, one of the brightest economists of this generation, especially his seminal work, *The Logic of Collective Action.*

Structural Problem No. 1: Motivation. Recall our rational voter or political participant. He/she would only take part in politics if the benefits at least equalled the costs of doing so. Now lobbying groups essentially are groups that pressure the government to deliver certain public goods which, as we have seen, are non-exclusive, i.e., can be enjoyed by anyone. This sets up a contradiction: if the lobby already exists, there will be little incentive for individuals to join, i.e., pay the costs involved in participation, as they will likely benefit without paying. Participation in collective action involves its own variation of the "free rider" problem.

Structural Problem No. 2: Lobby Size. Even is some way around the first problem is found, there remains a second problem, that of lobby size. Large lobbies, i.e., those that can claim some degree of representativeness of the interests for whom they are ostensibly acting, have a superior claim to legitimacy and may even be more effective in generating supplies of public goods than smaller, less representative ones. But this also involves a contradiction, for the larger the group, the smaller will likely be the share of benefits enjoyed by individual members. Yet clearly the fraction of the group gains enjoyed by the individual members must exceed the participation costs to the individual member to make participation worthwhile. Can any lobby of significant size meet this test?

Still, like bumblebees who persist in flying despite the laws of aerodynamics, large powerful lobbies exist heedless of the laws of economic analysis. How are they able to do this? There are three practical answers, all of which can, but need not, occur simultaneously.

First, there is a limit to the number of issues around which a permanent lobby can be organized. The stakes must be such as to enable the effort to be justified. They must be tangible, and realistic enough to permit short-term discounting by members who will make the sacrifices needed to obtain the future benefits. This is obviously going to be easier if members already enjoy a benefit and are threatened with losing it through government action than it will be to organize a group to get something new. *Threatened loss of private benefits* therefore provides an obvious way of solving both the free rider and size problems. Consequently, many lobbies and associations are defensive of the status quo and are suspicious of innovation, even if that innovation could be counted on to provide uniform benefits to all association members.

Second, large permanent lobbies must have professional staff and a permanent controlling board who manages activities on behalf of the membership. *There is very little, if any, spontaneous group action*, again because of Problems 1 and 2.

Third, lobbies must (1) provide other private benefits to members to make up the shortfall between group benefits and participation costs. These benefits typically include major economic advantages, such as malpractice insurance for AMA members or collective bargaining for union members, or other professional or social advantages of membership, for example, employment clearinghouses, professional journals, annual meetings, etc.

Or, (2) *lobbies must resort to coercion to induce solidarity*, through such measures, for example, as the closed shop, withdrawal of professional support, subtle business pressures, and the capability of causing serious losses of money and/or professional or community standing.

Generally speaking, therefore, lobby activity will be the reverse of spontaneous, aimed at protecting existing benefits, and able to control members' responses. From the standpoint of managing issues, these kinds of lobbies are bargaining agents for members, will command significant permanent support on issues of concern to members, and will likely dominate the flow of information to members.

What about comparatively disorganized interests who respond suddenly to attack? Examples are campaigns orchestrated by public relations agencies on behalf of special interests who face short-term specific threats either because of a conjuncture of economic circumstances or a piece of perverse legislation (e.g., "hide action" and "softdrink bottlers" cases, below). The stakes of the possible loss temporarily solves the participation and size problems, and coordination is provided by consultants and perhaps the larger corporate actors in the association. Over time, as the central association disseminates more and more information about the issue and takes steps to lower participation costs, the strength of the lobby will grow. If so, it will occur in a gradually rising straight line (according to theory of the rational voter calculation, $R = pb + c - d$) that eventually peaks as the limit of the susceptible population is reached. This reflects the increasing expected value of members' participation as industry awareness expands and the private costs of participation are systematically lowered by experienced organizers. Plotted against time, lobby participants on an issue, therefore resembles Figure V.2 on p. 83.

Since the motivation driving the increase is the expected costs of public policy, one should expect to see elected representatives one by one press the government to reduce these costs to zero as the lobbying effort brings

Figure V.2. Lobby Participation

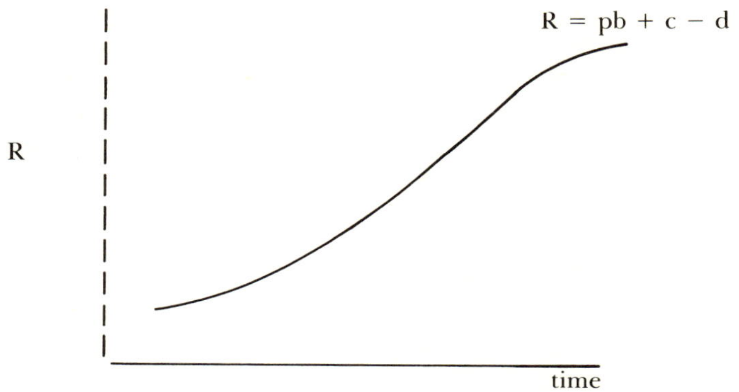

N_p equal or below N_r in legislators' constituencies. A rational legislator hates to lose one vote unless by doing so he can win one, or better, two. If the tax price (Q) of a measure can be reduced on one group without passing a cost onto another group equal to or exceeding its participation costs (P), that legislator is apt to favor the reduction of Q, other things being equal. Gradually, therefore, an effort of this sort can turn government policy around. But the organizers will have to solve the two structural problems mentioned earlier to create a truly permanent lobby. Unless the group or industry has been so frightened by the government that they judge a permanent lobby to be worthwhile insurance, the likelihood of a strong new lobby emerging is small.

The collective action model we have been studying therefore works within the political status quo. In terms of our equation governing the demand for public goods, f(Q,I,P), lobbies strive to minimize Q and P for members, while maximizing I. To the extent they can achieve this and at the same time reserve the gains in I exclusively to their members, they will grow fat in numbers and years.

However, there is a disturbing riposte that can occur to upset the political status quo, a form of group action that is much more difficult to predict or contain—"Critical Mass."

Critical Mass

Critical Mass is the reverse of the planned, permanent lobby. It is a wild brushfire of outrage that suddenly springs up to engulf corporate or government policies. So great is its effect that critical mass can:

- raise a local issue suddenly to national importance;
- force government and other key opinion leaders into the fray (against you);
- stop whole industries in their tracks and put individual companies out of business by directing a hurricane of hatred at them specifically.

Instead of simply a new bargaining configuration, the result of critical mass is often the imposition of a brand new political reality in place of the status quo.

Critical mass thus describes an explosion of public wrath, usually fanned by a smaller group of critics or political entrepreneurs. The link between the critics and their supporters is usually not the details of the grievance itself. More often it is a sense of injustice or bitter grievance against an institution or company, policy or practice. The grievance can be one of long standing, and may not be related specifically to the particular issue, except that the issue provides a long awaited opportunity to "get 'em at last." Critics fan the existing sense of grievance by showing that change is possible if enough people join in. As a graph plotted against time, critical mass looks like this:

Figure V.3. Critical Mass

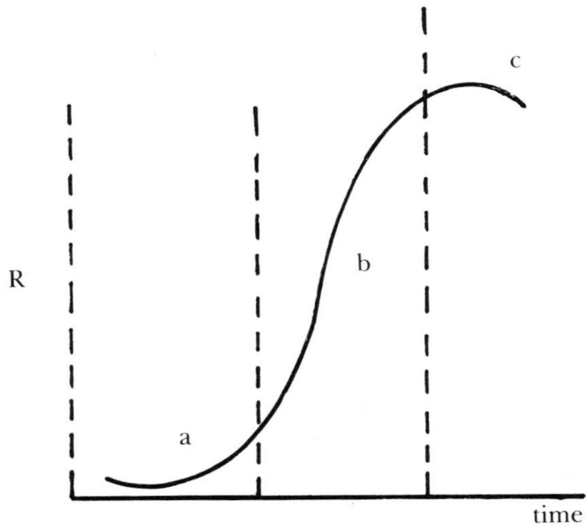

Note that in the diagram we have broken the critical mass into three phases: first, "a," in which the mass is building and which may be undetected, second, "b," in which the explosion occurs, and third, "c," when participation levels off, eventually to fall away.

As in the lobbying discussion above, the dynamics of participation can be explained by our rational voter calculation, in which the expected effect on outcomes plus the private benefits of participation induces people to pay the costs of participation.

The explosion in the "b" phase is caused by the exponential diffusion of awareness: (1) of outrage; (2) that the outrage is shared by great numbers; and (3) that personal participation can, through upholding solidarity, contribute to the long-wished-for effect. We can capture the effect of critical mass mathematically by rewriting our rational voter equation in integrated form, and adding (or making explicit) the effect of group interaction through persuasion:

$$R = \int_{t_1}^{t_2} pb^e + [c - d] \cdot dt$$

where the index "e" represents a conversion or persuasion factor, i.e., the number of others a new participant himself converts.

In words: Participation varies between t_1 and t_2 by the probability of personal influence raised to the power of the number of people persuaded on the issue by each new convert.

The effect of powerful mass media such as television is also discernible here. The critic reaches millions of viewers on the news, either through an interview or a demonstration designed to evoke sympathy. This in turn causes viewers of the program (1) to realize there are others who feel as they do and, prepared to take action on those feelings, (2) to tell others about what they have seen, who in turn react the same way. Result: an avalanche of public opprobrium falls upon the target.

Differentiating the equation above, we can capture the explosiveness of the rise in participation:

$$\frac{dR}{dt} = ep.b.^{e-1}$$

If a million viewers each put the case to two non-viewers, who discount the story by 50 percent, the result will still be an instantaneous doubling of support.

The type of diffusion we are discussing is word of mouth combined with constant source, about which there is considerable empirical research. Physicians adopt a new drug exponentially faster when word of mouth augments other linear (i.e., constant source) forms of propagation.[3] Computer studies comparing interpersonal diffusion with constant source diffusion in groups of small finite size show logistic shaped curves for both, but those curves are steepest of all—nearly vertical—with respect to time when interpersonal contacts are combined with constant source diffusion, the case most often encountered in these kinds of controversial public affairs issues.[4]

As explained in the section on governments, note the resemblance of our participation equation when written in integrated form with the "h" or hostility equation in the section on government:

$$h = \int_{t1}^{t2} pt\,(ct)\,[r(c)t - r(p)t]\,dt.$$

The chain of reasoning is the same in both, i.e.:

- hostile public memory (pt)
- fanned by critics (ct)
- both of which are affected by the evident difference between public values and those of the offending institution (r(c)t-r(p)t)

Our rational voter calculation ($R = pb + c\text{-}d$) lumps together hostile feelings and the effect of critics into the calculation of benefits from public policy (b), which in turn affects the community political discount rate.

The turning points or inflections in the critical mass diagram are now easily accounted for. In the "a" phase, hostility builds as individual stakeholders pile up grudges against the institution or company. In the "b" phase, an incident or demonstration unleashes that hostility. The hostility builds participation until either (1) the limits of the susceptible population have been reached, or (2) sufficient punishment has been absorbed by the offending organization that potential participants judge there is nothing for them to contribute, so R levels off and declines.

The explosively increased political participation raises demand for government output by (1) raising the "h" values in the government model for existing policy, and (2) showing the willingness of a possibly decisive number of voters to pay a higher tax price for stronger programs. When sufficiently powerful to affect the chances of reelection, critical mass also alters the relationship between N_p and N_r in favor of political action. It thus strengthens the politician at the expense of the bureaucrat; (3) it also in this way narrows the acceptable differences between the political discount rate and the community rate. For these reasons, the mass will "snowball," picking up support dramatically as its momentum induces more and more politicians to make the same calculations.

"Iron Triangles"

Another way of explaining the effect of critical mass on political decision making is in terms of "sub-governments" and sets of constituents. Normally, departments and regulatory agencies achieve an equilibrium balance among business, government and industry, with policies reflecting the relative political power of politicians, the industry, and its defenders and its users. Over time, these "iron triangles" allegedly become virtual "sub-governments" concerned with modification of detailed regulation within broadly accepted principles.[5] The effect of critical mass on these arrangements is (a) vastly to enlarge the power of one constituency over another, (b) thereby to expand the set of acceptable solutions over the hitherto dominant equilibrium set, and (c) thus often to force a permanent transformation on the sub-government relationship.

Critical mass achieves this effect by changing the pattern of political rewards derived under the pre-mass status quo from the permanent clientele.[6] One of the main pillars of resistance to critical mass is therefore the strength of established clientele relations. A key question is how sensitive is the relationship to override by (a) single issue concerns and (b) overlapping or competing jurisdictions—government committees and departments, or within a federal structure, between levels of government.

In a Parliamentary government, a critical mass that affects a possible decisive segment of the vote can dramatically override established department-clientele relationships unless the grass roots power and reputation of that clientele is politically more impressive and continuous than the critical mass. Under the American system of legislative committees, critical mass or even the less dramatic straight-line shifts in public opinion can circumvent or bypass established committee-agency-clientele relationships.

The effect of critical mass on "cozy" arrangements between legislators, bureaucrats and clientele can be illustrated as follows. Consider either of these situations: in a parliamentary system, a bill adjusting a regulation on, say, pollution control, is in committee. Or in a U.S. system, an oversight committee considering an agency proposal to ease pollution regulations on a particular industry. In either case, the cluster of opinions held by politicians, technocrats, and industry falls within a space considered acceptable by industry. In the diagram below, dots represent the ideal solution of each group; circles represent the areas of acceptable solution. The point of intersection X_o is the most likely outcome.

Suppose that, suddenly, after say a bad chemical spill in an urban area, public opinion becomes aroused and focuses on the bill or proposed

Figure V.4. Critical Mass and Iron Triangles

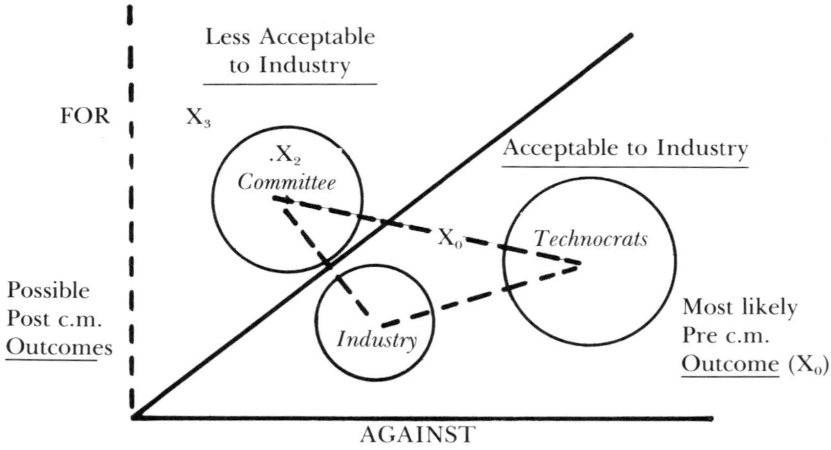

regulatory changes. For the first time, ordinary people feel threatened by those who draw up the regulations and want stricter controls no matter what the experts say. Long-time critics of the industry sense the new public mood and successfully canalize it into the legislature, arousing members/congressional leaders who have not been touched by the issue before. In Parliament, members of the governing party use caucus to bring pressure upon the minister and committee members to toughen the bill beyond the range of options it presently contains. In Congress, representatives or senators whose responsibilities overlap the jurisdiction of the committee threaten to hold hearings. *Result: either the committee outcomes shift above the line (in the diagram) or a new arena emerges which produces outcomes responsive to a different clientele-technocrat relationship.*

Company defensive strategies after the "a" phase of critical mass should therefore seek to strengthen any clientele relationships, ensure third party validation of any company claims, seek to reduce public perceptions of injustice, and to ensure political rivals have a thorough understanding of the company and its needs. As an offensive strategy, supporters of critical mass should aim at circumventing established alliances, dispensing rewards so at to bring down considerable distrust upon the status quo and strive to encourage government members and bureaucrats to take on "special interests." Key to the outcomes are the strength of the client-committee relationships vs. the ability of alternative power centers to capitalize on single issue pressure.

Analytical Treatment

The effect of successful critical mass on the governmental process can be set out analytically using the notation of set theory.

Before critical mass the cozy relationship can be represented by game Gm where S(x), the set of conditions favored by the in-group, predominates.

$$\text{Thus, } W(x) \cap S(x) = \emptyset \qquad (1)$$

In words, the x-beating set of solutions (Wx) is excluded from the favored set of solutions (Sx).

At the same time, the value of the game to the "in-crowd" is greater than to the larger number of people who would make up the set dominating S(x). In symbols:

$$V(s) > V(wx) \text{ and } \sum_{i \epsilon s} {}_{xi} > \sum_{i \epsilon - s} {}_{xi} \qquad (2)$$

Critical mass changes these relationships. Suddenly the set of x-beating alternatives becomes included in the government process, i.e., $W(x) \cap S(x) \neq 0$

Moreover, the "value" to those favoring the W(x) options now exceeds the value to those favoring the status quo set:

$$\sum_{i \epsilon - s} {}_{xi} > \sum_{i \epsilon s} {}_{xi}$$

Call these new relationships game Gn. It is clear that the outcomes of games Gn dominate (i.e., outweigh, are superior to) those of Gm. Moreover, the two games Gm and Gn stand in "zero sum" relation to each other:

$$V\,(Gm) + V(Gn) = 0$$

i.e., a victory for one is a corresponding defeat for the other.

The critical mass explosion has created the conditions of its own success by making it politically attractive to form a new coalition and impose a new set of solutions. Depending upon circumstances, the change could be permanent. In terms of our government model, the sudden increase of supporters changes the public opinion variables of the equations developed above, to generate a new payoff to individuals belonging to the set dominating the status quo:

$$\Delta R \rightarrow h\ f(Q,I,P) \rightarrow \overline{Wx_i{}^*}$$

In words, a change in R or participation generates a change in the demands for policy and the rate at which demand is discounted, which in turn creates a coalition of individuals prepared to defeat the status quo.

Guide to Symbols

$\cap$ = belongs to; Ø denotes a "null" or empty set; Σ = sum of; $i \epsilon s$ = individuals belonging to s; $i \epsilon - s$ = individuals belonging to the non-s set. For a brief treatment, see Mathematical Symbols Appendix below. For more comprehensive discussions, see Nigel Howard, *Paradoxes of Rationality: Theory of Metagames and Political Behavior*, 1971, MIT, or Anatol Rapoport, *N-Person Game Theory, Concepts and Applications*, 1970, University of Michigan, especially the introduction.

The transformations caused by critical mass can occur during an externality situation. They can also occur at any time to upset a continuing bargaining relationship. Indeed, the latter effect is far more common because most business-government issue questions are bargaining relationships.

Summary: Collective Action Strategies

Lobbying. The key to an analytical understanding of lobbying is the rational voter or political participant equation, R = p.b. + c − d. Successful lobbying requires organizers to overcome barriers to participation and attainment of representative size. Existing permanent lobbies appear to have overcome these barriers by (l) limiting concerns to issues in which the stakes are of sufficient size that benefits to members can approximate the costs of participation; in practice, this is more likely to mean protecting members against the loss of known and valuable privileges; and (2) providing significant side benefits in terms of professional, social and other advantages to that p.b > c-d. Remembering the demand function for public policy, f (Q,I,P), lobbies generally dominate information to members and can persuade elected representatives to support their positions in so far as Q approaches 0 for lobby members while not rising to or above P for non-lobby members. Depending on the issue, lobbies can be useful allies or extremely vulnerable.

Critical Mass. Where lobbies generally work within the status quo, albeit altering the allocation of resources and configuration of bargaining relationships among stakeholders, critical mass describes a hurricane of wrathful unpredictability that aims at overturning the status quo and establishing a new political reality. Again the rational voter model explains the dynamic of this type of collective action in which outrage combined with highly efficient information diffusion provide the driving forces. Optimal strategies involve (a) polling for the build up of silent resentment during the "a" phase, and if detected, then removing the grievance if possible, otherwise (b) seeking to change public attitudes before they reach the next stage.

Stage "b": earlier efforts having failed, you now face an outpouring of public hostility designed to add to the regulations currently dogging your business. So powerful is the indignation publicly expressed that every major political figure of the day has come out (a) to appeal for calm, and (b) to call for speedy fair trial of any accused. The best strategy is to seek to contain that outrage as fast as possible, or else canalize it onto different targets. Limit damage by presenting your case quietly to senior opinion leaders who remain uncommitted.

Stage "c": The conflict moves onto a more rational theatre, such as a court room or legislative committee room. At this point, those still ready to join a movement against your company are dissuaded by (a) the harm the company has already suffered, and (b) the diminishing need for public solidarity against company policies now that the issue is being investigated. The best strategy in the "c" phase is to tactfully draw attention to company activities designed to eliminate the hateful practice.

Bargaining is a process relatively well-understood by social scientists and managers alike. A small library could be built of books and monographs devoted to explaining how bargains are struck. The models in the next section are intended to distill from some of the available literature[7] points of practical interest to businessmen concerned with understanding how political bargaining works.

MODEL NO. 3: BARGAINING

Critical mass, it will have been evident from the last section, actually imposes new "community" optima after old ones are exploded. It does this by changing the rules of the road and creating new incentives so that, in effect, the public interest is redefined in such a way that it coincides with the political interests of new and more powerful groupings.

But only a few issues lend themselves to resolution by such means. Moreover, critical mass is a relatively blunt instrument for achieving relatively inexpensive settlements of comparatively technical questions. These latter questions are usually solved by bargaining.

In the real issues world, the main bargaining problem is how to protect legitimate interests with minimum damage to purse and reputation. Typical bargaining situations impinging on the public sector (so as to create public issues) include plant sitings, some acquisitions and some divestments, plus confrontation with public authorities.

As well, bargaining typically concludes situations that begin as externalities or critical mass.

The purpose of this section, then, will be to develop an analytical approach to the bargaining process that will help distinguish potentially beneficial situations from harmful ones, provide a guide to strategy pinpointing the way to quickest solutions and finally, shed some more light on the general issues problems of transforming private interests into public interest by consent.

To do this, some recourse will be had to game theory, analytical techniques developed by mathematicians, economists and other social scientists that relate strategies of individuals and groups to outcomes. Although extremely weak as a predictor of behavior, game theory is strong in the capability it provides for analyzing the logic of relationships between or among "players." This logic is fundamental in understanding the opportunities, threats, and traps intrinsic to particular bargaining situations.

Let us begin by looking at normal business bargaining deals between buyers and sellers, based on a straightforward "contract line," as displayed in an Edgeworth Box. (For a description of the Edgeworth Box, see page 22.)

Figure V.5. The Edgeworth Box

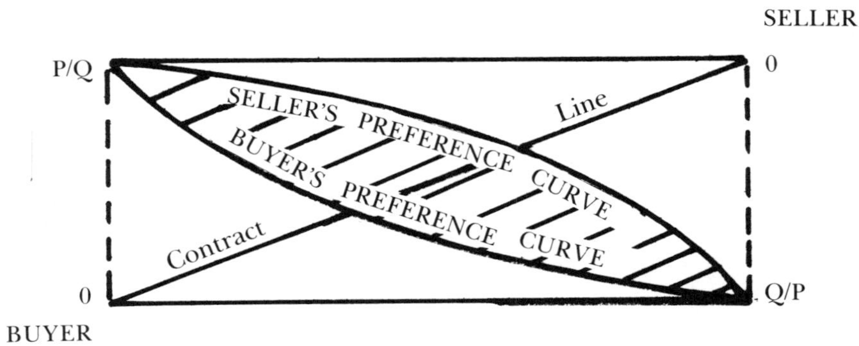

SIMULATION: Prisoner's Dilemma

Runthrough No. 1

Assume you are part of a two company foreign population in a small, Central American country in which a revolutionary tribunal has just taken over.

They have arrested you both and are holding each of you in isolation. You have no "rights," and there is no communication with anyone except the Revolutionary Prosecutor.

The Prosecutor offers you the following deal: *confess immediately*. You will be repatriated, no questions asked, and your company will be treated as though there had been little change in the regime. Moreover, the other prisoner will get 20 years in the camps and his company will be taken over.

Don't delay. If you both confess, there will be a show trial. You will get 10 years hard labor in the Jungle Gulag. Both companies will be nationalized.

If no one confesses, you will each get two years hard labor in the camps.

What is your response? Confess or not?

Runthrough No. 2

Same as above—except with an expanded foreign community. Instead of two CEO prisoners, there are now 21 CEOs under separate lock and key.

The Prosecutor offers the same escape for an immediate confession, and the same penalties for the other possibilities.

What do you do? Confess or not?

Runthrough No. 3

Proceed as in Runthrough No. 2, but with a changed ranking of outcomes. No confessions, all get off; one confession, the confessor gets off, then the others go to jail for the second-heaviest term. Otherwise the same. What results do you get?

In runthrough No. 1 and 2, from the prisoner's point of view, *win* means acting selfishly, while the other prisoner(s) act altruistically.

The *second best* outcome—total silence—results if both act *altruistically*, i.e., both resist.

The *second worst* outcome—if both confess—results if both act selfishly.

The *worst* outcome results from the reverse of win: you resist while the other confesses.

Ranking these:

Set Free	4	(i.e., I confess, the other(s) resist)
Light Term	3	(i.e., we both (all) resist)
Heavier Term	2	(i.e., we both confess)
Heaviest	1	(i.e., I resist, the other(s) confess(es))

As a matrix:

	Resist	Confess
Resist	3,3	1,4
Confess	4,1	2,2

As before, fear of the worst leads to the second worst. In a practical test, *resistance* (and thus light terms) is virtually universal under the conditions of Runthrough No. 1. There are only two players, and thus high confidence that resistance will be mutual. *(Nb. reputation is part of the logic of expectations!)*

Under conditions of Runthrough No. 2, *confession* is the option usually chosen. Because there are so many other players, the high confidence that *all* can be relied upon is missing. The second worst outcome is the usual result. Yet the same players conduct both runthroughs.

In Runthrough No. 3, the community outcomes outweigh even individual best outcomes. This produces a revised matrix.

The Revised Matrix

	Resist	Confess
Resist	4,4	2,3
Confess	3,2	1,1

Resistance, the best group strategy, is also the best individual strategy, and will almost always be preferred in actual play.

This exercise has some useful implications for issues management, based on the importance of *Expectations.*

First, companies with good responsibility records will, over time, find it easier to make their deals. Companies that win a reputation for "bottom line" narrowness can expect a tougher—and thus more expensive—time trying to achieve the same outcomes.

Second, a company (or industry) of which the public is probably suspicious *will make news* by anomalously trying to achieve second best. This will remind the public of that bad reputation. (Example: An oil giant's ad highlighting government findings that oil companies did not "rig" scarcities.)

A *sustained* turnaround will win high marks if sufficient to relieve the public's bad expectations. (Example: Firestone's comeback under new management.)

Third, therefore: Half measures are not enough. Contrary to the general belief that fairness is the mid-point between extremes, there must, on the contrary, be *convincing proof of commitment to the new course.*

Note that in the first two runthroughs, private interests outweighed group interest, but where the risk of betrayal is small (Runthrough No. 1), many will choose to take it. In Runthrough

No. 2, however, where the risk of betrayal is larger, the number of confessors is usually much greater. In Runthrough No. 3, the community outcome is as good or better than the individual outcomes, but achieving it is still riskier than in the first runthrough. Nevertheless, even with no communication among individuals, many groups will consider the risk worth taking.

These exercises underline the importance of the risk/reward relationship and, in that connection, the importance of information. For if the individuals were allowed to communicate with each other, formal collusion would be possible and the risk of betrayal minimized (with bluff and deceit matched by threats of revenge). In each case, allowing communication enhances the probability of the community optimum being chosen. This conclusion points to the value of extensive precautions to generate widespread public awareness and understanding.

Note that under business circumstances, several conditions have to exist or there will be no deal. First, if agreements are to be struck between buyer and seller, each must be better off as a result, or there will be no movement from the status quo. Second, the "utility units" for each participant are transferable: money. This makes adjustment easier. Third, the "game" ends when the bargain is struck: it is usually non-recursive. How much buyer and seller move is therefore a question of company "utilities" or "satisfactions." The point at which the deal is struck will be at the maximum combined utility for both players, within the shared ellipse in the diagram.

Business competitive relationships bear greater resemblance to business-political negotiations than does normal deal-making, in that competitive relationships are (1) non-Pareto-optimal, i.e., they can involve loss to the loser relative to the status quo; (2) recursive, i.e., can involve several replays before ending; (3) it is a condition of the game that information be kept imperfect, that is neither side can know for sure what the other is doing.

But business-government relations have additional properties that distinguish its process from that of a strictly competitive mode. (1) Utility is not necessarily transferable (each side can be playing for differently measured goals; their value systems are different), and (2) the process is studded with traps and pitfalls, with (3) the closely related danger of perverse outcomes. These damaging surprises are avoidable through careful analysis, requiring different conceptual tools than the simple box analysis.

There are three stages of development in business-government bargaining:

Stage 1. Statement of Terms. Each will try to get his own position on the table in the most advantageous way, forcing the disclosure of fall-backs and hidden agendas of the other, while demonstrating capacities to reward and punish.

Stage 2. The Search for Allies. If a stalemate results from Stage 1, contenders will move laterally, looking for support for themselves and denying it to the other side.

Stage 3. Resolution. The one with the most support now "forces" his preferred outcome on the other—or as much of it as he can. Success depends on how persuasive players have been in altering the preferences and/or expectations of each other and the strength of allies attracted.

Given the importance of allies and expectations in the process, some generalizations are possible. *Reputation*—a reputation for fair dealing will speed up adjustments and reduce transaction cost. *Attractiveness to Allies*—as allies can be crucial to success, it is clearly helpful to be at least as attractive to allies as one's own adversary. Critical mass can in this connection be viewed as a special case of alliance building.

Time is also an ally, if time pressure can be exerted on one's adversary. Perishables, for instance, are discounted over time and politicians become friendlier as elections approach.

Knowledge is an ally. Greater knowledge of your adversary than he has of you can also cut transaction costs and reduce possibilities of bluff and entrapment.

Strategic Breakdown

In bargaining situations with political or governmental or public opinion implications, there are special problems involved in utilizing one's resources to win favorable outcomes. Strengths can be transformed into weaknesses by a clever opponent. Apparently reasonable approaches can generate unreasonable results. Traps and pitfalls abound to confound rational, straightforward and direct bargaining approaches. "Utility maximization," for both sides, the usual result in good business between buyers and sellers of approximately equal power and skill, is unusual in the world of business-government questions. And where net gains for both do happen, it is usually the result of careful planning.

Understanding paradoxical outcomes and how to avoid them (or use them) can best be attained by looking at what some analysts[8] call "breakdowns in rationality," but as will be clear, are actual breakdowns for which strategy can have no useful answer.

Prisoner's Dilemma

Indeed, we have already discussed one such pattern, known as Prisoner's Dilemma (see Simulation). The model, a metaphor for unproductive conflict, describes the case of prisoners who are mutually dependent for survival, but forced by prison authorities into a competitive relationship. It has wide applications, from nuclear stalemate (international cooperation crippled by nuclear weapons competition) to labor relations, company vs. regulatory agency situations, etc. Virtually any situation in which fear of the worst outcome leads inevitably to the second worst outcome can be analyzed by a prisoner's dilemma matrix. In the diagram below, players A and B want to win, but will compromise to be fair. However, attempting to force either player to accept defeat will generate deadlock. Scoring preferences in terms of satisfaction, we get, of the four gross alternatives: Win 4, Compromise 3, Deadlock 2, Lose 1.

This pattern of interactions is characterized as "rationality breakdown" because the utility product that emerges (deadlock) is less than the maximum.

Note that according to theory, both players move simultaneously, in ignorance of each other's true strategies, like children playing "rock breaks scissors." The aim of this artificial condition is to establish that each player moves in ignorance of his opponent's strategic choices. In practice, business-government games involve sequential play, with each player, as in a duel, firing when he feels he has the best chance of winning. Governments thus usually "fire" or move first in questions of public policy, but are forced into a reactive mode when business decisions with issues implications become known. What matters for our analysis is the resultant outcome, irrespective of who moves first; we do not stress the point of simultaneous play, and in one or two examples actually abandon it, with no utility loss to the model, as the discussion of prisoner's dilemma shows. There is a simple mathematical technique of working out the best individual strategies. Take the column maximum for each player; take the row minimum (see diagram below). See, for each player, what strategies produce which. Clearly, for A, a hard strategy can win 4, and will guarantee a minimum score of 2. "Soft" strategies, on the other hand, promise a maximum of 3 and a minimum of 1 (defeat).

Note, too, the values are the same for both players so that there is a single minimum/maximum value (i.e., the highest of the "low" scores attainable) available for each player, namely 2—the product of a "least

Figure V.6. Prisoner's Dilemma

		Player B		
		C	D	Row Min.
Player A	C	3,3	1,4	1,3
	D	4,1	2,2	2,1
Col. Max.		4,3	2,4	

To find best strategies:
1. take col. max.
2. take row min.
3. see what strategies (a) risk least, (b) promise most.

risk," *hard* strategy. Since this is true for both players, it is an equilibrium point, where both minimum utilities intersect. It is the best minimum value of this pattern of interaction, and so the strategy designed to achieve it is called "maximin."

Two properties of the prisoner's dilemma pattern are of interest: The game has an equilibrium point (2); and the point is guaranteed to emerge if both players choose a single (i.e., pure) strategy, in this case "hard," and stick to it.

Yet by following the rationally correct strategy, the product of effort that results is "sub-optimal." Equilibrium is achieved at Deadlock, not Compromise. The combined value of the payoffs is 4 instead of 9. This is a paradox with many implications for political and other social scientists.[9]

But has it any practical implications for businessmen engaged in bargaining with regulatory agencies, government departments, labor unions or other contexts with political impacts or implications?

The answer is *yes*: (1) it explains why good compromises based on well-informed understanding are often unattainable without further strategic elaboration; (2) it demonstrates a potentially useful pattern for situations in which deadlock is truly an acceptable alternative (albeit not a "best") to gain time for new conditions to emerge that might make compromise possible.[10]

In short, a good strategic planner will put this pattern in his tool kit as (a) a warning, to avoid wherever possible, and (b) to use whenever necessary.

Avoidance and Usage

Here's how "game theorists" have "solved" prisoner's dilemma (i.e., explained why it doesn't happen more often). The key idea is that, over time, equal adversaries will demonstrate their ability to demand "fair" play and "punish" deception. Thus, an "undominated" equilibrium will emerge from "extensive" play, i.e., in a game lasting more than one move. Let us examine the thinking behind this by diagramming that extensive play.

Figure V.7. P/D Extensive Play

A \ B	C	D	Tit/Tat	Tat/Tit
C	3,3	1,4	3,3	1,4
D	4,1	2,2	2,2	4,1

Note that the "tit for tat" strategy generates an equilibrium that is better (i.e., dominates) any other alternative. Thus, for mathematicians, the paradox is solved, and there is a rational outcome after all. For those who might try to apply these results, however, there remain the same gaps as before: why shouldn't Player B "signal" a tit-for-tat strategy, then play "tat for tit" and win? In other words, extending the game supplies a theoretical solution that leaves out of consideration the details of actual play. The argument is often made that it is possible to preclude any other strategy than "tit for tat" by being sufficiently powerful to exact a price for deceitful play. But in practice, that argument must fail, since (a) the game will change if one side becomes powerful enough to "bully" the other, and (b) in the absence of such a lopsided configuration, the deception and victory may put an end to counter-threat (though victory). To avoid this result, instead of choosing compromise, both sides will compete in building strength while remaining in a deadlock position (such, arguably, has been the history of superpower nuclear weapons relations since 1952).

From a practical standpoint, then, prisoner's dilemma has no surefire solution. Instead, it should be regarded as a pattern of interaction, the establishment of which is in the interest of a player who prefers deadlock if he cannot compromise (e.g., the imposition of a new and painful regulation)[12]—assuming the relationship CAN be established.

For the player who would really like a solution and doesn't mind a good compromise, the answer to prisoner's dilemma is more difficult. He must, as Sun Tzu advised warriors of China a millenium ago, attack his opponent's strategy, i.e., so orchestrate matters that prisoner's dilemma becomes an impossible strategy to employ.

To avoid prisoner's dilemma, the executives in charge should structure the bargaining relationship so that (1) onus for deadlock would fall ineluctably and inescapably on the opponent; (2) alternatives to compromise (victory, deadlock, capitulation) are nearly impossible, and (3) there is time for the desired solution to emerge.

How to achieve this? Through long-range anticipation of issues and early attainment of a leadership position as the gold standard on the issue (e.g., IBM on privacy and storage of personal information). These are low-risk ways of avoiding prisoner's dilemma altogether. To be absolutely certain, however, one must do more: win support of public opinion such that a major reallocation of political rewards would be required before government could pursue deadlock over a reasonable compromise.

Strategic Breakdown No. 2

A second strategic or rational breakdown occurs in games in which there is no stable equilibrium point. Consider, for example, the case of foreign investment in a country determined to use public policy to capture the maximum benefit for the host country. Essentially, such policies create zero sum situations,[13] in which the harsher the policy, the weaker the investment, while the more lenient the policy, the greater the investment (but with leakages of benefits to home or third countries). This can be displayed as a diagram showing three combinations of two possibilities, worth 1 and 2 points respectively, and a fourth in which both sides lose (from reduced tax on reduced investment).

In the situation depicted in this diagram, there is no stable resting place. For no matter what cell or quadrant is considered, one player or the other will always believe he can improve his outcome by using his other strategy. In the fourth, i.e., bottom right, cell, both players believe a change in strategy will improve their side's results.

Figure V.8. Non-Equilibrium Game

		TAX	
		Up	Down
INVESTMENT	Up	1,2	2,1
	Down	2,1	0,0

In this type of situation, no single strategy can produce a durable settlement. Instead, policy and arguments chase each other from one extreme to another.

Again, mathematicians have an answer: each player should apply strategies in proportion to their probabilities of success. That is, apply strong solutions when they will win, i.e., when the adversary applies a compromise strategy, and vice versa.

In our example, each strategy has an equal chance of a productive outcome. Therefore, a random choice of one or the other (as opposed to "rational" and therefore predictable choice) will maximize each player's chances of winning. Translated into practical language: toss a coin.

Crucial decisions may sometimes actually be taken this way. Percy Schramm, for instance, tells us Hitler occasionally made decisions by tossing a coin (without, however, telling us which decisions).[14] However, this is clearly unsatisfactory for an elaborate, purposive, profit sensitive organization such as a modern business corporation.

A typical business response is to cut back on investment and insist on greater predictability of government policy as a precondition of reinvestment. Yet some gains are better than no gains, so governments believe that as long as their tax is no more harsh to profits than taxes in other jurisdictions, then investment will flow again. Only if companies can, through investment cutbacks, exert an effect on political benefits such that government is forced to change its approach, will this relationship be changed. That is extremely difficult to achieve in practice and in any case is fraught with ethical issues (should property, which is non-elected, dictate policy to elected representatives?). Very often governments will attempt to retaliate in response to shrinking revenues by tightening the tax screw, accompanied by much anti-big business rhetoric. And, as with much propaganda, the anti-big business stereotype thus created survives long afterwards to haunt business-government relationships.

This pattern of relations can arise on a smaller, more microscale. Consider, for example, the trading of charges and countercharges between consumers or environmentalists and manufacturers of long-used chemicals whose toxicology is too poorly understood for scientists to provide unequivocal guidance (e.g., saccharine, caffeine, some agricultural chemicals). Reasonable, unemotional criticism is effective but relatively unnoticed; loud, more emotional and less reasonable criticism attracts attention, but its effectiveness is undercut by the vociferousness of the attack.

The solution, usually acceptable to both sides, is to construct an impartial process for weighing all factors related to environmental issues and provide guidance to policy-makers. The process could involve an autonomous regulatory agency, as in the United States, or an ad hoc advisory committee as is a usual mechanism in Canada. If successful, the institutionalization of a process ends the unproductive cycle by (1) supplying a set of rules for settling disputes, and (2) supplying third party validation to whatever outcome is decided. But if the agency itself loses public credibility, this very important aspect can become critically weakened and the effectiveness of the institutionalization undermined.

Ending the cyclicity on the larger issue of tax and foreign investment is substantially more difficult. Policy can be made to vary with the business cycle, regulating more when investment pressure is high and relaxing when it is weak. The funding and establishment of economic institutes by one or the other of the contending parties can mediate government policy (e.g., change the political discount rate attached to the policy). Opposition parties can do the same. If the pro-international business constituency in the country is strong enough, it can erode the gains to the government once the costs of its policy can be felt.

Using the Pattern

Guidelines for business for this pattern include: (a) *Anticipation*, to avoid or discount; (b) *Positioning*, with creation of powerful constituencies and third party criticism to moderate cyclicity; (c) *Process*, of organized business-government consultations, even indicative planning, to create regulations and stability.

On the other hand, when deflection of decision would be useful, the cyclical pattern can be used. For low intensity conflict, in situations where time may provide the optimum resolution (e.g., when a new product or policy is about to come on stream that will eliminate a conflict), this pattern may, like prisoner's dilemma, provide a useful delaying strategy. An advantage is that the pattern itself takes time—usually several cycles—to detect.

Strategic Breakdown No. 3

A third strategic or rational breakdown occurs in the development of potentially self-destructive strategies. These can be grouped into a family of interactions related to "chicken," in which the potential for self-destruction inherent in "deadlock" acts as an inducement to compromise. The interaction diagram for Chicken looks like this.

Figure V.9. Chicken

Chicken

		Player B	
		C	D
Player A	C	3,3	2,4
	D	4,2	1,1

According to the pattern of play, a "hard" strategy (D) *can* generate a maximum gain of 4, but risks the minimum payoff of 1 (i.e., defeat); a compromise strategy (C) on the other hand, guarantees a minimum 2, but can only generate a maximum of 3.

The technique of play is therefore to play a "hard" strategy until the last possible moment, when disaster is averted by a compromise. The key strategic problem is how to induce a compromise before disaster occurs, in other words, how to accelerate the deterioration of preferences from win to compromise by proximity of calamity.

Inducing this deterioration of values is extremely difficult. In economists' language, the threat of calamity must be such as to ensure indifference between winning and compromise—the earlier the better. For once "on the run," an opponent may be induced to pay an even higher price to avert disaster. The knowledge that the price of compromise can increase if one flinches too early (appeasement), however, acts as a drag on the substitution rate: between skilled bargainers of roughly equal size and skill, calamity is a probable outcome, and will even "hang in the air" before, at the last split second, it may be averted—in its fullest intensity—by a hair's breadth compromise.

A usual form of bargaining between governments, chicken can also characterize labor relations, bargaining between industry sectors and governments, even hostile takeover struggles. Chicken games should not, but sometimes do, fit bargaining between single companies and governments, especially regulatory agencies.[15]

Preconditions for success include: (a) real power to inflict harm on your adversary and to withstand inflicted harm in return; (b) real assurance that your opponent is in fact playing chicken and not one of the other variants described below; (c) real communications expertise to ensure strong public support whatever the outcome. If any of the above is missing, think again.

Yet the game has its attractions. It is power bargaining, a way to achieve a compromise and preserve a reputation for toughness; it is challenging and, if the potential payoff is high enough to meet the transaction costs, it can pay dividends.

Guides to Handling: Strategy should concentrate on (a) enhancing strength; (b) denying suicidal and other non-chicken strategies to the opponent; and (c) building public support.

Let us now examine some of the chicken variants, note their warning signs, and look for methods of denying their utility to adversaries.

Leader

Preferences: (A) Chicken
(B) Win > Lose > Compromise > Deadlock

Figure V.10. Leader

Player (A) \ Player (B)	C	D
C	3,2	2,4
D	4,3	1,1

Like chicken, both adversaries dread deadlock, but the difference is that Player B values defeat above compromise. B will therefore make a "strategic capitulation," leaving Player A the satisfaction of his private wants, but reaping the gains that induced him (B) to have this set of preferences. Such gains could include a reputation for statesmanship, leadership, or the shifting of an onus onto Player A to deny him support and make him more vulnerable to a different attack later on.

Hero

Preferences: (A) Chicken
(B) Win > Lose > Deadlock > Compromise

Figure V.11. Hero

		Player B: C	Player B: D
Player A	C	3,1	2,4
	D	4,3	1,2

Like "Leader," this game will likely end in technical defeat for B. But in losing, B will be confirming his legitimacy as a hero to his constituents. Most dangerous of all, a "minimax" or compromise strategy by A will in all likelihood expose A to "D" responses that are more damaging to A than to B.

Both Leader and Hero strategies are useful approaches for weaker adversaries dependent upon broad-based public support against a more powerful adversary, less able to withstand public scrutiny. Although the Chicken player will likely win in terms of his private calculus, in the calculations of B, the defeat produces sufficient gains to make it his second best solution. Thus, the number of victories A can withstand may be limited. Denial of such strategies to opponents requires at least that the potential veto groups or powerful segments of the opponents' supporters be induced to withdraw support before or during the bargaining process.

The variations discussed above amount to a kind of political judo in which the strength of the powerful adversary is turned against him as he pursues short-run victory. The next variants of the chicken theme have the opposite property in common: the opponent in each case is prepared to take deadlock over compromise. The necessary deterioration of values essential to a successful Chicken outcome is not achieved, with attendant defeat for the Chicken player.

Called Bluff

Preferences: (A) Chicken
(B) Prisoner's Dilemma

Figure V.12. Called Bluff

		Player B	
		C	D
Player A	C	3,3	2,4
	D	4,1	1,2

In Called Bluff, although compromise is the second best result for both players, the different values for defeat and deadlock will determine the strategies and outcomes. As we have already seen, Prisoner's Dilemma rates deadlock as an acceptable payoff to avoid defeat; Chicken does not. Indeed, the similar valuation attached to compromise may cause a misreading that precludes a sufficient rate of value deterioration by A, the Chicken player, so his disaster (to him) may be inescapable.

The other two variations occur when Player B actually plays Deadlock as either his second best or his preferred alternative. The two diagrams below display the resulting patterns.

Bully/Big Bully

Bully
Preferences:
(A) Chicken
(B) Win, > Deadlock, > Compromise, > Lose

Big Bully
Preferences:
(A) Chicken
(B) Deadlock, > Win, > Compromise, > Lose

Figure V.13. Bully and Big Bully

		Player B	
		C	D
Player A	C	3,2	2,4
	D	4,1	1,3

		Player B	
		C	D
Player A	C	3,2	2,3
	D	4,1	1,4

In neither pattern does a chicken player have a chance of any outcome but defeat, either in terms of a punishing deadlock or capitulation. "Bully" strategies applied to Chicken may thus be maximally inducing, compelling the chicken player either to capitulate or accept an even worse result. Clearly, a misreading by a Chicken player of a "Bully/Big Bully" potential in his adversary would be calamitous. Once the game is started, the end is inevitable. Labor relations (such as the 1982 U.S. air controllers' strike that led to the decertification of the air controllers' union), business-government relations (U.S. Steel's confrontation with President Kennedy in 1962 resulting in a price rollback,[16] Revere Aluminum's confrontation with the Government of Jamaica in 1975 which led to the expropriation of the company's bauxite, mining, and alumina processing facilities)[17] are examples of such unfortunate interactions.

Denial of the strategies, either Called Bluff or Bully/Big Bully, can most simply be achieved by avoiding Chicken games with adversaries able to play them, perhaps instead employing Hero or Leader strategies against them. Success in these instances depends especially on thoroughgoing public support.

SUMMARY

This chapter illustrates the ways in which bargaining in the public arena can differ from the more narrowly focused problem of making a deal in the normal business environment. The traps and pitfalls discussed above occur because of the difficulties of constructing a clearly agreed upon "contract line" such as emerges virtually automatically in bargaining between buyer and seller in which values are transferable, results are usually Pareto optimal, and agreement is in the clear interest of all parties.

The problem in most organizations will be how to operationalize these strategies and gain sufficient control over policies so that effective strategies and policies can be generated. The requirements for this are easy to state and much less easy to implement. There must be a reliable issues monitoring service in place (this is discussed below); there should also be a public affairs specialist able to model the bargaining procedure and advise on positioning as the issue unfolds.

As to the procedure for employing the bargaining models discussed above, the following is suggested:

1. Having determined that bargaining (and not, say, Critical Mass) will play the critical role in determining outcomes:

   (a) *work out your priorities* and those of your adversary, rank ordering them in terms of outcomes preferences;
   (b) assign values (1 to 4 or other combinations if realistic estimates are available) to the outcome preferences and display them in a matrix that models the strategic interplay;
   (c) look for potential breakdowns in rationality, i.e., prisoner's dilemma, a game without equilibria, or the chicken case;
   (d) determine your success strategy, and that of your adversary;
   (e) work out positions that will render the adversary's strategy inoperable, except when playing into your hands;

Note: You will need positions for each phase: "Surfacing terms," "the search for allies," and "imposing a solution;"

Remember: Essentially you are either trying to achieve a situation such that a contract line is established, upon which a solution will emerge that maximizes the utilities of both players,

OR

You are trying to tie up and frustrate that procedure, to render it infeasible, until time deals you a better hand.

The next section will discuss putting together the observations made so far into a general model and developing a comprehensive issues track that will be useful to professionals now engaging in this sort of work.

Concepts and Terms

Issue models

(a) *Externality Problems*
  typical responses
  optimal response
  phase I and Phase II
(b) *Lobbies*
  Participation and size problems
(c) *Critical Mass*
  The inflections of each phase
  The R equation in integrated form
  Iron triangles
  Pre- and post c.m. outcomes
  Collective action strategies
(d) *Bargaining*
  Edgeworth Box
  Game Theory
  Three stages
  Minimax (maximin)
  "pure" strategies, "mixed" strategies
  Rationality Breakdowns
    prisoner's dilemma
    non-equilibrium games
    chicken and its variations
  Procedure for using the Bargaining Models

NOTES

1. However, if the costs to the community are such that they continue to escalate as, for example, with life-threatening emissions, then again swift settlement is indicated to minimize danger.

2. On the public affairs side, Edward Grefe, *Fighting to Win*, 1981 Harcourt, Brace, Jovanovich, George S. Dominguez, *Government Relations, A Handbook*, 1982, John Wiley, pp. 48-49. For an introduction to historical literature on popular protest, George Rude, *Ideology and Popular Protest*, 1980, Pantheon; Charles Tilly et al, *The Rebellious Century, 1830–1930*, 1975, Harvard; for theory, esp. Mancur Olson, *The Logic of Collective Action*, 1971, Harvard Economic Studies 124; Thomas C. Schelling, *Micromotives and Macrobehavior*, 1978, Norton, pp. 102-110. The discussion of collective action here relies heavily on Olson, 1971.

3. See James Coleman et al., "Social Processes in Physicians Adoption of a New Drug," Amitai Etzioni, *Social Change*; esp. Chap. 29, fig. 49-4.

4. James Coleman, *Introduction to Mathematical Sociology*, 1964, Free Press, Glencoe, pp. 500-505.

5. This seems to be a problem of perception with "horizontal" regulation rather than

a phenomenon that can be rigorously demonstrated. Cf Paul J. Quirk, *Industry Influence in Federal Regulatory Agencies*, 1981, Princeton. But with vertical, or industry specific regulation, there is considerable evidence. Cf. George J. Stigler, *The Citizen and the State*, 1975, U. Chicago.

6. What follows is based heavily on Barry R. Weingast, "Regulation, Reregulation and Deregulation: The Political Foundations of Agency-Clientele Relationships," *Law and Contemporary Problems*, Vol. 44, No. 1, Winter, 1981, 147-177.

7. For a summary of the literature, see: Robert L. Bishop, "Game Theoretic Analysis of Bargaining," *Quarterly Journal of Economics*, also, R.D. Luce and H. Raiffa, *Games and Decisions*, 1959, Wiley, and Raiffa, *The Art and Science of Negotiation*, 1983, Harvard. For applications of these games to international relations, see G. H. Snyder and Paul Diesing, *Conflict Among Nations*, 1977, Princeton.

8. See, for example, Nigel Howard, *Paradoxes of Rationality: Theory of Metagames and Political Behavior*, 1971, MIT.

9. In a different context, we have already used this pattern to justify public policy in general, arguing that the institution of government is practically necessary (if not always sufficient) to ensure the community optimum is attained in a timely fashion.

10. Cf. the situation with old and depreciated plant examined above.

11. Steven J. Brams, *Game Theory and Politics*, 1975, Free Press, p. 35.

12. e.g., Hoffman La Roche's resistance of a British government price rollback demand, described in Ingo Walters and Thomas Gladwyn, *Multinationals Under Fire*, John Wiley, pp. 350 ff.

13. A gain for player A = loss to player B so that the "sum" of winnings and loss = zero.

14. Percy Ernst Schramm, *Hitler als militärischer führer. Erkenntnisse und Erfährunge aus dem Kriegstagebuch der Oberkommandos der Wehrmacht*, Frankfurt am Main, 1962.

15. cf. Firestone 500 recall in Cases, below.

16. This case is described more fully in William T. Greenwood, *Issues in Business and Society*, 1977, (3rd edition), Houghton Mifflin, p. 100.

17. See Ingo Walters and Thomas Gladwin, *Multinationals Under Fire*, p. 277, for a discussion of this case.

Chapter VI

Putting it Together: An Issue Development Framework

We have now discussed in theoretical form (1) the origins of business government issues and some ways individual preferences are made to coincide with the public interest as decided by the political process, (2) the behavior of government, and (3) the characteristic patterns and strategies for resolving issues. The purpose of this section will be to put these observations together in a comprehensive management framework for the conduct of business-government relations. As our argument is primarily addressed to the issues management practitioner, the emphasis will remain on "what to do" rather than the management process for getting it done. Clearly, however, establishing a process for issues management is a significant responsibility that neither those with functional responsibility for issues nor top management, especially the CEO, should ignore.[1]

Let us begin by diagramming the track or sequence of development followed by all issues, plotting intensity against time and illustrating the main decision points (see Figure VI.1 page 114).

THE ISSUES TRACK[2]

Through time, the issue develops through three phases: origins (where it begins), resolution (where the contest occurs), and the outcome phase (where the results are played out).

Figure VI.1. The Issues Track

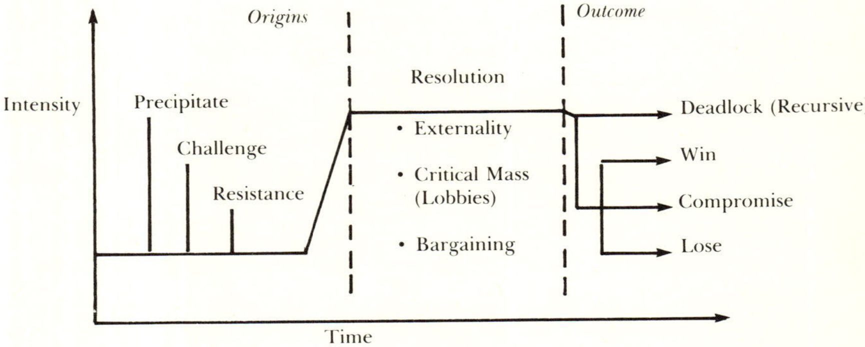

During the origins phase, there are three points for management decision: *First, the precipitate, or trigger*. Here is where the issue starts. It can be an accident (chemical spill, hotel fire, or other disaster) which will require a certain type of management response (such as clean up, containment, or evacuation plans, the activities covered under the heading disaster planning); it can be a government policy announcement (which government information officers will plan carefully for timing and effect); a new scientific discovery (a report on a forthcoming article or release of a major study); a company announcement (a takeover offer, a new profit figure, layoffs, or divestments). Each announcement will require decision about the effect to be achieved.

Still, the issue will remain at a relatively low level of intensity until the precipitate triggers a "challenge," i.e., *until a second event occurs that contests the position established by the precipitate*. The challenge is the second step in the development of the issue. How to make that challenge is another point of management decision for contesting issues. The aim would be to make it in such a way as to achieve the desired outcome, not only for the challenge, but for the issue as a whole.

Still, the issue remains relatively calm until the precipitating party responds to the challenge.

The response to the challenge is the third and decisive step in the developing intensity of the issue. If contentious, the response will intensify the conflict and lead to a contest that is resolved, ultimately, by the interactions of the stakeholders in the resolution phase.

Stakeholder interactions during the resolutions phase follow one or more of the interaction typologies or models discussed earlier: externality, critical mass (or lobbying) and bargaining. The pattern can be sequential: Externality → Critical mass → Bargaining; or one pattern can predominate. To stay on top of the issue, management should already have worked out correctly which resolution model or models will be followed in this phase and have devised appropriate strategies.

The final, or outcome, phase is the one in which the results of the issue become known. In this phase, intensity normally drops off and all sides try to salvage what credit properly or improperly belongs to them, at the same time making whatever economic adjustments are necessary as a result of the outcome.

The issues track highlights the key phases of an issue and the dilemmas posed for management. In solving those dilemmas, the following procedure should be adopted. *First, once the issue facing the organization has been identified, management should analyze the fundamental stakeholder relationships in the issue* and decide *which* stakeholders are allies, *which* are not, and *which* stakeholders, if any, have "veto" power over any of the outcomes.

Second, management should "model" the relationships, using externality, critical mass, or bargaining models as guides.

Third, select the best attainable outcome, based on the characteristics of the model. For example, an externalities situation requires direct compromise, with a special effort to affect "technocratic demand" in government. Critical mass, if strong enough to supplant cozy "sub-government" relationships, can enable a group or organization to prevail; bargaining outcomes must avoid traps and pitfalls, maximize allied support (especially "veto" groups) and impose or resist sets of specific terms.

Fourth, management should then structure the unfolding of the issue to achieve that preferred outcome. They should work backwards from the desired outcome to:

a. identify the key decision points;
b. choose strategies to generate outcomes desired at the main stages (P.C.R., key parts of the resolution phase, outcomes).

Fifth, operationalize the strategy as a program by:

i. predicting outcomes crisply, so success/failure and trends will become immediately clear;
ii. implementing the plan now prepared;
iii. monitoring closely to assess impacts and trends.

If results are as predicted, then no changes are needed. If results are not as predicted, then assess the impact of change on the fundamental stakeholder relations, i.e., is the model the right one, or should one's

Figure VI.2. Issues Management Procedures

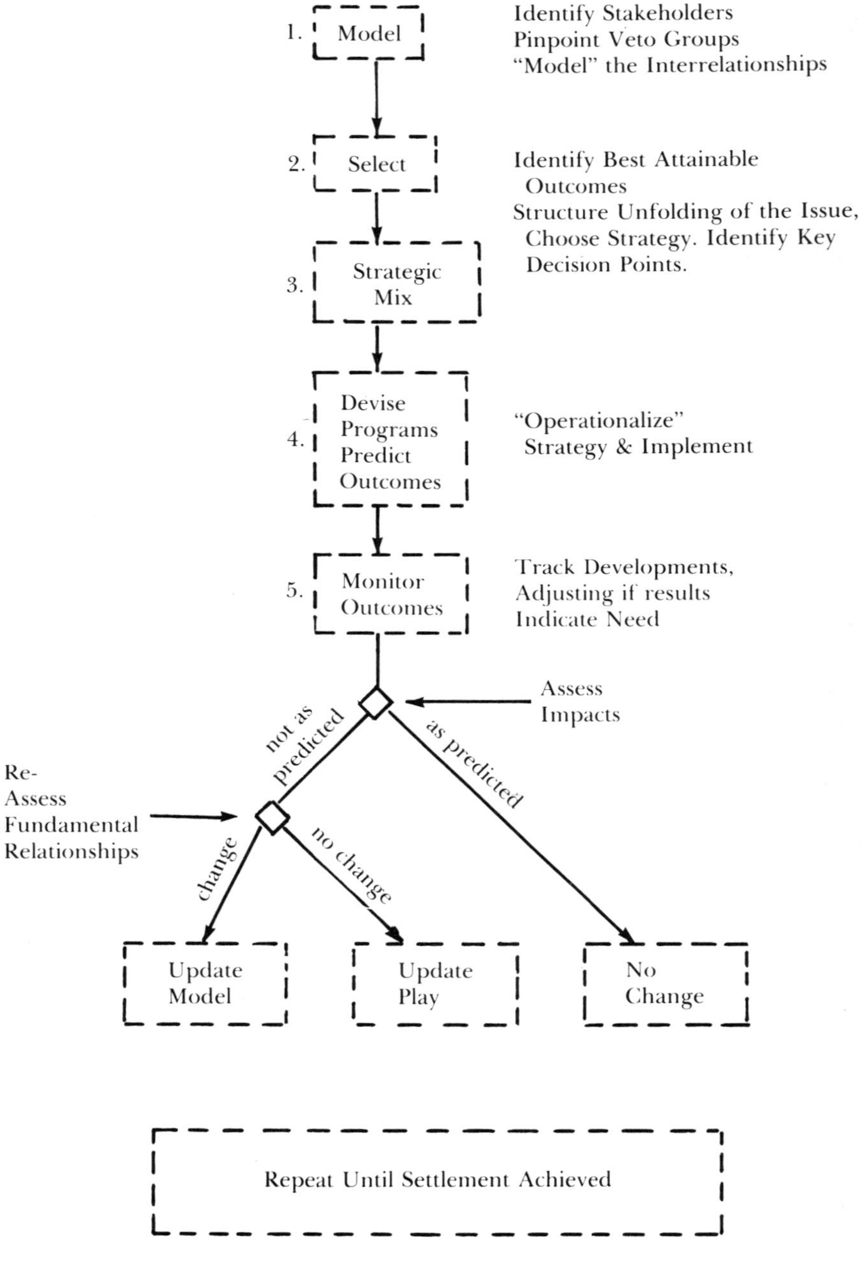

basic understanding of the issue be changed? If so (i.e., the fundamental relations have changed, or our initial understanding was flawed) then the model and strategy should be reviewed. But if the basic concepts are sound, then the effect of change on the program should be assessed. Any shift in events off the anticipated track will call for alterations in the program to make certain items stronger.

This monitoring and cross-checking should be continued until the issue is resolved. Figure VI.2 on page 116 illustrates these steps.

SUMMARY

From the standpoint of business, issues—public disputes in which the public interest is unclear—are debates about what constitutes wealth and how it should be created. Each issue outcome results in a new shift by firms to reoptimize the mix of production factors. Changing public values call forth new public policies, new public policies call forth new products, retire old ones and confront management with new decisions. Public affairs has thus become a management function of new importance.

This chapter introduced theoretical concepts designed to provide a framework for management decision-making in this area that puts together all the theoretical concepts set out and explored in earlier sections. How do issues emerge? How are they decided? How can winning strategies be chosen and losing strategies avoided? How can the models introduced earlier be used to develop issue handling programs? Those are the questions the section just completed has attempted to answer.

Concepts and Terms

The Issues Track
Origins, Resolution, Outcome
Precipitant, Challenge, Resistance
Resolution modes: externalities, critical mass, bargaining
Issues Track Procedure: 5 steps

NOTES

1. In this connection, W. Howard Chase, *Issues Management: Origins of the Future*, 1984, Issue Action Publications, Stamford, CT, especially section two.
2. cf. G.M. Snyder, Paul Diesing, *Conflict Among Nations*, 1977, Princeton, esp. p. 15.

Part II

CASES

Chapter VII

Cases

In this section, we will be comparing the insights of our theoretical analysis with actual practice of companies and governments in public affairs issues. The first set of cases will be externalities issues, the next set will examine the operations of critical mass and compare them with more standard lobbying examples. Then we will look at some bargaining examples and, finally, illustrate how to use the procedure set out above for making issues strategy by walking through an actual issues strategy document.

EXTERNALITIES ISSUES

Theory Predicts

According to our theoretical model developed earlier, environmental issues are most probably "externalities" issues, and therefore certain predictions about them can be made with confidence: first, government intervention will be inevitable, and cooperative rather than confrontational strategies will be more likely to generate optimum settlements. Second, behind the issue of pollution will lie questions of external costs, possible compensation, and appropriate policy to "internalize" most of the externalities. Third, the age of the plant in question may affect the willingness of the company to achieve a quick settlement, time being less important than costs for the old, fully depreciated plant. Fourth, key areas for government relations would be (a) technocratic demand (i.e., convincing officials), and (b) the political discount rate applied to policy by political leaders reflecting public perceptions (including perceptions of wickedness or value of the corporations involved and costs of political participation).

Rational companies, then, will want to work closely with government, prefer to settle quickly if the plant is new, and keep public debate to a minimum. Do companies actually behave this way in these situations? In the three cases below, two companies tried to meet the threats the issue raised. One company adopted a more confrontational approach, to its detriment.

Case 1: Mercury Pollution in Northwestern Quebec[1]

A major company's kraft pulp complex in Northwestern Quebec on the Bell river system used mercury in manufacturing chlorine and caustic soda for bleaching wood pulp. Without warning, the Canadian federal government suddenly, in 1970, announced it was closing the Cree Indian fishery established six years earlier in the lakes fed by the Bell (downstream from the paper company's facilities and from some 14 other companies with manufacturing complexes on the river system). The reason: high concentrations of methyl mercury had been found in the fish.

Note: The mill, which began operating three years earlier, had no mercury pollution controls. Only after the mill was completed did the company learn that mercury in waste water could be converted by the digestive system of the fish into a cumulative poisonous substance that could cause Minimata disease in those consuming the fish. A hideous nervous disorder, Minimata was first identified in Japan in 1956, 11 years before the plant in this case opened. Symptoms of the disease—loss of feeling, deterioration of vision, loss of muscular control—are irreversible, and often do not occur until 10 years after contamination begins. Moreover, confirmation of the disease is extremely difficult. Similar symptoms can be caused by snow blindness, vitamin B deficiency or diabetes, all of which exist in native communities in the region. The presence of the disease is, in fact, only verifiable with absolute certainty by autopsy.

The issue is complicated by shared jurisdictions of federal and provincial governments in Canada. Native bands on the Bell river system are the responsibility of the federal government. Inland fisheries are contested jurisdictions shared by both federal and provincial governments. Production facilities are within the control of the provincial government. Federal-provincial relations are, moreover, characterized by a competitive approach to the voter, especially in Quebec, where each issue is viewed by either government as a potential test of national or provincial loyalty.

The Company's Actions. The company (1) acted swiftly to reduce mercury discharges; (2) worked with Quebec and Federal governments to establish permissible levels of mercury emission (finally settling on .005 pounds per ton of chlorine, an average of .37 pounds per day or 135 pounds a year); (3) undertook research to study the contributions of other, chiefly natural sources of mercury in the river system; (4) rejected on cost grounds the option of using different, non-mercury discharging technology. Conversion would have cost around $20 million.

Outcomes. Despite these actions, the company was identified as a major source of pollution by a succession of government reports, subjected to attacks by environmentalists, and was among 15 companies sued by the Grand Council of Crees to get (1) an injunction halting all industrial operations involving mercury discharge, and (2) compensation totaling $8 million.

On May 15, 1978, the chemical plant was quietly closed, according to company spokesmen, "because of uneconomical operations." Thereafter, the company has purchased its bleaching agents from outside suppliers.

Analysis. This is a typical "externalities" issue, brought about by the discovery that the company's operations were introducing the risk of a new and frightening disease.

Companies caught in such situations usually feel singled out for attack, without realizing that they have become victims of a shift in society's ground rules. In retrospect, the company's actions appear to have gained time rather than achieved a quick and lasting settlement. Thus, it (1) moved swiftly to minimize damage; (2) tried to shift the onus through scientific research; (3) worked with governments to come up with realistic, enforceable legislation. Yet as the evidence mounted, it became clear that these efforts were insufficient. What else could have been done?

Issues, remember, are about people, namely the stakeholders of the issue, and the outcomes are the resultants of the choices they made which, in our models, are based on maximizing behavior.

Let's look at the stakeholders in this issue. They are, in addition to the paper company:

1. the native bands, whose fishery was closed;
2. the federal government;
3. the provincial government;
4. environmental groups;
5. other firms on the river system.

Of these stakeholders, only the provincial government likely has real "veto" power, i.e., can force the issue one way or another. But the direction taken by the province will be conditioned by (if not determined by) the federal government direction, as well as the need to appear sympathetic to the needs of its business constituents, as well as the countervailing pressure from the environmentalists.

To be successful, according to our models, an "externals" strategy must cooperate with provincial officials in internalizing costs related to the mercury discharges. The aim: to stimulate 'technocratic demand' for one set of policies over another. To be fully successful with the province, the strategy must also give technocratic demand the upper hand with respect to political inputs (i.e., forestall attempts by environmentalists to use political means to force unrealistic standards on industry). Yet another exposure lies with the native bands. A main food source and tourist attraction has been destroyed. The federal government will be under pressure from the natives and their sympathizers to find alternative food and income. If companies in the area can be held "responsible" for mercury pollution, then that alternative could be a straight cash transfer after a long court fight. Other options should therefore be introduced quickly.

The following steps address all aspects of the issue:

1. Stop mercury discharge until the issue is settled. Instead, purchase bleaching agents from outside suppliers. This is an *action signal* that the company takes its community responsibilities seriously.

2. Direct attention in a public statement announcing Step 1 above to the plight of the natives, and call on both levels of government plus business in the region to form a task force to find alternatives for the native bands until the river system waters can be reclaimed.

3. Remind the provincial government that the plant was built to their approval, incorporating state-of-the-art technology. If rules must be changed, request a low interest loan for installation of new, non-mercury using technology.

It is interesting to compare the actions of the company in the first case with those of the company in the following case.

Case 2: Mercury Pollution Control in Ontario[2]

In 1970, Dow Chemical moved under provincial government pressure to *eliminate* mercury discharges to the St. Clair River near Sarnia and at Thunder Bay, Ontario. The company developed new, more accurate techniques of measurement and analysis and, in May of the same year, began the substitution of non-mercury using technology, which was completed by the summer of 1973. Pulp mills in the Thunder Bay region were supplied with bleaching agents by ship and rail, using a specially built company terminal.

The province nevertheless launched a $25 million lawsuit against Dow, but in the months before the filing of the suit, the Federal Minister of the Environment singled out company performance in reducing emissions in a speech to the House of Commons. Subsequent analysis by the Ontario Ministry of the Environment predicted steady declines of mercury levels in fish to acceptable standards by the late 1970s (except for pike, which would take until 1983). Ultimately, the province abandoned its lawsuit against the company in return for Dow's total payment to the fishermen affected of $250,000 (less than $30,000 per fisherman), plus $100,000 to the province for water pollution research.

Case 3: A Chemical Spill in the U.S. Mid-West[3]

In this case, the company is a large American-based forest products company. A mill, located in a midwestern state, inadvertently released a mold inhibitor into the river system, resulting in a large fish kill.

The mill is an old facility constructed in the 1890s. The spill occurred from a leaking holding tank, and amounted to about 140 pounds of the chemical.

State regulatory authorities sought a conference with the company at which they presented a bill for compensation.

Other stakeholders in the incident also put pressure on the company. The Federal Environmental Protection Agency threatened prosecution under the Rivers and Harbors Act (1899). Environmentalists and the local news media attacked the company.

The Company's Actions. The company (1) paid the State's compensation bill as soon as it was presented; (2) stopped all production using the inhibitor; (3) established a new prevention program calling for a four-man 24-hour surveillance team to spot leaks and spills; (4) began design and construction of an emergency catch basin to hold up to six hours of the mill's effluent and installed a purification system to deal with any future spills of any other chemical; and (5) joined with the city authorities in constructing a secondary treatment plant to take advantage of a common interest: city phosphates, the residues from laundry detergents, helped to break down chemicals in plant effluent. (Note here a "lighthouse effect" from business-government cooperation.)

These solutions were expensive—but they kept the plant producing, while showing commitment to meeting local environmental concerns.

Recapitulation

These three cases of company actions and results can all be explained by the externalities model. In the first case, the company mistakenly equated maximizing behavior with defensiveness and consequently encountered the full weight of the community. In the next two cases, the companies concerned accepted public intervention and moved to cope with the problem as the model suggests is the most rational approach.

Interestingly, although the regulatory climate facing the Canadian companies was much less stringent than that facing the American-based firm, the management responses of Dow and the U.S.-based company were both cooperative with similar beneficial results for both company and community. No purely adversarial model of business-government relations can account for this similarity of approach, and no conspiratorial model can account for the generally beneficial outcomes. On the other hand, a "social responsibility" model based on essentially ethical and philanthropic considerations would be unable to express or justify the adversarial elements in the stakeholder relationships and how they were actually resolved. In reality, a joint approach is the hard-headed, businesslike manner in which to address an environmental problem. The externalities model explains why this should be so.

However, there is a problem with the model in respect to the "efficiency" of the chosen solution. The model predicts that, in externalities situations, the "issue" will be the internalization of external costs through government intervention. What is less clear is how efficient that intervention is.

Fully efficient intervention would result in an optimal solution such that (a) the benefits created by legislation would equal or exceed the benefits of the market or status quo solution, and (b) no better pattern of cost/benefit allocation could be achieved. Another way of saying this is that (a) substitution of public for private goods for each individual will occur at a point where the tax price of the public good equals the benefit from the private good, and (b) the benefits from the public good equal or exceed any benefits foregone by giving up the private goods. As a diagram, the relationship between cost and public goods and the solution points for the firm and the public can be displayed as follows:

Figure VII.1. Efficient Supply of Public Goods

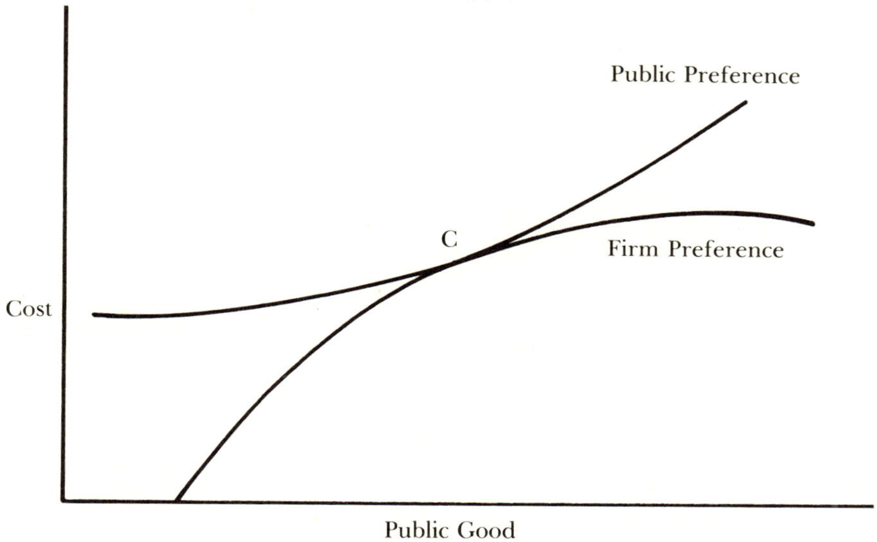

Clearly, if decision requires unanimous agreement, and that can be achieved, no other solution but the efficient intersection point is possible. Every other alternative to the optimum would be vetoed by the voter who stood to lose.

Under majority rule, however, the dynamic alters. Given that government intervention is inevitable, the firms affected and the public can be expected to produce different solutions and expect government to choose between them or resolve the differences in some way that provides optimal allocation of benefits among all three parties. The public will want a clean up at a price that is less than the expected benefit, with the offending firm making up the shortfall. The firm will endorse a solution that minimizes its costs, i.e., reduces adjustment costs to zero if possible while delivering enough public benefits to draw off support for the more costly (to it) solution. The Government will want a solution that leaves it with net political gains. These solutions are illustrated in Figure VII.2 on page 128.

This is in effect a restatement of the argument about the need for "strategic" behavior. Once the relationships have been established, and

Figure VII.2. Efficient Supply and Majority Rule

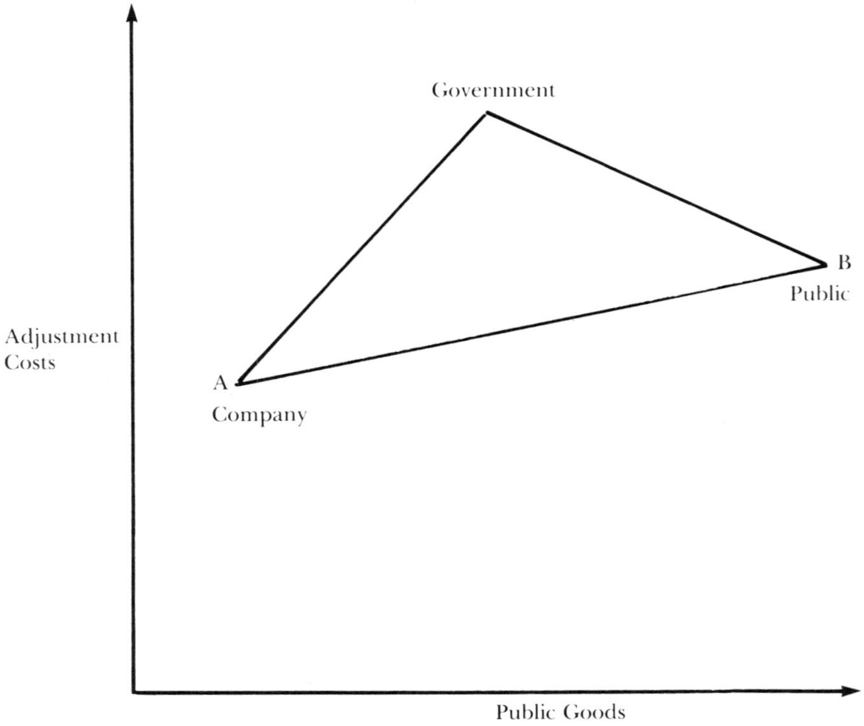

the two sides have put their proposals on the table, the efficient outcome will occur somewhere on the contract line AB. Where it actually occurs will depend upon the political skill and relative power of the two parties in making this solution attractive to government. If the outcome occurs, say, at B, the result would be a substantial defeat for the company, which would face tougher adjustment costs than it is prepared to pay. If the outcome occurs at A, the citizens group will lose significant amounts of the public good.

How this is worked out in practice is illustrated by the next case.

Case 4: The New York Bottle Bill[4]

The Bottle Bill issue arose first in Oregon in 1972, and has subsequently spread to seven other states (Vermont, Maine, Michigan, Iowa, Connecticut, Massachusetts, and in June, 1982, New York). Advocates of the measure are continuing to push at the state level hoping to generate pressure for a national bottle law.

These laws, aimed at reducing roadside litter, require five cent deposits on soda, beer, and other beverage containers including plastic, glass, or metal bottles or cans. Environmental groups sponsored and strongly supported the measure in each state as a quick, effective fix for getting rid of unsightly waste. The container industry opposed the bill with an externalities measure of its own.

Recognizing the externality represented by roadside waste, container companies, usually acting through trade associations (e.g., Can Manufacturers Institute) and in industry/labor coalitions, fought the bill by taking a more comprehensive approach to the problem. They introduced competing legislation directed at all roadside litter. Industry proposals championed either of two approaches: (a) the comprehensive litter bill, which used public education, enforcement, and recycling to reduce all types of litter, and (b) the Clean Community System (CCS), a voluntary, non-legislative anti-litter program backed by Keep America Beautiful, Inc. Both approaches mobilized community resources against all litter without putting deposits on containers.

Why fight deposits? According to industry, forced deposit laws raise prices, lower sales, and cause a net job loss for skilled workers employed in can and glass manufacturing. In other words, the deposit solution causes a loss of benefits conferred by the status quo solution. According to the anti-bill spokesman in New York, passage of the bill in that state was "an awful, cruel hoax" that would cost New Yorkers $400 million.

This, said industry, seemed a high price for an ostensible clean-up measure that would attack only about five percent of the total roadside litter problem. The comprehensive measures, in contrast, would reduce total litter by 45 to 58 percent, and could be paid for by a litter tax on all contributions to roadside waste. In other words, the comprehensive solution allegedly provided more public benefits at less total public cost.

The dynamics of this issue reflect the model discussed above: citizens' groups urging a measure with a high price for industry, with industry advocating a measure with lower adjustment costs for itself (but supposedly a larger amount of public good). Government chooses in such a way as to maximize benefits to itself.

In a nonstrategic world, the comprehensive bill might have won. Or a compromise might have been achieved that would weave together the best elements of both proposals (with, say, a longer adjustment phase for industry and labor). But, in the real world, the environmentalists won. Yet, it had taken 10 years for the bill to get as far as the governor's office, where, after heavy lobbying from both sides, the decision went against industry/labor.

The solution model only illustrates the problem. To understand the outcome, one must examine the model of government behavior. It will be remembered that tax expenditure was determined by the following formula:

$$E_t = k[B_t \; h \; f(Q,I,P)] + E_{t-1} + e^*$$

What shifted k to top priority for the environmentalists?

a. Participation had to be as high or higher for those willing to pay the tax price as for those opposed, so costs of participation had, of necessity, to be no barrier to participation; i.e., the environmentalists had to have good organization.
b. h had to be less for the environmentalists than for industry.
c. B_t had to favor the politicians so that either $N_P <> N_r$. In other words, the politicians either needed the votes or were sure they had them.

In other words, assuming rational (i.e., maximizing) behavior, the environmentalists won because, although both propositions were good, theirs was better for the politicians. In an election year, the proposition would confer benefits mainly upon nonurban, upstate voters who would remember the governor favorably each time they bought a deposit container: the price to be conferred on the container industry would generate political benefits from environmentalists.

What about efficiency? The bottle bill solution carries an economic price to the public. Higher prices for soda and beer, possible job losses, and additional tax expenditures. These costs, which would not be run up by the status quo or the comprehensive solution, would be mainly absorbed by the container industry. Thus, the political outcome, in effect, generated political benefits to the winners while passing the costs on to the losers. Recognizing government as a self-interested party to the outcome provides the key to the efficiency problem. The outcome is analogous to the "divide the dollar" problem noted earlier—efficiency boils down to a question of which outcome is dominant: equal division, i.e. V = 1/3, 1/3, 1/3 or V = 1/2, 1/2, − 1.

Clearly, in a majority rule setting, the latter alternative provides approximately equal total benefits (i.e., the environmental problem *is* addressed), but allocates them in a way that cannot be dominated. Neither the market or status quo solution, nor the comprehensive legislative solutions (both acceptable to the companies) could translate their economic soundness into greater political attractiveness. Thus, the environmental outcome is efficient (cf. the discussion on choice of policy instrument, *supra*).

However, consider the Carter Administration's efforts to enforce emission standards on two Cleveland Electric Illuminating (CEI) plants in 1979.[5] CEI sought to comply by switching from high-sulfur Ohio coal to low-sulfur Kentucky and West Virginia coal. Under pressure from Ohio coal producers, EPA enacted a provision of the Clean Air Act allowing the EPA administrator to order the utility to burn local coal (to protect jobs) and achieve compliance a different way—probably smokestack scrubbers. The utilities then undertook an effective public information campaign to tell utility customers the scrubbers would add about $4.00 per month to the average home utility bill. Result: in an election year, President Carter finally announced a relaxation of the emission standards for the two plants. Downwind states protested, but to no avail. In this case, the status quo solution represented the dominant configuration of political benefits. The company "won" by attempting to pass on costs of internalization to stakeholders who where able to reject them, and who did not feel harmed by the "externalities" government policy was designed to remove. In so doing, the company generated allies, whose participation occurred because the government policy proposals would have created perceived net disbenefits that outweighed the costs of becoming involved in the issue.

Conclusion

How well does the externalities model function as (1) a predictor of issue outcomes, and (2) an explanatory device? The model performed well in defining the terms of the issue, i.e. external costs and how to internalize them. The model also correctly suggested the most rational response: accepting government intervention, cooperating with them on a solution, resisting, where the facts warrant, the full cost of compensation. It also suggested the least effective technique, which in one case nevertheless appeared the most rational to management, namely failing to admit the existence of externalities, and treating it as a bargaining situation. Our cases, however, generally showed little management concern for milking every ounce of advantage out of these issues (i.e., in the case of old plant vs. new plant). Rather, the overriding management concern seems to be concern for the company reputation. Interestingly, too, the model applied in different regulatory conditions (Canada and the U.S.), although in Canada no formal "contract line" had been established in law, i.e., the rights and responsibilities of management had yet to be determined explicitly in such cases.

In the case of the bottle bill, the model crystallized the key problem. Its weakness was its inability to predict actual outcomes when the final determination was made on political as opposed to economic grounds. Thus, for an understanding of how outcomes are arrived at in political settings, recourse must be had to different models. The next set of cases, organized around the critical mass model, will look at that problem in more substance.

CRITICAL MASS

The critical mass model explains how a favorable status quo can be transformed, apparently overnight, into a disastrous political configuration for a company or other organization. An explosive public outcry alters the political benefits attending to a measure, causing what appeared to be acceptable not to be.

Historians, Bolsheviks, and others concerned with sudden social changes have debated whether such developments occur "spontaneously" or not. In our discussion, we assume the existence of a "prime mover," a special interest group or government agency or local citizens' organization. What distinguishes critical mass from the more familiar phenomenon of concerted lobbying is the explosive suddenness of the sympathy the group attracts.

Let us begin consideration of this model by examining two cases in which critical mass propelled an externality situation into a closing phase, in one case well handled, in another bungled by the company targeted. Then we shall examine in more detail the orchestration of a critical mass in a municipal store hours case. Finally, we will compare critical mass to concerted lobbying and, in a final case, show how critical mass was defeated by a well-focused lobby.

Case 1: Toxic Shock Syndrome[6]

In a restricted, narrowly focused way, companies are also "political" organizations, ones generally controlled by an iron hand from the top and stimulated throughout by competition among middle management for promotion based on top-down approval, in turn based upon previously agreed upon performance targets. As this case will show, in certain circumstances, public outcry can also alter top management calculations, just as it can for political leaders.

In this case, government officials in the Food and Drug Administration (FDA) generated the beginnings of a critical mass of consumer anxiety to bring additional pressure on a health care and food products giant.

The company, Proctor & Gamble, spent 20 years and some $75 million researching, developing, and marketing a super absorbent tampon, Rely. After one full year at full national distribution, the product had won 24 percent of the tampon market, and generated $45.7 million of the near $11 billion in sales rung up annually by the multinational company. But, in September, 1980, the company pulled Rely off the market, in part because of the careful use of the media by the FDA to stimulate consumer reaction. For the tampon had become linked to the deadly toxic shock syndrome, to which 25 deaths had been attributed in the U.S. between 1975 and 1980.

Here are the key moves in the case:

May

1. Atlanta Center for Disease Control (CDC) publishes first report linking toxic shock and menstruating women.

June

2. CDC asks Proctor & Gamble and other tampon makers for market information. Subsequent study confirms statistical correlation between toxic shock and tampon use, but does not recommend women stop using tampons, as the incidence rate seemed too low.
3. Proctor & Gamble conducts its own study, hampered by privacy legislation restricting access to CDC patient data. Findings confirm initial CDC conclusion that there was no link between toxic shock and any particular tampon brand.

July

4. New CDC study shows that, of women with toxic shock syndrome, more than twice as many used Rely as did a similar group of healthy women.

September

5. CDC study announced and confirmed by Utah Health Department some days later.

6. FDA plays up findings to ensure strong media coverage. Proctor & Gamble placed on the defensive.
7. On September 16, FDA contacts Proctor & Gamble for a meeting in Washington to discuss Rely. Under an Executive V.P., a task force is struck, comprising medical, research, legal, marketing and others (but not public affairs, directly).
8. Meeting between FDA and the company. Each measures the other's case. Proctor & Gamble decides its original position, a warning label, is insufficient. Company wins a week to study the CDC study more closely.
9. *Critical Mass ("a" phase) takes effect. Stacks of negative news and editorial clippings are passed to task force executives each day. Negative publicity threatens to spill over on to other company products.*
10. September 21 weekend. After expert teams conclude that latest CDC findings could not safely be ignored, despite uncertainties about the seriousness of Toxic Shock incidence, the company decides to pull the product.
11. Decision confirmed on Monday, P&G announces tampon withdrawal.
12. Proctor & Gamble meets with FDA for second round of talks. FDA views Rely withdrawal as a "preemptive strike" and, as such, a smart move.

In the session with the FDA, the withdrawal strengthened the company's ability to resist agency demands that the company admit it violated safety standards. (This has significant consequences for product liability suits the company would be facing.) FDA officials concede that admission of safety violations is unnecessary. FDA and Proctor & Gamble draft a consent agreement under which the company denies Rely is defective or that any federal laws were violated, but undertakes massive ad campaign warning against Rely and explaining toxic shock. The company also undertakes to buy back any unused Rely tampons in consumer hands, including free samples distributed in the $10 million introductory promotion of the product.

Surveys taken before and after the Rely incident by Leo Shapiro & Associates of Chicago showed the prompt withdrawal helped P&G boost consumer confidence. The first survey, taken just after the withdrawal announcement, showed negative reactions about Rely. The second, taken in mid-October, following the T.V. ads, showed public "admiration" for the company's swift action.

Case 2: Infant Formula Marketing in a Third World Setting[7]

Nestlé Alimenta, a major Swiss-based international food company with more than $12 billion in sales, in 1974 became the target of a consumer's boycott organized in the United States and Europe for the way in which it allegedly promoted infant formula in developing countries.

The U.S. boycott movement was led by INFACT, the Infant Formula Action Coalition, and other groups including the Interfaith Centre of Corporate Responsibility, an affiliate of the National Council of Churches, and the World Council of Churches. Both of the latter groups were especially concerned about issues linking multinational corporations and problems of development in the third world. So effective was the INFACT lobbying that the issue received two Congressional Hearings, in May 1978, called by Senator Edward Kennedy before his Subcommittee on Health and Scientific Research, and in January 1980 by Congressman Jonathon Bingham before his Subcommittee on Economic Policy and Trade.

At Senator Kennedy's initiative, the controversy was moved to an international forum, under the aegis of the World Health Organization, in October 1979. Consensus recommendations for marketing and distribution of infant formula products were taken by WHO for incorporation into an international marketing code, which was approved in 1981 by the World Health Assembly, the WHO governing body. Criticism continued to build, however. In May, 1982, the International Baby Food Network (IBFAN), a network of some 90 groups and organizations in more than 50 countries, published a report entitled *Breaking the Rules*, alleging 2,250 "violations" of the international code between June 1981 and April 1982 by 54 companies in 37 countries. Meanwhile, pursuant to the WHO code, Nestlé reached an agreement with an outside committee of church leaders and scientists (chaired by Senator Muskie of Maine) to provide third party validation of its own claims to be abiding by the code around the world. Following the report of the audit committee, INFACT, in early 1984, declared the boycott over.

The Issue. Simply put, the problem was that proper and safe use of infant formula requires clean water, good sanitation, adequate family income and a literate parent able to follow printed instructions. These conditions are, in the developing world, in notably short supply outside the most affluent urban areas. Yet the market able to use the products properly is large, and there is a real need for mother's milk substitutes and supplements.

Critics alleged that Nestlé and other formula makers tried to extend this "natural" market by promotional techniques which, while permissible in developed countries, could have lethal consequences elsewhere. For instance, the distribution of free samples in hospitals and clinics condition mothers to use formula who, for want of money or a sanitary environment could not use it properly once released from medical care. By then, however, their natural breast milk might well have dried up, so that there would be literally nothing with which to feed their babies. The use of detail personnel in quasi-medical uniforms in hospitals or accompanying health teams has a similar effect. Sophisticated print, billboard, and radio advertising further persuaded mothers who could adequately nurse their babies themselves that it was modern and chic to use formula. Alleged result: declining rate of breast feeding, and a rise in the improper use of formula.

Another aspect of this case was that facts were hard to get. Claim and counterclaim clashed in an atmosphere of emotional rhetoric; the absence of good official statistics on infant care made the debate almost impossible to resolve. Yet, studies completed by WHO and UNICEF indicated there was indeed a problem. The WHO background paper to the international conference in October, 1979, contained this paragraph:

> While it (the infant food industry) has met certain needs, it has also diffused new and often inappropriate ideas on infant feeding and has created an unnecessary demand with well-known health hazards. The advertising and promotion of breastmilk substitutes, particularly in health facilities, has contributed to the decline in breastfeeding. Promotion of breastmilk substitutes by commercial concerns has been more extensive and pervasive than the provision of information concerning the advantages of breastmilk and breastfeeding.

The WHO collaborative study on breastfeeding had this to say about the infant food companies and their policies:

> There was little evidence of policies concerning market limitation, market growth, market segmentation, or recognition of the various needs of different population groups.
>
> Most of the companies, however, had independently established or subscribed to codes of marketing conduct. . . . for the most part, industry appeared to be product oriented and primarily concerned with supplying the best possible infant food product with the best possible instructions to existing natural markets which, of their own accord, were growing.
>
> Most of the companies indicated they fulfilled a basic need. They did not feel it necessarily their task to restrict activities or to ensure that mothers who could adequately breastfeed did not buy their products.
>
> Few companies had undertaken studies of what possible adverse effects from bottle feeding there might be; no company reported the existence of an established system for monitoring possible adverse effects, or for researching potential ones.

Background: Phase I (1970–76). Interestingly, Nestlé had been involved with the infant formula issue since the early 1970s, when it participated in working out a code of conduct as part of the Protein Advisory Group. Known as Statement No. 23, and endorsed by food industry representatives, world health officials, and medical authorities, the statement outlined the problem as follows:

> Among lower socioeconomic groups, abandonment of breast feeding can be disastrous because alternative practices tend to be unhygienic and nutritionally inadequate.

The dilemma of the food industry, the statement said, was as follows:

> It is clearly important to avoid any action which would accelarate the trend away from breast feeding: at the same time, it is essential to make available to the mother the foods, formulas, and instructions which will meet the need for good nutrition of those infants who are not breast fed for various reasons.

To that end, the PAG conference produced a set of mutually agreed guidelines that *inter alia* called on industry (a) to undertake constructive involvement in solutions to the nutritional problems of vulnerable groups; (b) to stress the superiority of breast feeding in its product labelling and literature; (c) to undertake adequate training of its marketing personnel to avoid misuse by vulnerable groups; (d) to ban promotion in the postpartum period; and (e) to devote attention to standard ways of making dry and liquid preparation to minimize misuse. The statement also called on governments and U.N. agencies to recognize the problem and take action, including subsidies and educational programs about correct formula usage for the poor who, nevertheless, needed the product.

Nestlé subsequently went beyond the PAG requirements. It reevaluated its marketing policies to eliminate those that could adversely affect breast feeding, consulted with health ministries in developing countries to determine whether there was an educational role for the company in bringing nutrition education to mothers, and made the superiority of breast feeding an integral message on all its formula packages. It also played an important role in establishing the International Council for Infant Food Industries (ICIFI) to enforce PAG guidelines throughout the industry. This was the situation in 1975.

These actions were in keeping with the history of the company which pioneered the marketing of milk products in the third world using a strategy requiring the establishment of "a significant presence" in every national market—owning and upgrading existing dairy herds and setting up local processing facilities. (Its policies resulted in the doubling of milk production over four years in one region of Mexico, winning a commendation from the University of Guadalajara in 1976 for its contribution to developing countries.)

Phase II (1976–82). If events had stopped at Phase I, the outcome might have been different. But, in 1974–75, a scandal burst upon the developed world over the number of infant deaths attributed to the marketing practices of Nestlé and other food companies. Nestlé responded by launching a libel suit against a Swiss radical activist group for alleging in the title of an article that the company was committing infanticide. The case dragged on for two years, giving a forum to the critics, and a field day to their supporters. The suit ended with a verdict against the activists. But, in accompanying remarks, the judge said that the verdict was in no way "an acquittal" for the company's marketing practices.

The main effect of the trial and its attendant publicity was to make the issue a major concern of church groups concerned with international development and the role of multinationals. Almost immediately, these groups went into action, eventually organizing a boycott in the United States, although the U.S. division does not sell infant formula. The trial provided a focal point for the slow build up of a critical mass that made the problem a significant issue in the United States.

Nestlé Handles the U.S. A representative of the Swiss headquarters visited the U.S. in September, 1977 to meet with the boycott organizers, but no lasting understanding was obtained. When Senator Kennedy's hearings were held in 1978, Swiss headquarters viewed them as "an improper attempt to hold foreign companies accountable for their activities outside the U.S."[8] The company ignored its well-informed managers in White Plains, N.Y., and instead sent an executive from Brazil, who, despite his reputation as an authority of development problems, charged before the committee that the issue was an "indirect attack on the free world's economic system." This drew great sarcasm from the Senator, and made the company look ridiculous.

Analysis. The infant formula issue began as basically an externality issue: continuing unrestricted selling of infant formula products to people unable to use them safely hurt the community while rewarding the firm. And the company responded by involving concerned groups and working out a common approach to the problem through PAG guidelines. Although these did not go far enough to satisfy critics, and perhaps should have been more attentive to after sale consumer behavior, they were sufficient to win assent of groups on all sides of the issue. This could have bought time for further adjustments and saved the reputation of the company from the drubbing it subsequently took.

The public, however, was broadly unaware of both the problems and responses. When radicals were provided a public forum (the libel suit)—at a time of intense suspicion of multinational operations in the third world—they were able to awaken a sufficient critical mass of important segments of the American public with resulting Congressional hearings, all of which heightened the identification of the company with the controversy.

Presentations at the committee hearings (plus limits on jurisdiction of the U.S. government on an issue mainly affecting a European company) allowed the outrage to peak and got the matter referred back to an international forum. Here, however, the facts of the case and the power of the church-backed non-governmental organizations was sufficient to get guidelines adopted that effectively banned consumer marketing of infant formula products. The outcome, more importantly, served (1) to undermine company credibility while enhancing that of its critics, and (2) set the stage for possible restrictive legislation governing policies of U.S.-based MNEs. Only when company policy changed and was demonstrated to have changed by respected outside observers did the critics cease attacking the company.

Question. Could the company have fared better? In Phase II, the company was the target of vicious, misleading and emotional propaganda of a type that is difficult to combat effectively. Yet, even in Phase I, the company seems to have resisted facing squarely the question: is it responsible to sell products *requiring* adequate sanitation and education for safe operation in areas where those requirements rarely exist? In evaluating this lapse, it should be said that the company believed natural market segmentation prevented products from being purchased by families who could not use them correctly. However, as late as May, 1978, despite all the controversy, a company spokesman said it had undertaken no surveys to test that assumption.

Case 3: The Defeat of Early Closing Bylaws in Peterborough, Ont.[9]

In this case, we focus on the anatomy of a critical mass and its explosive development from the "a" to "b" phase. (See section on Critical Mass Model in Theory, above, for a discussion of the two phases.)

At issue is the question of retail store hours in Peterborough, Ontario, Canada, a matter which became controversial in the first months of 1974. A city of some 100,000, whose representative demography makes it a popular testing site for marketing strategies, Peterborough, like most cities in Ontario, has bylaws permitting retail stores to remain open six nights a week, Monday through Saturday.

On February 4, 1974, a group of "concerned citizens," mostly merchants from the downtown area of the city, urged the city council to enact bylaws restricting weeknight store hours to Thursday and Friday. Behind the proposal lay opposition to suburban shopping centres by merchants from downtown—part of a nation-wide campaign by downtown merchants against the competition posed by the plaza discount stores.

The trigger leading local merchants to support legislated restrictions was the adoption of plans for a downtown mall development giving the development the right to set tenants' operating hours. (Malls depend on optimizing business mix to attract customers, so mall management must be able to insist on performance requirements by all tenants. The performance of each is the condition for the prosperity of all.) Merchants in neighboring locations feared this would introduce extended hours into the downtown area.

The council tended to sympathize with the downtown merchants, who had enjoyed a quasi-monopoly on retailing until the arrival of the suburban stores. The problem for the discount stores in the plazas was to preserve six nights a week shopping (they did 60 percent of their business after 6:00 P.M.) and to avoid not only the restrictions suggested by the merchants but also any compromise proposal that the council might suggest as part of a political bargain.

The Company's Solution. The strategy the discount stores adopted was highly successful and was based upon the following insight. The stores realized that the success of their business rested on two dramatic changes that had occurred in society during the 1960s: the migration of city dwellers to the suburbs, and the desire of students, housewives, and others for part-time jobs. Proposals put forward by downtown merchants aimed at Plaza business were tantamount to a direct attack on the lifestyles of these groups. The solution, therefore, was to mobilize these groups in sufficient numbers to generate a critical mass that would convince the municipal authorities they had no choice but to preserve the freedom of choice of shopping hours.

Program:

1. *Demonstrate the fallacies of the opposition case.*

Action: A National Retailers Institute (NRI) had already been established to provide the best information on the store hours question. Arguments based on a NRI-commissioned study and tacitly endorsed by a provincial government discussion paper on the store hours question were presented to the City Council. These showed that evening hours did not cause a general extension of store hours; caused little hardship to established retailers; did not lead to a general increase in prices; did not force employees to work longer hours; and provided part-time jobs to those who needed them. Extended shopping hours represented a response to changes in life-styles.

2. *Provide leadership to enable the unorganized supporters of the company's position to identify themselves and demonstrate their opposition to early closings.*

Action: Stores alerted customers to threats to shopping convenience and conducted in-store balloting to allow customers to express opposition to the by-laws proposed. Form letters were handed to each adult customer entering the store. These explained the threat to store hours, and provided places for customer signature, address, and phone number under a prepared opposition statement: "I would like to express my opposition to a store hours by-law which would restrict week night store openings." The tear-off coupon was addressed to City Council. Care was taken to ensure there was no attempt to coerce or influence customer decision to sign a letter. Signed letters were collected in specially sealed ballot boxes located strategically around the store.

Result: Mid-week response of 8,900 signatures, verified by independent audit, were communicated to the City Clerk and media. Final results of one full shopping week—more than 10,000 signatures—were also communicated to City Council and media.

At the same time, full page newspaper ads were run, explaining "Reasons Why Legislation to Restrict Evening Shopping Hours is Unnecessary." The resulting editorial and letters to the editor showed the critical mass was at the threshold of the "b" phase.

3. *Council responded with a compromise intended to defuse.* The City Council suggested three night a week openings, and undertook to hear the public's view at special ward meetings.

Action: Plaza stores sought allies in other discount merchants. As well, concerned citizens presented themselves to the discount stores to act as leaders in what was becoming a real community dispute.

Result: Ward meetings were dominated by genuine opponents of the council's position. The meetings effectively offered a forum in which the built-up critical mass could show its potential. No longer were the discount stores in a leadership position. Their advocacy was overtaken by genuinely outraged citizens. Despite a relatively small turnout, the Council was effectively deterred, i.e., councillors' calculations of potential advantage were revised.

Follow-up: To gain maximum leverage, especially at the provincial level where there was still the possibility of province-wide legislation, a documentary record of the Peterborough case was prepared by NRI, presented to Council, then mailed to the provincial government. Its aim was to underline the lesson that "the public does care about store hours and will react to defend its interests when confronted with a specific proposal for restrictive legislation."

Note: Public response had to be at all times not only genuine, but, like Caeser's wife, "above suspicion." The sparking ingredient that aroused the normally quiet—not to say complacent—Ontario small town suburbanites to direct political action was the legacy of resentment built up by downtown merchants and the sense of injustice caused by their attack on evening shopping.

Note, too, the role of advocacy advertising. Here it was used to provide "leadership in print," i.e., it allowed the critical mass to generate by showing the legitimacy of the cause and possibility of a successful fight. But the second ingredient, the emotional content, was already there, the seeds of unpopularity sown by the downtown merchants, and the fact that the proposed bylaw would be taking something away.

The decision of the Peterborough City Council to back off the issue effectively disarmed the critical mass before it exploded in full force. Other City Councils were not so wise and suffered accordingly. The experience of North Bay, Ont. and Charlottetown, P.E.I. provide excellent examples of this: in both cities, councils faced angry mass demonstrations as a result of store hours legislation and had to rescind the bylaw.

Analysis

Specific cases so far examined conform to the model of critical mass discussed above. That is, under certain conditions, a small group of critics can manage to set off an avalanche of public support that ultimately reconstitutes the political "givens" facing rule makers who then adjust to the new status quo.

The necessary conditions usually include a legacy of ill-will, a sense of moral outrage, a commitment to change things, and an avenue of expression that is simple and direct. Given these factors, a critical mass can build up readily and, when it does, it is either decisive in itself in settling outcomes or else provides a significant contribution to the final outcome. Moreover, the possibilities of such events are increased by the power of contemporary mass communications.

In the first example, the FDA touched off a critical mass against Proctor & Gamble which hastened its decision to avoid a contest with the agency. In the second case, Nestle's Alimenta actually touched off its own critical mass against itself by providing its critics a prestigious forum—the law courts. Despite the company's record, the critical mass was able to undermine the company's credibility significantly, and set the stage for more control and regulation of MNEs. In the third case, a company that understood its business thoroughly, especially the social factors underpinning its business success, was able to generate a critical mass that defeated legislation proposed by its competitors, and thus preserve a satisfactory operating climate.

The cases also illustrate something the model does not show explicitly: namely, a critical mass at the end of the "a" phase is often enough to have the effect of a fully developed critical mass as one side or the other reads the signal appropriately and makes the necessary adjustments. Thus, the Rely tampons *were* withdrawn earlier than might have been anticipated to avoid the full effect of negative publicity, Peterborough city council dropped its original bylaw proposal for restricted store hours and went no further in order to defuse the store hours situation. True, some other city councils did not, until the critical mass exploded in full scale outrage; true, also, Nestle's Alimenta corporate headquarters failed to address quickly enough the case made by the critics with consequent damage to their image as a decent company.

However, these latter responses amount to serious miscalculations or sub-optimal results owing to the failure of the principal decision-makers to adjust their political discount rates in the face of concerted opposition. It would be realistic on this evidence to postulate a "rational expectations" interpretation of critical mass to explain the fact that adjustments occur *before* the critical mass explodes. "Rational expectations" would hold that, whenever a phenomenon closely approximates a critical mass near the end of its "a" phase, the balance of prudence is to act as if it was, in fact, genuine. In each case where adjustment was made, it followed corraboration by a third party or by direct experience of mounting opposition (in the news clips and mail monitored by Proctor & Gamble and in the ward meetings in Peterborough). Similarly, the failure of Nestlé to adjust rapidly to its emerging hostile public opinion environment may have had this explanation: a belief by its Swiss management that the company's critics were subversives duping supporters who would drop the issue if they knew the facts. (Hence, the opening statement by the company spokesman at the hearings by the Kennedy sub-committee.) The practical conclusion is that third party validation to *prove* the "a" phase is real can be just as powerful as the "a" development.

A further (and better-known) fact is that the third party validation used to demonstrate the "a" phase existence can also help to accelerate the development of that phase. A news story headlined, "Three out of Five Women to Vote Democratic, Survey Shows" will cause five out of five women to check their own political allegiances and perhaps feel more strongly about them if they are approved by the majority. In the Peterborough case, ads and stories highlighting the thousands of signatures and providing supporting arguments helped solidify opposition and give confidence to town residents who now knew they were not alone. That helped immensely in ensuring strong representation at the subsequent ward meetings.

The cases therefore enhance our understanding of critical mass by demonstrating the importance of the "a" phase. If the stakes in an issue permit adjustment (an important qualifier), then generating the "a" phase and demonstrating its genuine strength are all part of a seamless process of getting decision makers to revise their political calculations away from (or toward) a status quo.

The cases also show that critical mass forcibly overrides "cozy relationships" or status quo assumptions of decision makers. Peterborough town council would have preferred a compromise solution so that they could give their downtown merchant friends something. They revised their calculations. Proctor & Gamble would have preferred a warning label. But in the absence of decisive evidence in support of the product, mounting negative publicity led them to shy away from the confrontation that would have entailed. Instead, in both cases, a new set of preferences emerged. In thus forcing the emergence of a new set of preferences, and involving public opinion from groups or sections of the public beyond the publics normally involved in an issue, critical mass is subtly distinct from interest group lobbying.

The main difference is the spillover appeal, beyond the bounds of normal interest group pressure, that causes decision makers to revise their status quo assumptions. The following three cases illustrate the workings of interest group lobbying and the differences when compared to critical mass.

Case 4: Hide Action[10]

The Issue. In the spring of 1979, the American leather industry was faced with a sudden shortage of raw material. So serious was this scarcity that it was beginning to cause factory closings, tannery shutdowns, layoffs and extended vacations. The reason: foreign offshore manufacturers, mainly in the newly industrialized countries of Korea and Taiwan plus Japan, were buying up American cattlehides to the point where there were insufficient hides for American manufactures. The industry had made repeated representations to government and government agencies, but had received no satisfaction. So they had decided to form a coalition and go public with a national grass roots campaign that would raise the political priority of the issue, and thus gain relief from Congress or the White House.

Objective. The aim was to win enough Congressional support for a legislation imposing export controls on cattlehides to ensure that there was always sufficient domestic supply. At the time, only oil and cobalt were subject to similar embargoes.

At the same time, pressure would be brought on the White House to stimulate the Executive branch to negotiate with Argentina, Uruguay, Brazil and other hide-producing nations to sell a percentage of their hides on the world market. All of these countries had hide embargoes ensuring sufficiency of domestic supply.

Program. Phase I worked towards a Senate vote in July by stimulating grass roots workers rallies, letter writing campaigns, pressure from local and state officials, direct lobbying by industry officials, and direct communication with members of Congress. These efforts resulted in a close (46–38) vote on an export control amendment sponsored by prominent Senators Howard Baker and Edmund Muskie which surprised and encouraged the industry. The vote encouraged even more intense action in the House of Representatives, where a victory had hitherto not been believed possible.

The communications machinery was redirected to reach all 435 Representatives. Newsletters and letters were sent every few days from industry executives; the industry organized a "March on Washington," bringing executives and workers to Washington for personal meetings with their representatives. More than 150,000 letters from leather workers across the nation poured in containing pleas for action. As support mounted, it added pressure to the White House campaign.

At the same time, the industry indicated it was ready to enter New Hampshire around primary time to conduct anti-administration advertising and rallies.

Result. After the industry threat to intervene in the key New Hampshire primary, the White House speeded up the pace and increased pressure on the hide-producing nations. For the first time in seven years, Argentina agreed to make a hide supply available to the world market, adding 12 million hides and greatly relieving pressure on the American supply.

Case 5: Bottlers Bill[11]

From 1971 until 1978, the Federal Trade Commission (FTC) rumbled menacingly that the exclusive territories granted by soft drink bottling companies to their networks of independent bottlers violated antitrust provisions. Yet, the territories were a traditional business practice dating from the turn of the century. The industry contended that the territories provided incentives for small businesses to invest in independent bottling facilities in return for which the bottler got the exclusive right to bottle, distribute and market a soft drink brand within a certain market area. A change in the rules, the industry said, would mean fewer independent bottlers, attendant job losses, and greater concentration among large bottling firms: in short, less competition, not more.

The FTC contended that the trade practice amounted to unwarranted regional protection, and consequently higher prices to consumers. In April, 1978, the agency succeeded in outlawing the practice. The industry responded with a broad-based legislative campaign that unfolded according to the following chronology:

April, 1978

FTC outlaws exclusive soft drink territories on grounds that they are anti-competitive.

Summer, 1978

Soft Drink Bottlers Association forms a task force to combat FTC decision and create a grass roots campaign among soft drink bottlers. Soft drink companies help bottlers and employees to speak out against the bill. For a year, bottlers study how to make their power effective.

October, 1978

U.S. Court of Appeals hears arguments from industry and the FTC but, after two years, does not rule.

December, 1978

Bottlers hot line installed in Washington to give bottlers quick access to background on legislators and lobbying techniques.

April, Fall 1979

After months of lobbying, the soft drink bottlers bill permitting exclusive franchises is introduced. Senate sub-committee and full committee reviews are completed by mid-winter, 1979. House version stalls in the fall.

Fall 1979–February, 1980

Bottlers intensify pressure on Representatives. Finally, a discharge petition is introduced. Threat galvanizes House committee into holding hearings in mid-March and subsequent hearings in April.

May, 1980

Senate uses closure to pass soft drink bill and avoid destructive amendments.

June, 1980

Sufficient signatures (218) obtained for discharge petition. House Committee chairman reverses his position on the bill. House vote passes the bill on June 24.

July 9, 1980

President Carter signs the bill into law.

Case 6: Long Gun Control[12]

Issue. After three separate incidents in which maniacs used rifles to gun down families, policemen, and others (in one incident, an emotionally disturbed boy opened up in his Ottawa high school classroom), public pressure began mounting on the federal government to extend gun control laws to cover so-called "long guns," i.e., rifles and shotguns. (Existing laws provide strict regulation of handgun ownership and use.)

The government response to the public outcry was complicated by the following considerations: (a) a substantial portion of the Canadian rural population regards ownership and use of long guns as a natural aspect of life; (b) for most other users, long guns are for recreation only—

either competitive target shooting or hunting (for which licenses are already required and which is organized through gun and wildlife clubs); and (c) gun owners in Canada, although without formal Constitutional appeal as in the United States, nevertheless had an organized national voice in an association headed by a former RCMP commissioner.

The government handed the assignment of a new long gun law to a task force composed of personnel from the Solicitor-General's Department and the Department of Justice at work on a "Peace and Security Package" of amendments to the Criminal Code. These were designed to strengthen penalties against violent crime, while formally abolishing capital punishment for murder and high treason.

The "gun control" elements finally included in the package amounted to restrictions on the purchase of long guns whereby a form akin to a passport application (without a photo) had to be completed by a would-be gun buyer for a first purchase. The form required two testimonies of good character signed by someone in a list of 12 occupations (including clergy, lawyer, and other professionals but not, for example, factory hands, plant supervisors, businessmen, or bus drivers). The draft law also required safe storage of rifles and ammunition, but government legal experts were unwilling to provide explicit rules or standards to implement this provision. Essentially, if an incident occurred in which an unauthorized person seized a weapon and started killing, then the weapon would be presumed to have been unsafely stored.

Outcome—Phase I. The government announcement sought to play to the critical mass of urban dwellers supporting gun control while pacifying the most interested public, the rifle owners. The announcement stressed three themes designed to appeal to major stakeholder groups: (a) the danger to life of uncontrolled use of long guns (i.e., clear and present danger as rationale for the measure); (b) that the legislation encouraged "responsible" use of long guns (putting onus on opponents of the bill to demonstrate equal responsibility); (c) that, in practice, the new rules should pose no problems for those already using guns according to the safety procedures stressed by firearms clubs (designed to reassure long gun users).

Nevertheless, heavy opposition was encountered, not only from firearms clubs and associations, but also from hunting and wildlife editors, especially in Quebec. So vociferous was the outcry that government MP's from rural constituencies demanded changes in the bill before second reading. As a result, the firearms regulation part of the package introduced in April died on the order paper before the summer recess—despite objective survey data that showed a majority of voters favored the gun control provisions. In short, the interest groups had defeated the critical mass.

Phase II. During the summer, the head of the Peace and Security Task Force began marshalling support for the gun control provisions, tinkering with the details as necessary to win support from different groups. In this the government profited from a statement made during a T.V. talk show by a national firearms association chairman who said he recognized the need for *some* restrictions on long gun ownership. In a series of behind-the-scenes meetings, the task force and association executive agreed upon a modified ownership certificate replacing the character references with a police record of violent crime. When Parliament resumed after Labor Day, the government reintroduced the firearms measures package in modified form, based on the carefully worked out understandings, and secured relatively swift passage, despite charges of "sell-out" from Toronto and some other urban media.

Note: A vital element in the effectiveness of the opposition was the failure of the Task Force to communicate the details of the bill to fish and game editors across the country. This arose from the somewhat ramshackle organization of government communications whereby Justice analysts worked closely with the Task Force communications adviser, but both were divorced from implementation, which was jealously handled by the Solicitor-General Communications Branch. Extremely territorial, they resisted all attempts at change by the Task Force, including the careful implementation of Task Force communications strategies.

Also, the government did not try all options available before bowing to caucus pressure in Phase I, such as (1) a speaking tour by the Justice Minister to each "gun death" city; (2) advocacy ad campaigns or other attempts to strengthen urban support; or (3) any significant attempt to mollify opposition from wildlife editors. This was a product of the priority assigned by the government to the measure.

Analysis

Each of these cases is related to critical mass in that the interest group pressure was vociferous enough to look like a burgeoning "a" phase. In the long gun case, the urban critical mass was defeated by the more highly focused interest group opposing the measure. Yet, as these cases illustrate, interest group pressure is carefully controlled, directed, and regulated by professionals, and mainly related to normal political bargaining along a "contract line." Rifle users and the government reached a politically survivable accommodation. The White House responded to a vigorous lobby by strengthening its stance on trade concessions to hide producers. The soft drink bill permitting the status quo to continue was passed. The outcomes were questions of more or less. Nor is interest group pressure necessarily decisive, whereas a strong critical mass nearly always is. In the long gun case, the urban critical mass could not move rural MPs for whom the issue was far more salient and serious than it was for MPs in urban ridings. As it was, the bill nearly passed in its original form, and, had the urban mass reached critical proportions before Parliament adjourned for the summer, the original bill would probably have become law. Interest group pressure then had greater relevance to bargaining, which is discussed below.

What about efficiency? Does critical mass promote or undermine the efficient allocation of community resources? There, as with externalities issues, the answer depends upon whose "efficiency" wins political support. In the store hours case, critical mass supported the market solution; in the Rely case, critical mass favored the legislated solution; in the Nestlé's case, critical mass attacked and defeated the status quo solution. In another case not discussed here, the saccharin ban proposed by the FDA, critical mass overturned the government proposal in favor of a market solution based on informed consumer choice, information being supplied by warning labels. What our examples continually underline is that any outcome, whether market oriented, legislated, or a mix of market and administrative measures, must command public support to be stable. That public acceptability, in turn, depends on the decisions of stakeholders whether to intervene. At a minimum, therefore, critical mass can be seen as a dramatic check against large misallocations of public costs and benefits.

Conclusion

The externalities model brought us closer to a structured understanding of how issues emerge and where the settlement likely lies. Although suggesting optimum strategies for resolving the issues, the model cannot by itself account for the ultimate choice by legislators or other decision-makers of one alternative over another.

With critical mass, we move a step closer to a full understanding of how issues are resolved. Critical mass, especially the "a" phase, when detected, virtually dictates if not a new solution at least a new *set* of solutions, while eliminating the old status quo set. The development of a critical mass, we also saw, was a communications problem: how to give the unorganized yet passionate supporters of a point of view the opportunity to vent their feelings in a manner more persuasive than the pressure of the status quo interests. In our cases, this was done most successfully in the Peterborough store hours example.

This problem, of tapping the views of the unorganized and facilitating their expression, gives critical mass its kinship to interest group mobilization—and also distinguishes it from it. As with interest group mobilization, critical mass depends first upon lowering participation costs and raising expectations sufficiently that individuals will become involved. Unlike interest group mobilization, however, the critics elicit the support of ordinary people who belong to no association or group concerned with the issue. When these "publics" become aroused, the movement takes on a life of its own, beyond the power of those touching it off to control, literally forcing legislators to act.

Our cases show the chances are good that this can be accomplished whenever certain conditions are present by the use of certain sure-fire techniques. There must be (1) a sense of injustice, or legacy of ill-will; (2) a belief in the possibility of change; (3) an opportunity for those outraged to express their outrage; (4) a way of monitoring the outrage and (5) strengthening it by reporting back to those who share these feelings that there are many, many others who agree; and (6) when the pitch of outrage has built to the point where its effects demonstrably reach beyond those most directly affected by an issue, there must also be a way of communicating that sentiment to the decision-makers involved. When this occurs, the result will usually be a decisive shift in favor of eliminating the injustice.

However, as we saw in the last case on long gun control, critical mass can be frustrated by strong sectional or other client-government relationships. Not all issues can anyway be settled by critical mass, and there can often be contests among the special interests themselves. In those other instances, our general issues model indicates, bargaining will be the method of resolution. The next set of cases will examine issues resolution through bargaining in a business-government context.

BARGAINING CASES

Theory Predicts

The bargaining models described negotiation as falling into three stages: the announcement of terms, the search for allies, and, finally, imposition of terms. The general process has the effect, it was argued, of deciding where on a contract line the final result would occur.

Our discussion then contrasted political bargaining with other forms, and drew attention to "breakdowns in rationality" that were particularly likely to occur in business-government bargaining confrontations. These, it will be recalled, included second worst outcomes emerging from unflinching pursuit of the best, bargaining patterns in which no single strategy could produce optimal results, and, lastly, traps of self-destruction. Awareness of these pitfalls, it was argued, could improve bargaining performance.

In this section we will look at actual company government performance to see how well the models correspond to and predict reality.

The Bargaining Process: Gun Control Again

The three cases discussed in the last part of the previous section (Hide Action, Bottlers Bill, and Long Gun Control) illustrate the crucial importance of allies in political bargaining. But the gun control case is especially interesting. In that case, the government's failure (a) to touch off a real critical mass of vocal support for the bill, or (b) to assuage the anxieties of gun owners, transformed the issue into a bargaining one between urban and rural interests.

The search for allies during the summer created a problem for each side analogous to that of an ideological (i.e., non-broker) political party: victory required more support than their own most fervent partisans could offer. But the base support had to be broadened without weakening or alienating the core supporters. "Fuzziness" or ambiguity, the method favored during campaigns to cope with this problem, was not sufficient for what was, after all, a narrowly-focused, specifically targeted government program. But, as the public debate continued, the competition for support caused each side to shave its positions that were most offensive to the other side. Thus, the rifle users association accepted the principle of regulation, and the government modified its regulatory mechanism to be least offensive to law abiding rifle owners. Rural elements in the governing party caucus were thus mollified, and the government succeeded in getting a law on the books embodying the *principle* of controls on long guns. There was disappointment among the *arditi* on both sides; but the result allowed both sides to claim a modicum of victory that satisfied the majority of their respective supporters.

Case 1: Firestone vs. National Highway Traffic Safety Administration (NHTSA)[13]

Issue. A government agency, the NHTSA, recommends recall of the company's entire 500 line of steel belted radials, some 11 million of which are still in use. Total production cost of the free replacement that recall would entail would be $275 million and more than $300 million if private brand similar tires are added to the recall. Company net income in FY 1977 was $110.2 million, gross revenue $4.4 billion. In the first half of FY 1978, the company lost $37 million. Compliance therefore could cripple the company, but failure to settle the issue could undermine public confidence in the company beyond its ability to recover.

Origins. The issue emerged in 1976, four years after the company began production of the tires, when the Center for Auto Safety (a Washington based consumer group once associated with Ralph Nader) alerted the NHTSA to the large volume of complaints they had received about the product. The NHTSA responded by initiating a survey in 1977 which indicated widespread consumer dissatisfaction, but whose findings were undermined by the weakness of its methodology.

The Government Case. The Government case against the tire rested primarily on inference from the relatively high incidence of accidents (hundreds) and deaths (at least 34) associated with the tire. At the heart of the agency's data was a flawed study of 6,000 consumer reports of 14,000 separate tire failures and the so-called adjustment rate (ratio of returns to sales) which, for the 500, was twice the average of other radials.

The Company Case. Despite its sweeping investigation, the agency had failed to pinpoint a single defect in the tire. The company maintained that consumer mishandling—over-inflation, frequent rough contact with curbs and speeding—were behind the accidents and complaints.

The Issue Choice. If the tire was truly defective, then the issue was an externality situation, and company cooperation with public authorities was advisable. There is no issue in an unsafe tire: both the company's and society's interests are best served by the product's disappearance from the marketplace.

Possibly, however, full knowledge of the tire was concealed from the corporate officer responsible for handling the issue. In that circumstance, the company would appear to be in a bargaining situation with the agency, with customers, Congress, and ultimately, the voters looking on.

A Bargaining Analysis. As a bargaining situation, what are the possible outcomes? In gross terms, they can be reduced to four: win, lose, deadlock, and compromise. For the agency, loss would be the second against

Firestone, and thus, one could conjecture, unacceptable. A deadlock, with its attendant publicity, might be preferable to a compromise, as it conceivably could lead to wider regulatory powers. But a compromise would be better than an outright loss. These preferences can be ranked and scored as follows (giving the most preferable four points): win (4), deadlock (3), compromise (2), lose (1).

For a company, a win is best, a deadlock that keeps the issue in the media but unresolved is worse than anything but a total capitulation, thus making compromise second best. Therefore: win (4), compromise (3), deadlock (2), lose (1).

Diagramming the outcomes gives this result:

Figure VII.3. Firestone 500 Case

		Agency C	*Agency* D	*Row Min.*
Company	C	3,2	1,4	2,1
Company	D	4,1	2,3	1,2
Col. Max.		4,2	2,4	

The diagram also shows column maxima and row minima. These show the outcomes for hard strategies and soft ones, "D" and "C", respectively. The squares show the actual outcomes and their respective worth the the players based on the schedules prepared above. Thus (C,C) a compromise (two compromise strategies) is worth 3 to the company. A clear win (D,C) to the company, or (C,D) to the agency, is equally preferred by both. (D,D), the deadlock outcome, the result of hard strategies by each, is the second best outcome for the agency (3), the second worst outcome for the company (2).

But now look at the maxima and minima. These show that, for the company, a "hard" strategy has a theoretical possibility of delivering an outright victory (4), while risking only (2) as low score. By way of contrast, a conciliatory policy might only win (3), but could result in total defeat (1). Apparently, therefore, a tough bargaining stance is called for.

But look again. The diagram makes clear what would happen if the company decides to tough it out and play D. The agency might capitulate, but would more rationally play "tough" right back. The result would be the second best outcome for the agency, and the second worst for the company. We are thus in a pattern that amounts to a "breakdown in rationality": an apparently best course is actually a worst course. For the company, although a win is preferable, it is clearly impossible to achieve. Instead, the challenge to the company strategist is to induce the agency to make concessions with a view to landing the outcome in the top lefthand (C,C) quadrant, the second best for the company. The problem, from the company standpoint, is how to bring about the necessary deterioration of agency preferences so that compromise becomes possible.

This becomes even clearer when one remembers the likely stages through which the conflict will pass. Bargaining follows three stages, as we have seen (terms, allies, imposition of settlement). What allies are possible for a company that plays confrontation games against a regulatory agency with a *prima facie* case? Moreover, the agency has the power to give consumers a better break than they could otherwise get from the company: new tires for old. Under these conditions, a confrontational response might even generate a critical mass response against the company.

Both "externality" and "bargaining" analysis urge a generally cooperative thrust for best results.

Actual Outcomes. Historically, Firestone chose confrontation. The company went to the mat with the agency, and failed to cooperate fully with its requests for data. It attempted to suppress an agency survey of radial tire owners that was unfavorable to the product, taking the agency to court when it might have been better to wait until the survey was released and then demolish it in a public statement. The company also failed to make a good showing before a House of Representative subcommittee that intervened and finally ran afoul of the Securities and Exchange Commission. The company even inadvertently held a major clearance sale of the 500 radial just before the government investigation got full publicity. Not until every avenue of resistance had been exhausted did they voluntarily recall the tire.

Documents subpoenaed from the company showed that, at the same time the company president (who later resigned) and top executives were receiving detailed reports of the tire's defects from their own production experts and major corporate buyers like General Motors, Atlas Tire Company, Shell, and Montgomery Ward, "they still assured the public that the 500 had no safety defects and were not telling stockholders of the problems." Beside alienating major customers, the company faced staggering liability suits, and, worst of all, evidence of management's cover up of the defect risked sharp reductions in the company's product liability insurance.

Conclusion. This case illustrates some of the traps into which a company can fall through failure to act in a fully rational way in accordance with the dynamics of bargaining. True, superficially, a confrontational strategy provided the best chance of maximizing gains and minimizing losses. But closer analysis should have revealed the breakdown in rationality that led to those results.

The outcomes were as predicted by the model. The company's actions in the opening phases were too defensive to inspire public confidence. In using the courts to suppress a damaging study, the company played into the hands of the agency, adding to government credibility on the issue. The opportunity presented by the congressional subcommittee hearing was also mishandled. Instead of using the forum provided to eliminate the grievance, the company continued to expose itself to public doubt and criticism.

The case also illustrates how choices lead to conclusions. The main issue at the outset was consumer complaints. Had the company been monitoring this aspect of their business satisfactorily, government intervention could have been avoided. However, the complaint monitoring was not taken that far. So the issue was then translated into a question of the reliability of survey data. Here the company created allies for its adversary and isolated itself (by suppressing the survey through use of the courts). The issue was then replayed before a Congressional subcommittee. Here public attention could focus upon a doughty federal agency trying to police an apparently shifty corporation. Throughout each stage, the "issues space" favored by the impartial majority was moving steadily away from the company position. As negative publicity mounted, the company's main private brand distributors effectively withdrew their tacit support. The company then faced powerful inducements to settle quickly and reestablish its good name. The federal agency was, at that point, able to impose terms.

Could a different strategy have produced a different outcome? First, it appears from the final events of this incident that the company was seriously mismanaged, and that there was actual readiness among some top management when under pressure to try to hoodwink the public. That this failed is to be applauded.

A better managed company caught in a similar situation might have achieved a better outcome, i.e., might have succeeded in achieving a more limited recall than the 10 million ultimately required.

The recall ultimately negotiated with the NHTSA covered tires constructed during a 12 month period in 1975–1976, as well as private brand equivalents from the same period. The company was also required to offer 50 percent discounts on new tires to customers trading in Firestone 500s built before March, 1975. Total pre-tax costs were set out at the head of this case, based on 100 percent return. True, company negotiations reduced the initial NHTSA demand by threatening to tie up the issue in court when the agency wanted a quicker solution. Thus, the bargaining approach generated some benefits. But the true costs involved the reputation of top management and the company. Bearing in mind that the actual rate of return in most recalls in the tire industry usually settles at around 25 percent, the value of the outcome may be questioned.

Using the courts to try to suppress the agency survey was also inappropriate; the survey's flawed methodology was an ally in disguise. A better approach would have been to have allowed its publication and then demolished it in a statement afterwards—the agency's credibility could have been harmed and some political allies perhaps won. Perhaps, too, the Congressional hearings could have been avoided. A more forthcoming position, at that point, might have delivered added benefits in goodwill and consumer confidence. Compare, for example, the Proctor & Gamble Rely Tampon Case above. A generally cooperative "Let's get at the truth" approach might have had significantly better results. Such a strategy was used in the Canadian subsidiary of Firestone (where Public Affairs instead of Legal Affairs made the decisions) and achieved good cooperation with government, a more limited recall and little publicity.[14]

Case 2: The Inco Layoffs

Issue. Consider, from the standpoint of the company, the following situation. Inco. Canada's third-ranking industrial corporation in terms of assets, producer of 40 percent of the non-Communist world's nickel, is helpless to overcome sagging markets and faces cash losses of $700,000 a day. Already the firm has lost its top-rated investment status in Moody's, Standard and Poor's, and Dominion Bond's investor services. One immediate objective must at all costs be achieved: conserve cash. Action required: cutbacks of 15 percent in operations, and layoffs of nearly one-fifth of the 21,500 person work force, most of whom live in a single community. How should this be handled?

The Company's Solution. The company decided to adhere strictly to the law by making a flat announcement in a statement issued to news media following the third quarter board meeting. The letter of the law, Regulation 251 under the Ontario Employment Standards Act, which requires 16 weeks notice be given of layoffs of 500 or more employees, and U.S. and Ontario financial reporting regulations requiring that all shareholders get the facts at the same time to avoid insider trading, was respected. Inco also consulted the federal government two weeks before the announcement.

Result: Although the actual layoff plan minimized damage to the community, the outcome was a PR debacle in which the company was excoriated in the press, dragged before a provincial commission of inquiry, denounced by opposition party leaders, and subjected to a series of suggestions by the federal government. Could this outcome have been improved?

Bargaining Analysis. Feelings are normally intense between mining companies and their employees, the mining communities and, therefore, the government and the press. It is a combustible mixture and the potential for the development of a critical mass of anti-company feeling is so great as to border on certainty.

However, despite the volatile background in which the layoffs occur, the situation is, like all divestment decisions, *primarily* a negotiating one, involving the cooperation of the unions, the town and the government to make the slowdown a success. The preferred outcome of the stakeholders, in order of preference, would be: (1) to make the company cancel its layoff plans (Win); (2) to make the company reduce the numbers to be laid off (Compromise); (3) to have no solution—i.e. avoid any suggestion of capitulation (Deadlock); (4) last of all, would they yield to the company's view of the situation and concede. Stated grossly, and ranked with 4 as the highest of the four possibilities: Win (4); Compromise (3); Deadlock (2); Yield (1). Inco's preferences were the same, except it preferred a deadlock in which layoffs would proceed to any compromise. In other words: to achieve the desired layoffs without cost (win); layoff without any solution (deadlock); compromise if it meant changing plans; finally, yield and abandon the project. Thus, Win (4), Deadlock (3), Compromise (2), Yield (1). Figure VII.4 on page 158 matches the preferences and outcomes.

Comparing column maxima and row minima, it is clear that a "hard" strategy opens the possibility of a win, while exposing them only to a second best outcome as the worst possible result from that strategy. Moreover, when inspected for signs of a "rationality breakdown," it is

Figure VII.4. Inco's Layoffs

	Others C	D	*Row Min.*
C	2,3	1,4	1,3
D	4,1	3,2	3,1
Col. Max.	4,3	3,4	

Remember: squares stand for outcomes: C,C = Compromise, D,D = Deadlock, C,D or D,C a win for "others" or Inco, respectively, "D" moves are "hard", "C" moves are "soft".

apparent that no such signs exist. The company will be playing D against (assuming maximizing behavior on the other side) a C strategy.

This analysis illustrates the extreme difficulty of the company achieving an impression of "responsible" behavior. Should the company show signs of compromise, with a "C" opening move, it would risk being entrapped in an unacceptable alternative or a stiff return that could produce defeat. The temptation then is to play hard, and if the result is deadlock, so be it. From the stakeholders' side, the likely reply to a hard company move will be attempts to "compromise," or if that fails, to reach a "deadlock," especially against the volatile background of opinion we have described. This is essentially the game that was played, but, as we have seen, the outcome was ragged.

The problem from the company's viewpoint is mainly one of "packaging." To achieve its desired outcomes, the company has to play "D" in such a way that the stakeholders capitulate or else play "D" back again. The key to achieving this is communicating the *inevitability* of the layoff: *the Company has to be seen to have no choice.* If this is accepted, the stakeholders then face difficult options. They must either cooperate with the company in the manner in which the company chooses to proceed, come up with a better alternative, or else oppose the company so strongly that they (the stakeholders) seem unreasonable.

The Program. One way, perhaps, to have communicated inevitability would have been to announce (1) that the company would have to cutback production, and that this would inevitably mean some layoffs, and (2) that the company was studying ways of achieving this in such a way as to minimize effects on the community. Second, immediately initiate consultations with union leaders, provincial, civic, and federal governments on the layoff plans. Third, make the public announcement, with (or without) the cooperation of the other groups, about the manner of the layoffs. The announcement should be accompanied by a full explanation of why the layoffs are inescapable, and how their impact is being minimized.

Dangers in this approach include: (1) occupation of the work site after first announcement: offset by invitation to cooperate; and (2) government or union interference with right to manage once consultations begin: offset by (a) cost to public purse of government bailout; and (b) improbability of union acceptance of work sharing.

Finally, there is the slight chance that one or more of the parties to the discussion might come up with a better or acceptable alternative. This would achieve the company's goals and could result in a joint announcement.

This case also illustrates how outcomes emerge from initial events. The list of news stories set out in the box (below) shows how the issue actually proceeded from the way in which the company handled it. Clearly, first impressions were that the company had violated the public interest. Nor was that impression wholly alleviated by the Provincial Commission of Inquiry. Its first report severely castigated the company, and had to be rewritten at the command of the Provincial Government.

These results corroborate the suggestion of the model of the overriding importance of strategy in a bargaining situation and how it governs the development of outcomes. Inco's apparent "public be damned" confrontational approach set the beat to which all the other actors danced, virtually locked in their adversarial roles. Neither company, nor union, nor government—only to some extent the town of Sudbury—benefitted from the way the event unfolded (Sudbury won the attention of the southern part of Ontario long enough to make a case for better economic development assistance). True, the company achieved its work reduction on time, but in a way that did little for its long term interests or those of the industry. A different approach, with more attention to public explanation, might have achieved more optimal outcomes.

List of News Stories

20 October 1977	*Toronto Star,* "Inco to drop 3,450 jobs and cut production."
21 October 1977	*ibid,* "Two Governments battle to save Sudbury jobs."
"	*ibid,* "Heartbroken Sudbury, Everyone's been shafted."
"	Edward Clifford, *Globe and Mail,* "Mine output to be reduced as Inco plans massive cuts."

21 October 1977	*ibid*, "Lewis blames Queen's Park for Inco layoffs."
"	*ibid*, "Worst blow hits Sudbury as Inco cuts out 2,800 jobs."
22 October 1977	*ibid*, "Nickel cartel studied as way to raise prices."
"	*Toronto Star*, "Cartel could have saved Sudbury: P.M."
"	Rudy Platiel, *Globe & Mail*, "Mine layoffs have almost become way of life in Sudbury, regional chairman says."
"	editorial, *ibid*, "Bad Day at Sudbury."
23 October 1977	*Sunday Star*, "Broadbent: ' "Stockpile unsold nickel.' "
24 October 1977	editorial, *Toronto Star*, "Inquiry needed on Inco layoffs."
25 October 1977	*Globe & Mail*, "Nickel dumping cited as reason for layoffs."
"	Jack McArthur, *Toronto Star*, "Is big Inco bad for Canada or vice versa?"
"	*Globe & Mail*, "Ottawa may take nickel dumping case to GATT."
"	*ibid*, "Davis to meet Inco chief to discuss layoff problem."
"	Ronald Anderson, *ibid*, "The real world."
26 October 1977	*Toronto Star*, "Don't give us welfare, save the jobs, Inco union tells government officials."
"	*Globe & Mail*, "A month ago Inco denied layoffs coming, minutes show."
"	Wilfred List, *ibid*, "Cure is to prevent Inco layoffs, union tells bureaucrats."
"	*ibid*, "Inco management 'arrogant' as industrialists of the 19th century, Sudbury mayor charges."
"	Elmer Aoplia, *ibid*, "Mood in Sudbury."
27 October 1977	George Bain, *Toronto Star*, "Six-month notice could have cushioned Inco layoffs."
28 October 1977	Robert Sheppard, *Globe & Mail*, "Trudeau misled Commons over Inco, made 'serious errors,' Broadbent says."
28 October 1977	*ibid*, "David sees investment menace in criticism of Inco layoffs."

28 October 1977	*Toronto Star*, "Inco to discuss delaying, layoffs for 3 to 6 months."
29 October 1977	Donald Turnbull, *Financial Post*, "Union wants stockpiling."
"	*Globe & Mail*, "Inco stand dashes hopes for any delay in layoffs at Sudbury."
"	Roger Croft, *Toronto Star*, "Safer to fire Canadians Inco admits."
31 October 1977	*Toronto Star*, "Foreign operations not a factor in layoffs."
15 November 1977	*Globe and Mail*, "Mines stage 3-city marches on Sudbury layoff."
22 November 1977	Rudy Platiel, *ibid*, "Legislature group on layoff looks over Inco operations."
23 November 1977	Rudy Platiel, *ibid*, "Early pension retirement plan would cushion mining layoffs, Inco inquiry members told."
24 November 1977	*Financial Times* of London, quoted in *ibid*, "New producers of Nickel blamed for world surplus and price cuts."
1 December 1977	Wildred List, *ibid*, "OFL convention urges nationalization of Inco."
3 December 1977	Victor Malarek, *ibid*, "Inco pollution-control order extended."
9 December 1977	Rudy Platiel, *ibid*, "Sudbury reels from further cutbacks in mining industry."
14 December 1977	*ibid*, "Joint union–Government effort could avert Sunday layoffs, Trudeau feels."
20 December 1977	*Toronto Star*, "Inco defends job cutbacks and warns of new actions."
21 December 1977	*Globe & Mail*, "There could be further layoffs, Inco bosses say."
12 January 1978	*ibid*, "Union proposals to avoid layoffs rejected by Inco."
13 January 1978	*ibid*, "Should have slowed in 1975–76, Inco says."
9 February 1978	Robert Williamson, *ibid*, "MPP's urge subsidy scheme to delay Inco layoff."
"	Elain Corey, *Toronto Star*, "Halt Inco layoffs 60 days MPP's say."
11 February 1978	Johnathan Manthorpe, *ibid*, "MPP's fight Inco layoffs with hot air."

11 February 1978	*ibid*, "Sudbury: From lush green hills to slag and layoffs."
1 March 1978	Lawrence Walsh, *Globe & Mail*, "Inco predicts gain in demand; hints at more cutbacks."
4 March 1978	*Toronto Star*, "Diversify industry Sudbury is advised."
8 March 1978	*Globe & Mail*, "Mine tax changes needed to save jobs, Miller says."
15 March 1978	Hugh Windsor, *ibid*, "Layoffs will be boon, Sudbury official says."
17 March 1978	Ronald Anderson, *ibid*, "Nickel Outlook."
"	Peter Mosher, *ibid*, "Queen's Park report is at odds with budget on nickel-refining jobs."
18 March 1978	Peter Mosher, *ibid*, "MPP criticizes failure of Miller to give committee nickel report."
19 March 1978	Charlotte Montgomery, *Sunday Star*, "Mines may lose 1,300 more jobs."
22 March 1978	*Toronto Star*, "Falconbridge needs tax break, Davis says."
29 March 1978	*ibid*, "Mine layoffs: 'We never used to squabble.'"
19 April 1978	*ibid*, "Inco's earnings show faint glimmer of hope."
7 June 1978	*Globe & Mail*, "Layoff problems not as bad as feared, Sudbury officials say."
9 August 1978	Rudy Platiel, *ibid*, "Gloomy forecast for Sudbury area turns into smiles."

Case 3: National Energy Program (NEP) and Multinational Oil Co. X[16]

In October, 1980, the Government of Canada introduced a National Energy Program that dramatically changed the rules of the energy business. The program aimed at setting new directions for the Canadian economy, realizing Canada's vast energy potential, achieving security of supply, and reducing the foreign-owned share of the industry, from 70 percent to 50 percent. Although a statement on energy policy had been awaited for more than a year, the new policy went further than virtually anyone inside or outside the industry anticipated. The main points of the program were:

Price—a blended oil price, made in Canada, to rise slowly to 85 percent of world or U.S. oil prices, whichever is lower, "so as to preserve a competitive advantage for Canadian industry" and natural gas prices to be held below oil to encourage consumer substitution.

New Production Taxes—a new federal tax on natural gas and gas liquids beginning immediately for domestic sales and, on February 1, 1981, for export sales, increasing over the next three years; plus a new 8 percent tax effective 1 January, 1981 on net revenue from oil and gas production in Canada.

Canadianization—at least 50 percent ownership of oil and gas production by 1990; Canadian control of a significant number of major oil and gas corporations, and an early increase in the share of the oil and gas sector owned by the federal government.

This to be Achieved Through—a Canadian ownership levy at the pump; a change in depletion allowances to favor Canadian companies (phase out of depletion allowances outside frontier areas by 1984; a new system of incentive payments structured to encourage investment by Canadian companies and individuals, with added incentives for off-shore and frontier exploration).

Other Measures on Federal Lands—the Crown reserves a 25 percent interest applicable to all existing interests, however acquired; minimum 50 percent public or private Canadian ownership required for any production from Canada lands; high Canadian content rules, with special training and employment rules for native Canadians where applicable; a Progressive Incremental Royalty (profits tax), based on the profitability of each producing field, in addition to basic 10 percent royalty.

New Agencies—Creation of the Petroleum Incentives Board to administer the incentives program, plus more power for the Petroleum Monitoring Agency, particularly to determine ownership and control; creation of a natural gas bank, to purchase natural gas from Canadian producers unable to bring their product to market.

Federal Dominance in the Energy Sector—Petro-Canada (the government oil company) to become the largest oil company in Canada with acquisitions financed by a Canadian ownership tax on consumption; extension of the natural gas pipeline system to Quebec City and the Maritimes, with gas price held to Toronto and Montreal level; a new Petroleum Compensation charge on oil refiners (the federal government had, up to now, been paying Atlantic provinces the difference between world and domestic prices) to shift the burden of compensation from the federal government to refiners; a new split of revenues from petroleum production; 24 percent federal, 43 percent provincial (who technically owned the resources), 33 percent industry; (the previous split had been: 10, 45, and 45 percent, respectively), plus a $4 billion economic development fund earmarked for spending in the Western provinces.

Background. The National Energy Program was the most interventionist and controversial policy launched by the Government of Canada since the imposition of wage and price controls in October, 1975. The roots of the program had as much to do with the central government's wish to cope with the centrifugal forces within the Confederation, from Quebec nationalism to so-called Western alienation. Economic and political advice received by the government held that meeting those challenges and keeping Canada viable until the end of the century would require large-scale national adjustments: first, to maintain national unity and, at the same time, maintain Ottawa's role as the fiscal balance wheel and central administrator of confederation (vs. a collegial administration of Canada by all 11 governments), and, second, to strengthen Canada's economic base and improve its international competitiveness.

From Ottawa's perspective, the new policy would provide assured energy supplies at bargain prices, pumped through pipelines that hooped the staves of the country together like an enormous barrel, the whole package intended to position Canada to reap maximum advantage from the global marketplace of the 1980s.

The NEP increased centralization by destroying the long-term resource-based political power of all the oil producing provinces and transferred it to the federal government. At the same time, it allocated economic rents from oil and gas production to favor, *inter alia*, consumers (and voters) in Central Canada. It also encouraged economic nationalism by creating new investment opportunities for Canadians by discriminating against foreign-owned oil and gas firms.

Company X

Company X was an exploration and producing subsidiary of a large U.S. multinational oil company. Company X was one of the top five producers of crude oil in Canada, one of the top 10 natural gas producers, and it employed more than 1,000 people. Its relations with Canada went back 30 years, to the opening of Western Canada's oil industry. The company had significant interests in the high arctic and North Atlantic oil and gas exploration activities.

The company was therefore seriously impacted by the new government policy. The new taxes throttled cash flow, eroded profitability and, together with the federal government's announced back-in or take-over of a 25 percent interest in off-shore projects, made it impossible, in the opinion of the company, to realize fair market value for any assets it might consider "Canadianizing."

The effect of the NEP proposals (for price and revenue split) are given in the following exhibits. Exhibit I shows the netbacks to the industry from 1975 and the netbacks that could be anticipated after the program took effect. Exhibit II shows the effects of the NEP on the relative profitability of exploration in Canada compared with other jurisdictions.

NEP CASE: EXHIBIT I. Industry Netbacks (Company x Statement)

	OIL – $/BBL					
	Alberta		*Saskatchewan*		*British Columbia*	
Year	*"old"*	*"new"*	*"old"*	*"new"*	*"old"*	*"new"*
1975 July	1.65	2.40	.17		0.72	
1976 July	1.77	2.68	.80		1.02	2.35
1977 January	1.84	2.83	.74	1.91	1.62	3.04
1977 July	2.02	3.15	.85	2.19	1.86	3.45
1978 January	2.13	3.40	.87	2.39	2.96	3.81
1978 July	2.31	3.71	.80	2.55	3.28	4.20
1979 July	2.43	3.96	.81	2.68	3.58	4.58
1980 January	2.44	4.11	.79	2.83	3.83	4.91
1980 August	2.80	4.71	.78	2.99	4.40	5.62
1981 Post-NEP	1.62	3.74	Lloyd.	(.48)*		
			S.W. Sask.	(.86)*		
			S.E. Sask.	(.01)*		

*Reflects anticipated netbacks for Company X-operated properties only since at this time it was extremely difficult to predict industry netbacks.

NEP CASE: EXHIBIT II. Comparative Profitability of Investment in Oil Exploration and Development (Company x Statement)

Recently proposed Canadian energy policies will severely impact on the financial attractiveness of oil exploration and development investment opportunities. Compared to other countries, investment in offshore resources in Canada will be generally less attractive even at the most favorable price level accorded other production, i.e. oil sands prices. Other countries permit production to be sold at international prices and provide accelerated amortization of investment for tax purposes. Only giant fields in Canada with reserves of one billion barrels or more would approach the profitability standard of the poorest of the other countries studied. With expected field size and lower price levels, e.g. the prices established for conventional onshore production, investment in offshore resource development would not be attractive...
Profitability of investment in onshore oil exploration and development in the United States is substantially greater than in Canada. This is due to decontrol of oil prices which more than compensates for higher unit investment costs than in Canada...

NEP CASE: Comparative Profitability (Company x Statement)

		1981 Prices and Costs			*1985 Price and Costs*		
OFFSHORE	*Field Size (Million Bbls)*	*Profit ($/Bbl)*	*Profit Ratio* ($/$)*	*Gov't Take***	*Profit ($/Bbl)*	*Profit Ratio* ($/$)*	*Gov't Take***
US Gulf of Mexico	20	10.74	1.07	74 %	16.96	1.53	70 %
Norway	1,000	7.28	2.30	82 %	10.19	2.07	82 %
UK	400	5.62	1.38	85 %	7.91	1.32	85 %
Indonesia	200	5.36	1.59	85 %	8.01	1.65	85 %
Canada							
Expected Field Size:	250						
Conventional Prices		1.18	0.22	84 %	2.91	0.40	81 %
Oil Sands Prices		6.01	1.13	77 %	8.60	1.15	77 %
Giant Field Size:	1,000						
Conventional Prices		1.76	0.39	81 %	3.77	0.61	79 %
Oil Sands Prices		6.61	1.48	77 %	9.45	1.50	77 %
ONSHORE							
U.S.	1–5	12.16	1.53	67 %	17.32	1.56	66 %
Canada—Alberta	1–5	1.24	0.23	89 %	3.04	0.46	85 %

* Profit Ratio—Dollar Profit per Dollar Invested

**Government Take—Percentage of Gross Revenue taken by Governments through Taxes and Royalties.

The Company Response. Yet the program and the way it was introduced virtually hamstrung the company's ability to fight back.

At first glance this seems surprising. The NEP antagonized most sectors of the oil industry because its planned taxes bit so heavily into cash flow and profits that it made Canada appear a relatively poor place to do business. Indeed, the months after the program was announced witnessed a massive exodus of drillers to the United States and elsewhere.

The program also appeared to discriminate massively against foreign-owned, especially American-owned business, which did in fact prompt extensive reaction in Congress. In addition, it antagonized the oil producing provinces with taxes that appeared to encroach on provincial jurisdiction (taxes on provincial crown corporations and export taxes on provinces at less than they deemed reasonable). No agreement was reached with the producing provinces until September, 1981, nearly a year after the program was introduced.

Business outside the energy sector was also adversely affected by the slowdown in the energy boom the program caused and by the sopping up of scarce capital diverted to Canadianization.

Yet, all had been anticipated by the federal government with the result that bargaining during the course of the program's passage into law was restricted to relatively minor adjustments. No changes in principle were considered. The program, disastrous as it appeared for Canada and its oil industry less than two years after its introduction, was passed into law in approximately 18 months of debate during which the government yielded virtually nothing. How was this achieved?

Policy Development. Work on the policy began towards the end of Prime Minister Trudeau's government in early 1979, and resumed again when Trudeau regained power after the Conservative eight-month interregnum. The program was conceived in constitutional and political terms: no sovereign nation could afford 70 percent foreign ownership of an essential resource; Ottawa could not remain dependent on Alberta and other producing provinces if it was to retain its pivotal role in confederation. As well, it appeared to some officials, Ottawa should adopt a strongly confrontational policy to hasten settlement of the constitutional issue by 1982.

Policy development was entrusted to a special group within the Energy Mines and Resources Department, who worked feverishly in isolation, short-circuiting normal departmental procedures, and consulting extensively with senior officers of the government oil company.[17]

Preparation of the policy announcement, which normally would have involved pre-announcement consultations with the main stakeholder groups, was reviewed only by the Cabinet Committee on Priorities and Planning as part of the budget package.

Initial Results. The initial announcement knocked 40 points off the New York Stock Exchange share price of U.S.-owned oil and gas companies with extensive holdings in Canada. This was followed by an exodus of drilling operations to the United States (where a new pro-business administration had just been elected), and a massive flight of capital, up to C$10 billion in nine months vs. normal outflows of $2 billion a year).

The Game. The confrontational model chosen by the federal government shows that a pure confrontational strategy against a clearly defined "villain" (OPEC, foreign domination) articulated in terms of national values (patriotism, energy security, economic development) can hobble effective opposition.

The government preferred, after outright win, continued deadlock to compromise, and may even have felt that being forced to capitulate would be better than fundamental compromise. Industry would have preferred a return to the status quo, but failing that, a compromise over deadlock or capitulation.

Ranking these as Government: Win (4), Deadlock (3), Capitulation (2), Compromise (1); Industry: Win (4), Compromise (3), Deadlock (2), Defeat (1), we get the following matrix:

Figure VII.5. NEP Case

		Multinational Industry C	*Multinational Industry* D	
				Row Min.
Canadian Government	C	1,3	2,4	1,3
Canadian Government	D	4,1	3,2	3,1
Col. Max.		4,3	3,4	

Given the preference schedules above, it is clear that the government's best strategy was to play as tough as it could, for it then risked only a deadlock, which was its second best option. Equally, it is clear that industry's minimum risk strategy was to try for confrontation, but that this would almost certainly have placed it in a losing deadlock. Also, the favored treatment given Canadian firms by the program would likely have ensured their isolation if they were moved to deadlock at that time.

Essentially, the foreign-owned sector of the industry was virtually paralyzed unless it could attract Canadian allies with a common interest in defeating the program.

At the outset, this appeared extremely unlikely. Multinational companies were the victims of growing Canadian distrust through the 1970s, to which the government had responded with increasing regulation of direct investment (notably the Foreign Investment Review Agency).

Suspicion of multinational oil companies had risen especially following the oil crises of 1973 and 1978–9. Company X, in particular, was especially isolated on this point, having done little to accommodate Canadian nationalism or establish much of a Canadian identity for itself. Thus, when suddenly victimized, it was too isolated to respond effectively, except in technical language. Although the economic case it presented in a low-key delivery before both Commons and Senate Committees considering NEP legislation was correct, that case was not widely believed. Nor did it attract much media attention.

Indeed, six months after the program was introduced and many of the initial negative consequences had already been felt, there was still an absence of potential allies.

The federal government buy-out of Petrofina at high settlement that added 3.5 cents a gallon to the pump price of gas was greeted favorably by consumers, although it did not result in a single extra drop of oil for Canada.

Current public opinion overwhelmingly favored Canadianization, distrusted multinational corporations, and welcomed massive government intrusion as a countervailing, protective power—especially in Central Canada (Ontario and Quebec).

Even Canadian businessmen favored the program. The financial community expected to do well from financing Canadianization. Middle management outside the financial sector hoped to profit from the hobbles on "foreign competition" or to use the growing nationalism to win more responsibility from the head office.

Reports commissioned by segments of the oil industry showed that the main business reaction was uncertainty. Much of the domestic slowdown from the easing of the energy boom was made up in exports or cutbacks of planned expansion rather than reductions of current operations. Although businessmen were expecting 1982–3 to be the year of maximum losses from NEP, executives were unwilling to talk about how large the losses would be. That unwillingness to discuss bad news stemmed not only from financial circumstances, but also from political ones. As one confidential report put it, manufacturers were "extremely reluctant" to be identified directly or obliquely with an issue perceived as a source of contention between the Government of Canada, the Governments of the producing provinces, and the petroleum industry. Several companies surveyed in the study indicated great unwillingness to say anything that could result in their becoming "political fodder."

In other words, the cost of political participation outweighed other inducements to get involved. As a result, Company X adopted a Fabian strategy, waiting for the economic news to worsen and for others to emerge who could more credibly carry forward responsible opposition to the unworkable aspects of the plan. Their position was, in effect, silent acceptance of deadlock.

Could they have done more? Our model of government behavior indicates that the bargaining power of officials in other economic ministries besides Energy might have been strengthened with sound information and more detailed projections they could use against Energy later on. But the tight Ministerial discipline, for which the ruling Liberals were especially noted, ensured that this, too, would have had to be a long-term strategy.

Economic Downturn. By mid-1982, as predicted, the economic arguments began to bite, especially since the Constitutional questions had been temporarily settled with the "patriation" of an amended British North America Act on July 1, 1982.

By then, the presuppositions that had informed the NEP lay in disarray. OPEC notwithstanding, the international oil price stabilized at around $34.00 a barrel, below economic rates of return for tar sands and frontier oil production. The "mega projects" with which Ottawa hope to stimulate economic activity lay at a standstill.

Oil company profits fell 50 percent in the first year of the program, and 50 percent again in the second. Canadian companies that had used highly leveraged debt to "Canadianize" their assets and those of U.S.-based competitors now found their cash flow squeezed to pay the service charges on their debts. The high debt positions of major Canadian oil and other companies put pressure on the major banks who had financed the transactions. Meanwhile, the anticipated revenues from oil had failed to materialize in sufficient quantities, sending the government deficit to twice the levels anticipated by the NEP budget. As Dome Petroleum,[18] one of the chief beneficiaries of the program, tottered on the brink of receivership, the ability of the government, whose own credit was stretched to the limit, to guarantee the loans of its corporate supporters was becoming a question. As a consequence, popular approval of the government slipped to 24 percent, an all-time low.

Policy Turnaround. The erosion of the economic underpinnings of the NEP and, with those, the erosion of the economy in general and the support for the government, transformed the payoff matrix with which the government began. They were no longer able to profit politically from continued deadlock and lack of progress. On the contrary, the deadlock had become as destructive to the government politically as it was to the oil companies economically. Events were transforming the government side of the game into "Chicken" without appreciably altering that of the companies. The resulting configuration ("Called Bluff" in our discussion of theory) is shown in the diagram below:

Figure VII.6. NEP Ending Phase

		Multinational Industry C	*Multinational Industry* D	*Row Min.*
Canadian Government	C	3,3	2,4	2,3
	D	4,1	1,2	1,1
Col. Max.		4,3	2,4	

This is a closing game configuration in that the inducements are now set for a settlement of some kind. The government appeared to recognize this in announcing a series of tax changes for the oil and gas industry on May 31st. The measures which included reductions in the PGRT and tax credits against future earnings would, it was estimated, increase industry revenues about $2.05 billion over two years, or about 2.8 percent of the $74 billion estimated total for the period. The federal tax changes echoed a variety of tax concessions announced in April by the Alberta government, estimated to total $5.44 billion through 1986.

Also included was a one-year elimination of the incremental oil revenue tax and adjustments to the administered price of oil from tertiary recovery projects, some experimental oil recovery schemes and oil discovered between 1973 and 1980. The Canadianization incentives, and the 25 percent back-in provisions, remained unchanged.

Meanwhile, Company X entered into farm-out arrangements with Canadian companies on offshore leases, reducing its interest on leases under Canadian control to below 50 percent (down from 75 percent).

Observations. The NEP case further underlines the power of the opening position. Carefully chosen, with an eye to deeply-rooted attitude trends, the opening position can be decisive in defeating an opponent's strategy from the start.

The Fabian strategy of Company X equally showed how the market economy can itself act as a corrective to hasty political actions and force the actors in a business-government issue to reposition themselves in such a way as to make compromise possible. The source of strength for Company X was its relative obscurity in the debate. As an E and P company, with no marketing operations in Canada, the company was relatively inconspicuous so that its silence, as it happened, was not noticed. Secondly, its commercial power was such that it could afford to wait out the government. This made it a potential winner whichever way the international oil price moved. If it went up, then the company would profit. But, if it went down, then it would be up to the government to make production viable.

The case also illustrates the importance of keeping a cool head. Had Company X rushed headlong into print—an ad campaign, a round of indignant speeches—it then would have played up its deadlock with the government, to the advantage of the government, as the model shows. Wisely, it chose to wait and watch, very carefully, for any break in support for the government, the first sign of a deterioration in the values of its preference schedule.

Conclusion

The three bargaining cases confirm the insights of our models into how issues are actually resolved. They emphasize the importance in a democracy of finding allies, and of the workings of the marketplace as a corrective when government has miscalculated but no allies can be found. The cases also show the importance of choosing strategy carefully and being especially alert for "breakdowns in rationality." The Firestone 500 case demonstrates the importance of analysis before the fact, and how outcomes develop stage by stage from the opening phases of play. The Inco case shows the usefulness of the models in capturing the complexities of a company's position. Yet it does not answer the question of why the company did not lead off with a thorough public explanation of the need for a layoff and the manner in which it would be achieved. The NEP case confirmed the importance of opening moves. But it also showed that commercial power and a cool head can help to minimize damage and perhaps over time help regain lost ground.

PUTTING IT TOGETHER

Case: Issues Track Strategy Paper[19]

This case is designed to illustrate how to use the issues analyses we have presented to put together a useful strategy paper.

The Client

The client is the Chairman of an about-to-be established Canadian government committee of scientific experts examining recommendations to restrict the use of one of North America's most widely used fungicides.

The Requirements

A strategy paper is needed to lead the Chairman through the public policy process so as to maintain maximum credibility and give his committee's recommendations the weight they deserve. Note that his scope for flexibility is enormous. The chairman can negotiate his own terms of reference and rules of procedure.

Method

The method is that summarized above on page 116:

1. *Identify stakeholders, pinpoint the veto groups and model the relationships.*

   Chief stakeholders: Environmentalists, including scientists and lawyers; producers, including farmers and chemical companies; farm workers, organized and unorganized; wholesalers and retailers of fruits and vegetables; customers; federal government departments (Health & Welfare, Agriculture); provincial governments; and other jurisdictions, especially the U.S.A. and Sweden.

2. *Model the Relationships.*

   Issue: Whether or not an externalities model exists. Environmentalists may say yes, agricultural and business interests may say no. Others will be in between looking to the committee for guidance, but also to other jurisdictions, who may be making the same decisions.

   Note: Between environmentalists and producers, a gain for one is perceived as a loss for the other and vice versa.

   Best position for the committee: above the conflict, even handed, especially between environmentalists, producers, and organized labor.

3. *Define Best Attainable Outcomes.*

   1. Win confidence of both sides from the outset of investigations.
   2. Maintain that confidence during the course of hearings.
   3. Draw equal criticism from both sides after results.

4. Leave attentive publics (consumers, editorialists) feeling that the job has been thoroughly and honestly done and that they can have confidence in the findings.

4. *Structure the Unfolding of the Issue.*

    1. Design the optimal committee (use research on procedures in other jurisdictions).
    2. Build in corrections for sub-optimal committee design. Fix bedrock (i.e., *sine qua non*) requirements.
    3. List any key decision points:

        (a) negotiations with Minister to get committee design.
        (b) recruiting members.
        (c) working out procedural rules.
        (d) announcing to press.
        (e) literature research phase.
        (f) call for submissions.
        (g) public hearing(s).
        (h) report writing.
        (i) announcement or handover of final report to Minister.

5. *Operationalize Strategy. Include Critical Path.*
    See strategy paper below.

EXHIBIT: STRATEGY PAPER

I. STRATEGIC OBJECTIVE

TO WIN AND MAINTAIN PUBLIC CREDIBILITY SO THAT THE PUBLIC INTEREST MAY BE IDENTIFIED AND SERVED.

II. RECOMMENDATIONS

1. CONSTRUCT THE COMMITTEE AND CONDUCT ITS AFFAIRS ACCORDING TO THE OPTIMAL CASE.

    OR, IF CONSTRAINED IN ACHIEVING "1," THEN MEET THE FOLLOWING GOALS:

    (a) HAVE BEDROCK PREREQUISITES APPROVED: Terms of reference, membership, burden of proof;
    (b) REDUCE PUBLIC EXPECTATIONS of Committee's mandate and ensure high public awareness of importance of Minister's role;

(c) WIN PROFESSIONAL AND OTHER UPSCALE PUBLIC SUPPORT for articulation of pesticide problem and problems of weighing scientific data;

(d) IF "SUB-OPTIMALITY" GIVES COMMITTEE A "PRO-INDUSTRY" APPEARANCE, CONVINCE ENVIRONMENTALISTS of (1) Committee's separateness from undue Department of Agriculture influence, (2) Committee's willingness to weigh *environmentalist values* in considering evidence.

III. THREATS

ANALYSIS OF MEDIA COVERAGE SO FAR REVEALS THESE POTENTIAL MISUNDERSTANDINGS THAT GNAW AT THE COMMITTEE'S CREDIBILITY:

- Suspect Terms of Reference;
- Failure to Ban—Even Temporarily;
- Attacks on Excessive Secrecy.

AN ADDITIONAL POTENTIAL EXPOSURE TO CRITICISM AND EROSION OF CREDIBILITY IS THE POSSIBILITY THAT E.P.A.[20] WILL CONCLUDE ITS HEARINGS ON THE SUBSTANCE AND REACH A DECISION BEFORE THESE HEARINGS ARE COMPLETED.

IV. THE OPTIMAL CASE

ALL THREAT OF POTENTIAL MISUNDERSTANDING COULD BE EFFECTIVELY OVERCOME IF THE "OPTIMAL CASE" COMMITTEE WERE CONSTRUCTED: THAT IS, A COMMITTEE ARMED WITH RECOMMENDED POSITIONS ON:

- *Terms of reference*
  Authority to subpoena, burden of proof on maker, environmental as well as human consequences
- *Structure*
  "Wise Men"
- *Burden of proof, implemented*
  Temporary ban on household use and in-store warnings

- *Procedures and rules of evidence*
  Explicit statements of (1) treatment of scientific evidence and (2) use of cross-examination
- *Public access to information*
  Conforming to *spirit* of government guidelines on access to information

ACHIEVING THIS COMMITTEE STRUCTURE AND MANDATE WOULD (1) POSITION COMMITTEE *ABOVE* BOTH ENVIRONMENTALISTS AND INDUSTRY; (2) ELIMINATE MOST OF THE CONSTRAINTS ON WINNING PUBLIC CONFIDENCE; AND (3) GIVE COMMITTEE THE TOOLS IT NEEDS TO SERVE PUBLIC INTEREST AND BE SEEN TO SERVE IT.

V. SUB-OPTIMALITY

WHILE THE "OPTIMAL" CASE WOULD, VIRTUALLY AUTOMATICALLY, SUCCEED IN WINNING PUBLIC CONFIDENCE, IT IS POSSIBLE A LESS-THAN OPTIMALLY ARRANGED COMMITTEE COULD SUCCEED (ALBEIT TO A LESSER DEGREE) THROUGH A STRATEGIC MIX OF MEDIA RELATIONS AND COMMITTEE PROCEDURES.

BASIC DILEMMA, WHICH STRATEGY MUST RESOLVE: *A 'ZERO-SUM' RELATIONSHIP BETWEEN ENVIRONMENTALISTS AND MEDIA ON ONE HAND, AND INDUSTRY AND GOVERNMENT ON THE OTHER*. IN SHORT:

A GAIN FOR ONE "SIDE" IS AUTOMATICALLY PERCEIVED AS A LOSS FOR THE OTHER.

THE "MANAGEMENT" TASK IS *TO ENABLE THE COMMITTEE TO PROCEED, BY FORESTALLING THAT IMPRESSION OF "LOSS"*.

Prerequisites for Success:

(1) *Terms of reference:*
Must include (a) evaluation of environmental as well as human health consequences; (b) placing of burden of proof on manufacturer;

(2) *Membership:*
Must absolutely avoid all conflicts of interest.

GIVEN (1) AND (2), *THE FOLLOWING STRATEGIC GOALS MUST BE ATTAINED:*

(A) *Reduce public expectations.* Stress themes of thorough, even-handed review of existing information in government hands;

(B) *Win professional and other upscale public support.* Stress themes of identifying gaps in existing knowledge, general questions of risk/benefit assessment, need for continuous professional review through new, yet-to-be-created government machinery;

(C) *Mitigate suspicions* (of environmentalists, unions, opposition). Stress themes of independence of Committee members, willingness to consider their evidence, and terms of reference permitting evaluation of environmental considerations.

Attaining Those Goals Will Require:

(A) Strong use of committee chairman (Interviews).

(B) Occasional use of whole committee (Travel, open hearings).

(C) Structure of committee procedures into phases (with accompanying media activities): (see *Critical Path*)

I. Literature review (Startup announcement, interviews)

II. Other test evidence (Interviews, reflections on social discounting of risk)

III. Collection of other data: environmentalist and industry output (Announcements, travel, receipt of data, questions to witnesses)

IV. Writing and report ("No comment")

(D) Speed in completion of task and handing over advice to minister (60–100 days maximum).

(E) Publication of committee evaluations, *as a minimum*, as a discussion paper accompanying minister's recommendation.

CRITICAL PATH

Objective:

To identify threat and suggest responses and positions affecting the Committee in sub-optimal condition over the time required to complete its mandate.

Critical Path

Point One: ***Start Up***

Threat: Skeptical media, disappointed stakeholders, political opposition (Parliament)

Response: Terms of reference (comprehensive, no arbitrary exclusion)

Temporary ban (if possible) and Burden of Proof on manufacturer

Committee Membership (no conflict of interest)

Point Two: ***Literature Review***

Threat: Skeptical media, disappointed stakeholders, potential claimants, political opposition (Parliament)

Response: Committee is receiving written briefs

Interviews with Chairman emphasizing comprehensiveness of terms of reference and Committee objective: a calm, even-handed review of existing information

Point Three: ***Test Evidence***

Threat Skeptical media, aroused environmentalists, political opposition, especially as budget debate tapers off through November.

Response: Chairman and other interviews, stressing gaps in existing knowledge, general questions of risk/benefit assessment, need for continuous review of chemical use through new, yet-to-be created machinery.

Point Four:	***Collection of Other Data***
Threat:	Skeptical media, political opposition in Parliament, aroused environmentalists.
Response:	Public hearings in five selected cities (with participation limited to 15 minutes, plus written submissions), "paper trials" to permit testing of scientific evidence; questions to witnesses, to focus attention on difference between facts and values.
Point Five:	***Writing and Report***
Threats:	Premature leaks, indiscretions
Response:	Coded drafts, strong moral suasion from Chairman
Point Six:	***Hand Over to Minister***

Total working days: 100 (9 October, 1981–1 March, 1982)

CONCLUSION: CASES

The cases, grouped by issue model, illustrate the application of theoretical issue analysis to the real world of issue contests.

The value of theory is that it explains why some approaches work and others do not. As the cases themselves illustrate, no single approach is always correct. In some cases cooperation was the optimal approach. In others, confrontation. In yet others, a wait-and-see approach was needed. Judgment and experience may indicate that one course or another would be best. Theory identifies the critical points early, and allows the relatively quick testing of one's conclusions.

The cases are written to show how outcomes conform or depart from the conclusions of logical analysis and where the analysis might have improved performance of one side or the other. The final case, the strategy document, is intended as a walk-through of the analytical method set out at the end of the section on theory. It is perhaps worth noting that the final product makes little explicit use of the analyses behind the document.

The aim is to prepare a clear, crisp, swiftly actionable instrument, not a complex theoretical edifice. But, to ensure that the conclusions are sound and that the client can have confidence in its recommendations, it is useful to have some conceptual tools to allow one to check the issue all around and ensure there are no gaps in one's own understanding.

Lest these cases give the impression that the world of business-government relations is one crisis after another, the next part examines ways to anticipate issues and incorporate a sensitivity to the non-price signals of the environment into business planning.

NOTES

1. Based on Richard Asinof, "The Poisoning of the Indian Waters," *New York Times Magazine*, 21 Oct. 1979; discussion with Government of Canada Officials.
2. D. M. Young, "Anatomy of an Environmental Crisis: Mercury in the St. Clair River," *Dow Canadian Insight*, November, 1978; Ross Howard, *Poisons in Public*, Case Studies of Environmental Pollution in Canada, Toronoto, 1980, Lorimer.
3. Private study by a company manager.
4. "Carey Signs Law Requiring 5¢ Bottle Depoist," and "How the Law on 5¢ Deposit Should Work," *New York Times*, June 16, 1982; "Is the Bottle Bill Solution Going Flat?" *National Business*, May, 1980; "The Michigan Experience, Why Deposit Laws Don't Work"; "Forced Deposit Laws: They Aren't Working"; Publication of The Can Manufacturing Institute. "The Bottle Bill, an idea whose time has come . . . and gone," Address by Judd H. Alexander, Sr. V.P., American Can Company, March, 1980.
5. Dianne Dumasostis, "Acid Politics," *Technology Review*, October 1982, pp. 64-5.
6. "Killing a Product: Taking Rely off Market Cost Proctor & Gamble a Week of Agonizing," *The Wall Street Journal*, 3 November, 1980; "State of Alarm, Tampon Industry Is in Throes of Change After Toxic Shock," *The Wall Street Journal*, Feb. 26, 1981.
7. *Official Sources*: WHO Collaborative Study on Breast Feeding, MCH/793; Background Paper Prepared by WHO and UNICEF, for the Meeting on Infant and Young Child Feeding, Geneva, 9-12 October, 1979. FHE/ICF/793; Marketing and Promotion of Infant Formula in the Developing Nations, 1978, Hearing before the Subcommittee on Health and Scientific Research of the Committee on Human Resources, U.S. Senate 95/2, May 23, 1978;

   Nestlé Company:

   WHO International Code of Marketing of Breast Milk Substitutes, Instructions to all Companies of the Nestle Group and to agents and distributors . . . Feb., 1982; Nestle press releases on Infant Formula Subject Commission (3 May, 1982); "The Nestle Boycott as a Corporate Learning Experience,"

   Secondary Sources:

   "Marketing of Consumer Goods by Multinationals in the Third World, Is it a Scandal?" *Economic Intelligence Unit*, Autumn, 1979; "Infant Feeding: Breast is Best," *Newsweek*, October 22, 1979; Herman Nickel, "The Corporation Haters," *Fortune*, 1 June, 1980; John A. Sparks, "The Nestle Controversy—Anatomy of a Boycott," *Public Policy Solution Fund, Inc.*; Richard A. Barovick, "Activism On A Global Scale," *Public Relations Journal*, June, 1982; "Keeping Track of the Code," *Development Forum*, June, 1982.
8. Herman Nickel, *op. cit.*
9. From "The Public's Verdict," a case history prepared by the National Retailer's Institute.
10. Based on PRSA summary of Golden Anvil Award winners, 1980; Hill and Knowlton was the winning agency.
11. "How the Soft Drink Industry Said NO to the FTC," *Issues*, PepsiCo Campaign; C.J. Louis, Harvey Yazijian, *The Cola Wars*, 1980, Everett House, pp. 334-349.
12. Interview with Government of Canada officials.

Robert D. Hay and Edwart R. Gray, eds., *Business and Society: Cases and Text*, Scott Wilson Publishing Co., 1981, pp. 297 ff.

14. Company officials.

15. Guy Stanley, John Eichmanis, "The Inco Layoffs, A Case Study in Corporate Responsibility," *Financial Post*, 4 Nov. 1979.

16. See, *National Energy Program*, Energy, Mines & Resources, 1980; The National Energy Program, *Update, 1982*, Energy Mineral Resources, 1982; "Canada Cuts Levy on Energy," New York Times, 1 June, 1982; Guy Stanley, *Canada Faces the 1980s*, Business International, pp. 66 ff.

17. For a detailed account of the development of the NEP, see Peter Foster, *The Sorcerer's Apprentice*, Collins, 1982.

18. Dome, "The Cornerstone of Canada's Energy Policy," was spending about $100 million a month on debt service and dividends on preferred shares. It had little left over to cover day-to-day operating expenses. All lines of credit were exhausted. All cash-generating assets were pledged against loans. The company placed $2.27 billion in bank drafts coming due before or on 31 March, 1983. It owed Canada's five largest banks $4.5 billion, i.e. 40 percent of their total equity and reserves (*Wall Street Journal*, 22 July, 1982, p. 1.)

19. This case is based upon discussions with Government of Canada officials and a project conducted by Public Issues Group Division of John Doherty & Co., Ottawa.

Part III

ANTICIPATION

Chapter VIII

Anticipating Issues

Kings may be slaves to history, as Tolstoy said. But corporations that are responsible for maximizing returns on the investments of others cannot afford to be. Yet can the future be predicted? How else can a company avoid unpleasant surprises and threats to business in the form of potentially dangerous issues? The list of whole industries (not just businesses) crippled, laid waste or dramatically transformed by issues is a long one: steel, automobiles, nuclear power are among the most important. Taken together, they affect more than one job in six in the United States, still the largest single economy in the world. Myopia about issues on the part of these industries thus has serious implications for virtually every other business in the free world.

DEFINING THE PROBLEM

Of course, one cannot predict the future without causing it to happen, as Sir Karl Popper, among others, pointed out long ago. The most one can do is to generate some more or less plausible scenarios about the way society, the economy, politics, etc. might develop and weight these by estimates of probability. This is a procedure we look at in more detail below.

However, less than 20 percent of the issues of real concern to business fall into the category of such long range future or strategic issues. By far the greatest concern of business is current issues—that is legislation currently before legislatures or about to be introduced, court cases pending or currently at trial, and new or proposed regulations. By far the greatest effort in terms of money and other resources should be and is devoted to the area of current issues.

Rather less is spent on tracking the development of *emerging* issues, although here is where detailed scanning activities on a reasonably small scale can produce warnings up to two years or more in advance of events. Companies probably spend too little on evaluating emerging issues and properly utilizing the results of such scanning in relation to the adjustment lead time this activity can provide.

In terms of the ratio of resources to results, on the other hand, companies are increasingly trying to peer into the future and assess the likelihood of longer-range threats to business. Particularly in capital intensive business with a lot of overseas involvement, the pressure to factor assessments of political risk into project evaluation is intensifying. Whether this effort really makes sense as currently understood we shall examine below.

We can therefore break down the problem of anticipating issues into three levels: current issues (those now before us); emerging issues (issues the traces of which are now discernible and which are likely to be current issues in two to three years); and strategic issues (issues that can be predicted with trend analysis, scenario generation and other techniques) that will likely emerge as issues three to five years from now. We can display the ideal resource commitment as a pyramid.

Issues and Resources

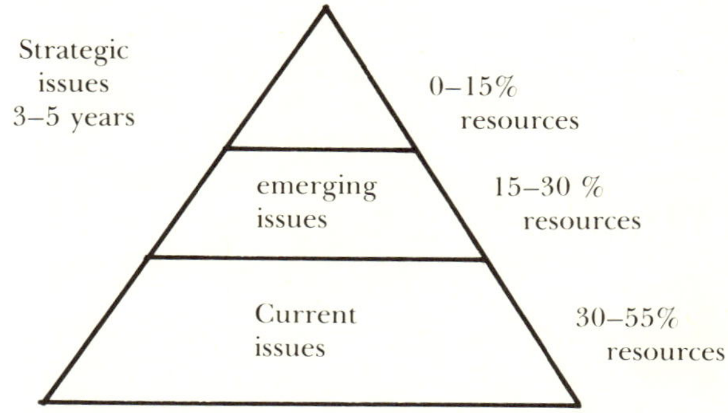

The diagram also indicates the basic priorities in anticipating issues. These are:

1. That the most important issues are current issues, i.e., those now developing. Anticipation of these issues boils down to working through

the models discussed in the theoretical section with a view to forecasting the stakeholder relationships, the main resolution mode and the best strategy for the organization to follow. This amounts to around half the total issues anticipation effort.

2. That emerging issues are the second most important area of concern and should consume about 30 percent of one's issues anticipation. Together, current and emerging issues should account for 80 percent of these issues anticipation efforts.

3. Finally, the real future issues, those five years away: a relatively small commitment of resources will show the shadows on the cave wall, i.e., trace some possible outlines. But save your money. Doubling the resources committed here will in no way even approach a commensurate return on forecast reliability. There are just too many unknowns interacting with each other to produce more than a suggestion of the broad lines of issues.

Anticipating issues therefore is mainly a matter of grappling with current and emerging issues. The models discussed in the theoretical section above will suffice for anticipating the structure and development of current issues. Emerging issues and long range strategic issues require companies to scan the socio-political environment as well as the strategic business environment.

SCANNING

Fundamental to issues anticipation is an activity known as "scanning,"[1] the first step of which is to divide reality into observable categories. Categories increasingly favored by planners are the following:

Economic—macro and micro economic environment, the "leading economic indicators" plus the indicators of the commercial environment of the firm (industry outlook, comparative advantage of the company, its new opportunities, its competitive threats.)

Social—demographic and other changes in population (such as patterns of family formation, economic facts such as workforce participation rates) relative positions of minorities, together with changing public attitudes.

Political—changes in government priorities ("k"-values and discount values of our government model) political leadership, party divisions, including ideology, leadership and support, the mechanics of the political system.

Technological—breakthroughs in applied knowledge and resulting new goods and services and the public policy choices they present.

Other—(usually ecology or human resources) changes in the natural environment, developments in employee-management relations.

Some of these categories have potentially more direct significance to a business than others. Technological and political changes can transform a business overnight. Social, economic and ecological factors are trends more likely to be detected relatively early before they seriously affect a company or an industry. All the factors are interrelated, parts of a whole picture. The trends in the areas listed above must be interwoven and the cross-impacts charted for an understanding to emerge of the total effect of change on a business or industry.

Scanning Techniques

Scanning is the first step in marshalling issue-related information for management in an action- or decision-oriented form. From the outset, trends should be classified, as we have already done with issues, according to time. *Strategic* trends are those that will impact the company within the strategic planning time frame, say, three to five years; *Emerging* trends are those that will affect the company within the *operational* planning time frame, say up to two years. *Current* issues, those happening right now, should be monitored as they unfold.

Costs and reliability are both related to time. Strategic trends are difficult to assess and their cross-impacts tricky to chart. Special techniques are necessary to relate the trends to the specifics of the firm. As mentioned above, emerging and current issues are the best investments for early warnings.

Strategic Issues

Strategic issues, the choices a company or organization must face in say three to five years, are impossible to predict, if one uses the word "predict" accurately, that is: stating the precise time and place of confrontation together with the form the issues will take. However, careful scanning, using a variety of specialized techniques, can enable companies and other organizations to detect trends that could develop into emerging and current issues half a decade from now. The value of such analysis lies in (1) the fact that it compels senior management to be future-oriented and think over their businesses on large lines; and (2) the assistance it provides senior managers in answering the question, "What kind of company must I be to prosper in the time period ahead?"

Techniques

Techniques most often utilized by planners in large companies or the specialized firms that serve them are:

1. *"Core" attitude surveys.* These are surveys of "opinion leaders" or "trend setters" or a combination of such a survey with a more universal sample.

The aim is to assess values judged to be critical over the time and space of the planning period (e.g., attitudes to foreign investment, relative confidence in business, government and labor leadership, attitudes to work, leisure, salary levels, authority, the credibility of different categories of "opinion leaders," etc.). The techniques are based on the assumption that what "opinion leaders" believe today, the public will come to believe within a few years. As society has evolved since World War II, that is no longer so widely true. Instead, people draw their opinions from different leaders on different subjects so that the ranking of future concerns becomes more difficult. Still, geography and demography can help. There are certain "bellwether constituencies," e.g., what New Yorkers and Californians think today, the rest of America may believe in three to five years; and fundamental attitudes may vary according to generation—attitudes widely held by those in the 23–35 age bracket—especially basic values related to authority and personal fulfillment—could well affect the prevailing government policy framework and hence demands on business for a generation.

2. *Trends Evaluation and Monitoring (T.E.A.M.) and Trend Analysis Program.* This technique explicitly links line and staff. Volunteer "scanners"—usually line officers—are assigned a short list of publications each. Any article showing environmental trends or discontinuities of long-range concern to society and to the particular business is clipped or abstracted. Every eight weeks the abstracts or clips are analyzed for trends by staff specially assigned to the task. Every 12 weeks, a trend report is prepared for senior executives by a staff/line committee.

Advantages of this method are mainly those of "process." It involves line managers and provides cross-links among departments that build management awareness. It is, however, time consuming and error prone and needs strong incentives to keep participants sharp. Useful sources for TAP programs with regard to strategic issues include publications of permanent debates, reports and newsletters of stakeholder/watchdog groups and opinion leaders.

3. *Authority, Old Hand, "Genius" and Delphi Forecasting.* The first three of these techniques amounts to commissioning a report, tailored to the needs of the organization, from an outside expert or authority (e.g.,

Argentina in 1990, or the Oil and Gas industry in 1995). Such reports are useful mainly as validators of in-house work or for sparking company imagination. "Delphi" is a specialized version of authority forecast, named after the most famous authority of all time, the oracle at Delphi in ancient Greece. (Noted for its ambiguity, the oracle advised King Croesus that the result of his planned attack on Persia would be the destruction of a great army: it was—his own). This technique involves identifying several oracles, asking them to develop a list of strategic issues, circulating the results, among them and asking again for a consensus list. The technique automatically corrects for bias or individual perspective. In a modification of the technique, the oracles are chosen according to their known biases or perspectives and generate separate scenarios that are compared on a matrix according to the known ideological position of each oracle.

4. *Scenario building, cross-impact charting.* These are techniques for coping with the effect trends have on each other. If population ages, economic growth stays a steady 0–1 percent, inflation persists at double-digit levels, and more people take advantage of office of the future technology to work at home, how will these trends interact to affect my business? What if Britain gets a centrist permanent government party, France shifts leftward for the same period, and Germany goes dramatically conservative? How will that affect the business climate in the European Community? Such questions can be answered by constructing scenarios in which possible trends are assumed to happen so that specific choices can be crystallized for the company. To do this, it is necessary first of all to visualize the connections between developments.

This process usually involves input at both corporate and division headquarters for "coordination" into a strategic plan. Too uncertain to provide positive guidance to management, socio-political forecasting at this level can nevertheless alert management to potential threats and opportunities and potentially fruitful trend lines to monitor (or to affect) with a view to inclusion in operational plans.

Charting the Cross Impacts: Some Conceptual Approaches

One way to approach this one is to analyze the links from the point of view of public choices. What will the public choices of the future involve? How will they affect my business?

Answers to these questions can be visualized and systematically approached by applying a "linked economies" model to the variables discussed earlier.

Treating those variables as "The Environment," we get a sequence as follows:

Figure VIII.1. Cross Impact Charting Using Linked Economies

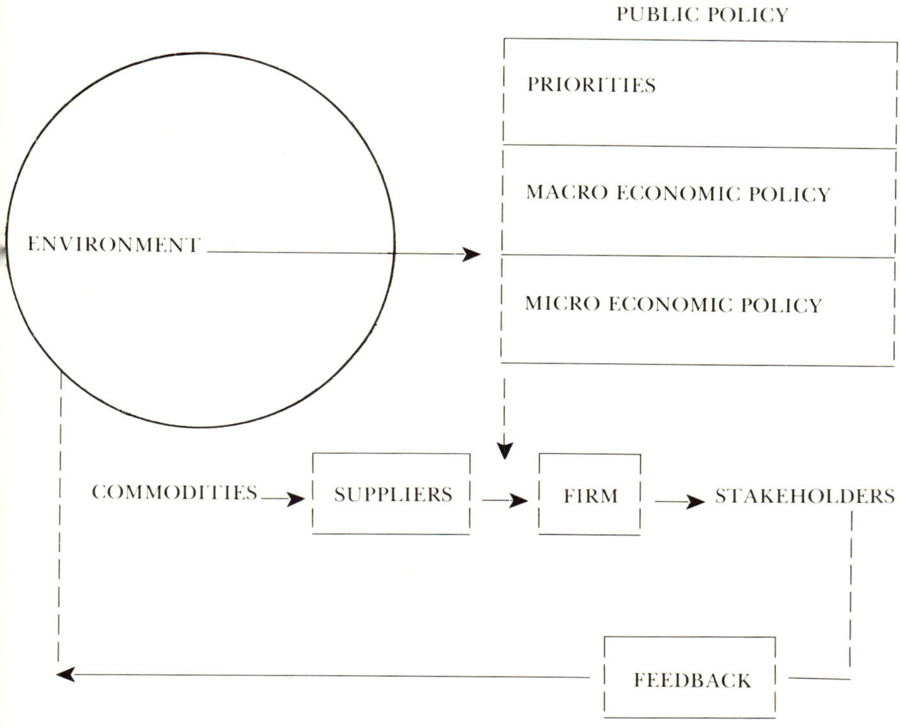

Notice that in this approach, public policy is taken as the main conditioning factor for each element of importance to the business.

Putting the diagram into words, the public policy "box" responds to environmental pressures earlier described (economic, social, political, technological, other). The policy will affect and be affected by commodity supplies and suppliers, their effect on your suppliers, the factors that are combined in the firm, and stakeholders including the community in which the firm is located. As always, the time taken for the system to absorb stimulus and change is a critical variable.

The firm in this model is thus positioned as a pivot between its suppliers, stakeholders and customers on the one hand and public policy on the other.

This approach does not answer any questions. On the contrary, it is designed to set up certain questions—to bring into focus the questions that will affect the balance sheet and suggest where to look for answers. For example:

1. What will be the main environmental changes over the next planning period?
2. What will be the main political priorities as a result?
3. How will these be reflected in macro and micro policy?
4. How will that affect the main elements of the business: costs of suppliers, factors, stakeholders, and ability to earn returns on these assets?

GAIL System

Another way of charting the cross impacts of environmental factors is to apply to the problem a system analysis, based on GAIL.[4]

Meet GAIL. GAIL is an acronym that describes all the properties of a system, large or small:

G = Goal setting mechanism (e.g., "polity" or political community)
A = Adaptive mechanism (e.g., the economy, which allocates resources among demands)
I = Integrating values (i.e., those that keep classes, or groups together—team spirit, class consciousness, ethnic solidarity, political loyality, etc.)
L = Latent over-arching, or 'bonding' values, conflict resolving beliefs (national vs. group or class loyalties, etc.)

GAIL is designed to chart the cross impacts of the elements of the system in a coherent and logical way. Note how the four boxes or elements of the system are interlinked. Issues arise as the system acts and reacts on itself across the boundaries. Here's an example:

- A new political priority (get Britain moving again) puts fresh claims on the economy.
- Both place demands on the "group values" of society (appealing to loyal supporters of the government, antagonizing the opposition, perhaps pitting labor against management).
- Equilibrium is maintained (i.e., conflict is constrained) by "latent values" (patriotism, social norms), by the political system (using ballots, instead of bullets, to resolve issues).

In the process, what new demands will be placed on the company or on management: will new management militancy increase shop floor

Figure VIII.2. Cross Impact Charting Using GAIL

G POLICY	A ECONOMY
I VALUES (GROUP)	L VALUES (LATENT CONFLICT RESOLVING)

tensions? Will class loyalties outweigh or become fused with national values to the detriment of market forces?

In other words, the diagram allows analysts to trace relations between demands for new government policies and constraints. Simply put, the technique for using this approach is this:

Ask These Questions:

a. What are government priorities for the planning period?
b. How will the economy react?
c. Will values help or hinder?
d. How long will it take for the different cells to change?
e. How should my particular business (a) adjust? (b) contribute to the fulfillment of these goals?

Looked at in this way, the growing influence of environmentalists during the late 1960s to 1970s can be viewed as a process in which the ecological values held by a relatively small group became transmitted to a larger group and thus transmitted into government priorities, which in turn dominated the adjustment mechanism, i.e., the economy. Subsequently, in the early 1980s, although the values held by that group have not changed, the operation of the economy has generated other competing values that are moderating the priorities assigned to factors at the national level.

It will perhaps be clear that the forecasting of strategic issues can be quite a labor-intensive job, demanding specialists with a great deal of accurate knowledge about the issues, areas and industries they are analyzing. And even with such expertise—which almost certainly will carry a high price—the results can be difficult to assess and to use in the solution of specific business problems.

Some companies therefore prefer to leave strategic issues forecasting alone and instead focus on the risks over a specified time frame that the political environment could pose to the returns on investment or business profitability in different locations: so-called political risk. Some of the techniques and information bases are similar to those of issues forecasting. But as explained below (pp. 204ff), the objectives are significantly different.

Emerging Trends

Scanning for emerging trends is one of the most cost-effective early warning mechanisms available. Emerging trends are relatively easy to spot with a high degree of certainty; scanning for them lends itself to a management process and specific goals and objectives can be defined. For emerging issues, the following is a good breakdown of targets for scanning:

- watchdog groups and agencies (e.g., Common Cause, Environmental Defense Fund, Union of Concerned Scientists, etc.), political debates and speeches; trend setting jurisdictions should be watched and charted by the capital city office, by trade associations and outside consultants;
- emerging problems with stakeholder groups can be detected inhouse by analyzing mail from customers and by regularly surveying field personnel and unit managers for their perceptions;
- scholarly journals and expert debates can help pinpoint emerging new knowledge. These can be followed inhouse, according to management discipline (marketing, finance, production, product development, and legal) and scientific specialities (chemistry, biology, etc.).

This forecasting will work because issues emerge as stakeholders develop awareness and succeed in interesting politicians, and, in some instances, the courts. In an open society, watching what stakeholders are saying and how opinion leaders react is thus to watch the process of public choice in action at its formative stages. As Earl Newsom said more than a generation ago: "Today's headlines can be tomorrow's legislation." Detecting emerging issues means going behind the headlines and detecting tomorrow's headlines today. It is mainly a matter of tuning in and listening. Instead of *what* to scan, the problem facing organizations concerned with emerging trends is *who* should scan.

Line management is usually better placed even than news media to hear what everyday people are saying about a company and to pick up how it is regarded in the community. Heads of operating divisions in regions or host countries are usually well-enough connected to know what some government ministries and the business community think of national developments. Like diplomats, management should be encouraged to file periodic reports on the moods and opinions they encounter. Meanwhile, the changing picture at the political level can be picked up by the capital office and/or trade associations. These reports can be sent to and correlated by the public affairs department, whose chief or designate can provide regular briefings on emerging issues and corporate responses to senior company decision-makers.

Current Issues

These are issues that are happening now. Knowing what's happening, and making sure that information reaches senior management in actionable and timely form are the chief scanning challenges posed here. Main sources for current issue developments are news, legislative debates, other political speeches, reports of studies by policy institutes and official publications. Too often, despite considerable time and effort devoted to issue anticipation, a specific piece of legislation will suddenly surface, with the main source of knowledge about it being the news media. If the event or issue happens away from the national capital or major news center (e.g., Los Angeles, New York, Miami in the U.S.; Montreal and Toronto in Canada), headquarters may have to track the matter by telephone.

Atlantic Richfield's systematic tracking program uses a computer-assisted information system developed in consultation with line managers who need the information the system can provide. Personnel supervision, for instance, needs to keep current on OSHA requirements, financial managers need the latest in tax information, etc. In the field, meanwhile, trade associations and Washington office personnel keep the company abreast of developing situations. The information from all sources is matched in a computer with the specific interests expressed by middle and senior management who receive a weekly report edited to their professional interests. The reports identify the legislation, summarize its contents and the implications for the company, and list company people working on the bill together with the names of the people in the

Figure VIII.3. Atlantic Richfield's GAMIS

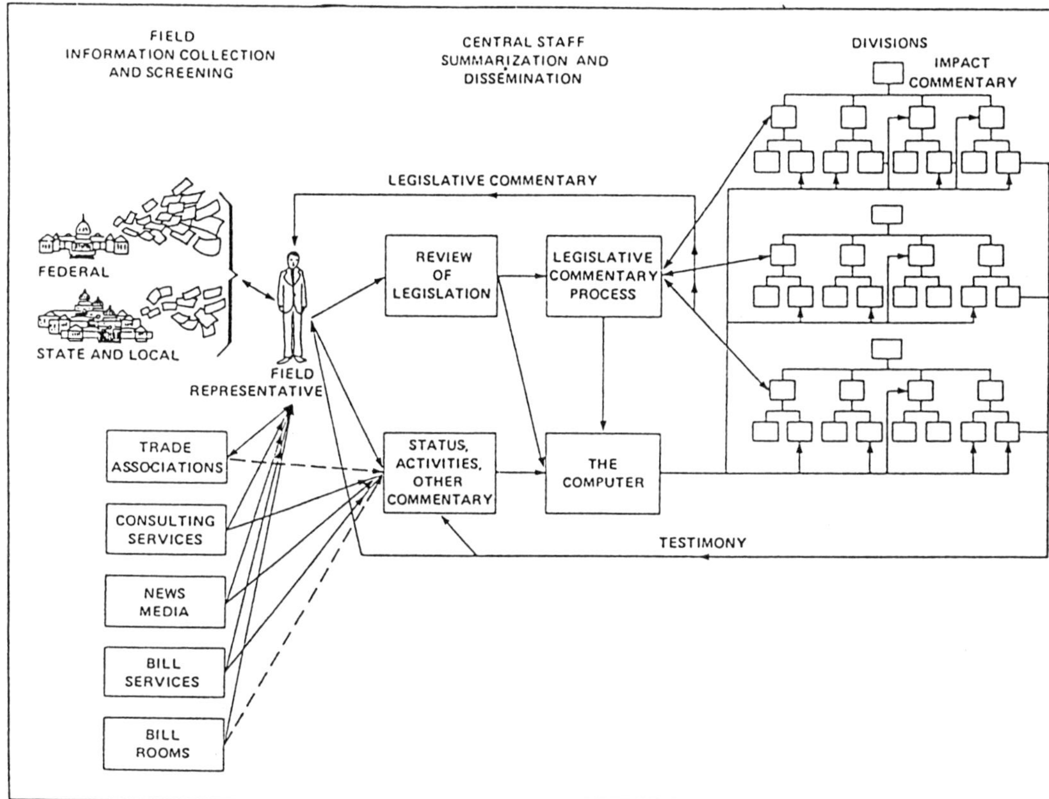

Source: The Conference Board, Action Plans for Public Affairs, Report 733, 1972

government relations department to contact for more information. The diagram illustrates the process.

Although elaborate, GAMIS contains all the elements of a legislative and current issue tracking process. (GAMIS is an acronym for Government Activities Management Information System.)

Pivotal in the system is the Issues Adviser who supervises an analyst and reports on government relations to the manager. The adviser gets a respectful hearing, although there is no certainty that any actions will result from his advice. Generally, the adviser's experience is with the political process rather than the main business of the company. His primary expertise is tactical. Assessment of the business impact of policy and draft legislation is carried out by the managers of divisions affected by the proposals who must respond within a tight time frame.

The strengths of the system are its immediacy and bottom-line relevance, linkage of line and staff, and the fact that it is a continuous process that permits a "proactive" response. It puts together the elements required to cope with current issues, especially in areas where short response times are essential, that is, tracking of policy options through the legislative process, assessment of policy and impact of options, reactions of stakeholders and assessment of probable outcomes, input to the company, response development, service to line management.

In other companies, the scanning of current issues is less well developed. Some centralize scanning and try to decentralize response by using line management as spokespersons. Others involve the whole company "family" by providing timely issues information to employees who, if sufficiently concerned, can express their views directly to legislators (such as Pepsico's Employees Political Action Campaign (Empac)). In all cases, issues developments should be presented in crisp, brief, actionable form, either showing what is being done and results achieved or where senior approval is necessary, a *brief* outline of the options, with advantages and disadvantages of each.

Structuring the Results

Especially when scanning is part of a corporate planning process, the issues detected by the scanning methods employed above should be compared according to (1) effect on the company (high, medium, low) and (2) probability of occurrence (high, medium, low). This can be done as a matrix:

IMPACT

HIGH

PROBABILITY

x		

LOW

Time lines can also be added to the basic matrix structure and trends plotted over a total planning period (i.e., near term/operational and long term/strategic).

IMPACT

HIGH

PROBABILITY

x		Issue (b)
		Issue (a)

TIME *LOW*

Breaking out these trends is the first step towards crystalizing the choices affecting a company as a result of social change, i.e., towards answering the basic question, "What kind of company will the public interest require?"

The exhibit on pg. 199 illustrates the issues, sources, and detection methods covered above.

The next step in predicting issues is to decide which of the trends will result in public choices that the firm must address.

Turning Trends Forecasts into Issues Forecasts

Negative issues—public choices that might add to the costs of business—arise, as we have seen, from external costs that the community is unwilling to pay any longer, and on which the community is prepared to act. Drawing up warnings of them is a matter of identifying emerging "Externalities" situations. Trends of the sort discussed above are helpful, but they are not enough. Trends are developments over time. But issues become issues through events. Events are discrete developments occur-

1. List current issues likely still to be issues during the medium term (e.g., energy, inflation, productivity, foreign competition, composition of government, regional balance). Use the scanning reports your company has developed on emerging issues.

2. Construct a timetable of institutional meetings at which each issue could be articulated prominently—e.g., the legislative calendar including State of the Union Address, Meetings of Governors, major party meetings, meetings of provincial premiers, Throne Speech, etc.—or annual or semi-annual meetings/conferences of think tanks and institutes, professional societies, or stakeholders' associations—or annual meetings of "lead" companies and assocations. These are the potential external "precipitates" that could make an emerging issue into a current one.

3. Now refine your timetable of potential external "precipitates" by trying to identify possible "flash points" that could, through "Critical Mass," accelerate or decelerate the emergence of issues. These could include elections and the run-up to elections and visible court cases, and, as well, *Company Plans*. Company operations can also set off issues. So planning for emerging and new issues should indicate the effect, if any, of company developments. For this, a special approach using the "Product Cycle" is described in the box below. Remember, you are looking for events that could change the "k" value of the issue you have identified.

4. Now you want to factor "new" issues into the projection of current and emerging issues. Consult your list of trends, looking for developing Externalities situations affecting the company and possible arenas for articulating these issues (scholarly journals, specialized magazines and political or governmental task forces). These will be "new" issues. Look also for crowding at the end of legislative sessions (which could impede surfacing of the issue) as well as other forces that might obstruct emergence (government priorities). How are the "k" values of departments and ministries likely to be affected?

The emergence of new issues and the effect on continuing ones can be displayed on a probability/impact matrix or even a PERT diagram, or a written report. In practice, only high impact scenarios should be considered. For those high impact issues, however, this kind of staff work can provide an accurate critical path of development.

Anticipation Using the Product Cycle[2]

This approach relates the concepts of critical mass, Externals, and bargaining to the main stages of the business/product cycle. (This is done in the chart below).

Figure VIII.4. Anticipating Using Product Cycle Approach

Cycle	Social Expectations	Possible Situations
1. R&D, Testing	Thoroughness, safety reliability	Bargaining, Critical Mass
2. Plant siting Construction	Jobs, environment city, province or state	Bargaining, Critical Mass
3. Expansion Acquisition, Dominance	Stakeholders interests management track record, work force community & national interests. (Social/political opposition from competition or public interest groups)	Externals
4. Obsolescence	Work force, community transitions	Bargaining, Critical Mass

MONITOR:
Changing Social Values

KEY QUESTIONS:

1. What social and political factors matter to my business?
2. This year (or planning period) what company developments will affect those relationships?

Here is how the chart should be operationalized. Let's illustrate it step by step with the following exercise:

> You are advising the CEO of a new company about to introduce a line of microfiche readers.[3] The company wants to win a government contract worth $10 million. As part of its pitch, the CEO wants to include a sketch of the company's approach to the relevant issues of the next two or three years and how the company would handle them.
> Your job: draft the document.

First, start with the point on the cycle. Between now and the years 3 to 5, the company will certainly pass through Points 1 and 2.

Second, analyze social expectations at the cycle points. Social expectations and thus the broad issue categories are listed (product reliability, thoroughness of testing, etc.).

Third, identify the likely issue situations. Corresponding possible issue situations or resolution modes (Externals, Critical Mass, etc.) are listed beside the appropriate expectations.

Putting these steps to work in the microfiche company of our example:

Cycle Point 1: *Product Safety. Have you a program of testing and follow-up?*

- what government agencies (if any) must be satisfied before you bring the product to market?
- Is the end use readily acceptable in terms of social values, or is public explanation or policy adjustment called for (to avoid "critical mass").

Cycle Point 2: *Plant Siting. Job environment, company acceptability.*

- What are the centers of power and influence in the proposed location?
- What government and legal requirements must be met?
- Other considerations: can a critical mass *in support of* the company be generated?

Information Requirements

To fulfill the needs indicated by this analysis, the necessary information must be developed for the company to use, both in policy considerations and its approach to the community. This should include thorough, detailed descriptions of the product testing process, and the benefits brought to the community by the plant. There must also be the equipment required to present this information effectively, so as to encourage third party endorsements.

Will the company reach Cycle Point 3, dominance, during the planning period? If so, it can expect to become a target for a critical group. Anticipating this, it is a good time to review (a) social values, and (b) effects of a change in scale. If the microfiche producer in our example is still serving military or government 80/20 by the time it reaches this point on the cycle, it would then be vulnerable to:

- changing government programs and priorities
- charges of favoritism
- charges of overdependence on the "military-industrial complex."

Besides the grass roots data the company would normally generate for public affairs purposes (jobs provided, community approval, etc.), the company should also begin developing explanations or programs related to the relative lack of private sector business: positive statements about the contribution made by the company to national well-being—e.g., microfiche readers as a vital contribution to essential research.

Also, having identified the key publics of the company in the course of these analyses (e.g., municipal, state, federal, governments, unions, researcher, etc.), you will keep watching and monitoring any changes or new developments to stay on top of any implications for your business.

How to use the "Cycle" approach chart
(1) *Identify your location* on the product/industry cycle (start-up, dominance, devolution);
(2) *Read across* to identify social expectations at that stage. Check to see whether those expectations still apply or whether they will continue to apply for the life of the project;
(3) *Read across* to identify the type of issue most likely to be met. This will enable you (1) to identify arguments and information requirements in advance, and (2) to flag any policy implications the issues may raise.

Putting together these four levels of analysis—unresolved current issues, timetable of external precipitates, surfacing of "new" issues, and "effect of company plans"—should enable a comprehensive appreciation of emerging issues to be produced. The study should stand up for the period of operational planning, i.e., 18 months to two years.

POLITICAL RISK ANALYSIS

Political risk analysis differs from issues forecasting in two critical respects. First, the focus of political risk analysis is narrower. While experts differ about what constitutes a political risk,[5] the aim of the exercise is clearly to assess the likelihood of political developments affecting the profitability or other goal of the business.[6] One advantage in this precisely defined mandate is that the cost of information gathering can be reduced. Another is that the level of analysis can be rudimentary in comparison with issues analysis. Indeed, as we shall see, in many companies a questionnaire prepared in-house and circulated to line chiefs in different countries suffices, perhaps with occasional "validation" by an outside country expert.

Second, in order to perform this mission, political risk analysis identifies in advance the developments which could have the harmful effects mentioned above, then evaluates the likelihood of any of them occurring.

As a result the analysis is usually passive and under emphasizes anything a company could do to affect events and outcomes. Although virtually every political risk specialist would agree that the quality of a company's relationship with its hosts can have a dramatic effect on its success in that country, political risk analysis as such rarely takes that variable into account.

The primary goal of political risk analysis is to enable planners to make systematic comparisons of political risk within and across different countries. Methodologies therefore self-consciously strive for systematic rigor and in many cases try to reduce historical, political and cultural specifics of a range of countries (insofar as those factors contribute to political risk) to a single number on a scale of 1 to 10. Such approaches obviously devalue the kind of deep, practical knowledge and networks an "old hand" in a particular country may have. But then good managers will rarely rely on a single source of information (they can call on "old hands" any time) and the impersonal, reductionist risk value or index provides apparently clear unequivocal comparisons.

In actual practice, most companies are still relatively unsophisticated and appear not to have bought very much of the risk analysts' arguments, although there are some signs this may be changing. Many companies use sporadic "grand tours," discussions with peers, advice from banks, home governments and informal media reviews before committing to a major foreign investment. Increasingly, companies combine such techniques with the use of a standard checklist of questions provided to overseas managers. Some go considerably further, and attempt to develop quantitative models. In nearly all instances, however, political analysts within companies do not have a continuous interface with senior management and therefore can provide only occasional "snapshots" of a company's foreign environment.[7]

Conference Board surveys suggest that 46 percent of companies studied use some form of qualitative analysis and another 25 percent some quantitative techniques. But interviews with the respondents suggest a basically ad hoc approach with overlapping responsibilities between planning, public affairs and international credit. A recent survey of American banks, for instance, showed loan officers having final say over credit worthiness assessments by political analysts, with resulting overcommitment in loans to Latin American countries.[8] Canadian banks, more prudent abroad than at home, restrict foreign lending according to simple decision rules, e.g., no participation beyond existing country market share. Nowhere is there a single pattern of practice one can point to and say, "that is how political risk assessment works." Nevertheless, informal conversation confirms scholarly analysis to the extent that management systems are increasingly requiring analysts to prepare findings in quantitative form that planners can use more or less mechanically in taking investment decisions.

State-of-the-Art

Let us therefore "walk through" an example of a fully developed political risk assessment method, one pioneered by a major oil company and now used with modifications in other oil companies, financial institutions and some consulting firms.[9]

The Political Risk Decision. The aim of political risk evaluation is to enable executives to weigh the consequences of various alternatives based upon conditions of uncertainty. The rational method of choosing the optimum course is to assign (a) values to consequences and (b) probabilities to events. Then the "best" choice is the alternative with the highest expected value. In a diagram, the process looks like this.[10]

Risk Evaluation Process

Events (uncertain, expert-estimated probabilities)
|
v
Action (decisions by executives:
invest, don't invest)
|
v
Consequences (expected value; profits or losses)

The role of the political risk analyst is to generate a probability p for predetermined risk events in each of a list of countries. These values allow executives to determine the relative attractiveness of the different investment locations.

Method. Consider, therefore, the political risk that could impede the success of a 10-year resources contract in country x.

Step 1: "Decompose" political risk into political risk events capable of impeding the venture's success, e.g.:

- sudden expropriation;
- creeping (or gradual) expropriation;
- adverse changes
- civil disorder;
- war;
- production restrictions;
- repatriation limitations;
- domestic price control;
- devaluation risk;
- export restrictions

Step 2: Identify political risk factors, i.e., circumstances influencing the occurrence of a political risk event:

- sudden ideological change;
- visibility of foreigners in economy;
- "imperial" identification of firm;
- demonstration effect;
- factors affecting host country ability to run business (e.g., marketing ability, bureaucratic development, supply of managers, scientific technology);
- relations with firm home country;
- lack of reciprocal dependence (i.e., few opportunities for home country retaliation in kind)
- economic performance.

Step 3: Generate Probabilities of Risk Events

(a) *Elicit Subjective Estimates*
Circulate a questionnaire to members of a Delphi panel of country experts. The rules defining "experts" should be explicitly established and followed. For statistical reliability, the panel should consist of five or more experts and each should have derived his expertise from separate sources of information and disciplines. In the first round, the questionnaire asks experts to assess the risk of political factors and events in the country under consideration.

(b) *Deriving a Common Estimator*
(i) *consensus.* For the next round, recirculate the questionnaire so that each expert can see how the others answered

the questions (without necessarily disclosing names), and use this as a basis for forming consensus. This is the most preferred method, by far. Most people doing political risk achieve consensus this way.

(ii) *weighted average.* (a) Total up the probability estimates, assuming equal reliability weights, and take an average. Or (b) assign a weight to each experts' reliability, total the weighted probabilities and divide by the number of experts to take an average, or (c) allow each expert to weight the reliability of his own forecast. This is sensible if the expert acts sincerely, because he is likely to be more aware than anyone else of the reliability of the data underpinning his opinion.

(iii) *Computational Methods*
A more sophisticated approach is to combine the consensus forming feedback with statistical analysis so that each expert is clear about the full implications of his probability rating. An advanced method is to ask each expert to assign a confidence rating to his forecast consisting of the number of similar events witnessed or "trials" that produced the outcome forecast. By combining the subjective probability estimate and the reliability estimate, a curve can be drawn to express the distribution of probabilities for the event under consideration, i.e., the probability density of the event. The curves can then be circulated to the Delphi panel and reconsidered so that a consensus curve emerges or the density functions can be combined sequentially to yield an aggregate function of the event's probability. The main advantage of this procedure lies in the strict division of responsibility between the country analysts and the statistician so that the quantified risk estimates that emerge are the results of clearly specified statistically appropriate decision rules with hidden cost indications revealed and investigated (see Panel Paradox in the box on page 210).

Cross Impacts. The computational method can also be used to derive scenarios of the "if a then b" type to show interrelationships between events using the probabilities already derived. This can be done through the following simulation process.

1. Arraying the political events along the vertical and horizontal axes of a matrix,
2. select a row event at random;

3. determine the occurrence or non-occurrence of the event by generating a random number and comparing it to the original probability of occurrence;
4. recompute all other (column) probabilities using the cross-impact conditional probabilities;
5. Repeat steps 1–3 until the occurrence and non-occurrence of all events are determined. This sequence will generate a scenario in the sense that each cell of the matrix will show a revised probability of the column event if the row event occurs.
6. Repeat steps 1–4 for the number of runs desired.
7. Calculate the frequency of each scenario in the runs.

D.W. Bunn and M.M. Mustafouglu, whose method we are following, report that 10,000 simulations resulted in 240 scenarios. Consistency checks ensure that the marginal probabilities of each event tested are the same as the originally assessed probabilities so that the original risk profile remains unchanged. What happens, however, is that the decision-maker can see the implications of those probabilities on composite developments.

Other panel methods chart cross impacts by asking panelists directly to assess the contribution of factors to events under different scenarios. When the single event and composite risk assessments are complete, they are returned to the experts for additional comments.

Using the Political Risk Assessment

The pressure for quantification within a large corporation is akin to pressure on a visitor to speak the local language. Numbers, even subjectively derived, can be used easily, whereas judgments qualified in words are more difficult to factor into business decisions. Even in companies that really know better and are fully aware of the limitations of political risk indices, political judgments must be quantified.

Unlike words, numbers can be directly applied to a business decision. Probabilities multiplied by potential profits and losses respectively permit the construction of payoff tables, and these in turn facilitate the rational selection of projects or strategic alternatives. Rationally, executives will attempt to maximize profits while minimizing expected losses (bearing in mind that the expected losses in question are so-called opportunity losses, i.e., the difference between losses actually realized and the cost that would have been realized had the best decision been followed).[11]

To illustrate: suppose project x has anticipated profits of \$10 million, project y of \$8 million. Opportunity costs of y therefore equal $profits_x - profits_y$ = \$2 million. Opportunity costs for x (best alternative) are zero if x is successful, but if unsuccessful, equal to anticipated losses$_x$ + any minimum profits from a less profitable but safer project whose failure would still show positive returns, e.g., Losses$_x$ + Gains realized from project z even if unsuccessful. To factor in political risk, weight anticipated gains or losses by values derived from risk analysis: A 75% chance of serious adverse tax change would diminish anticipation of fully realized gains from project x to 25%, one chance in four. Assume for illustration the adverse tax anticipated is confiscatory. There would be only a 25% chance (1-p) of realizing full value. Therefore the expected value of both projects would be: (.25)(10 million) for project x, and for project y, (.25)(8 million) = 2.5 million and 2 million respectively. These results also affect opportunity costs of y, reducing them to .5 million, and of x if unsuccessful, reducing them to (.25)(minimum gains from project z). Remember, these values are estimates of realizable gains in the face of uncertainty. If the values were based on certainty, then the highest certain gain and no losses would be preferred. Estimated opportunity costs should be viewed as the price of uncertainty—and like all costs, should be minimized as far as consistent with overall goals.

As well, political risk assessment allows managers to determine a "best" strategy for single projects. For example, suppose a company requires project payback over five years, that is at an annual rate of 20 percent, and analysts have attached to the project a warning that there is a high risk (say 75 percent) of say, adverse tax changes during the life of the project. Other things being equal, the company may respond in any of several ways, e.g.:

a. by insisting on local participation and rates of return based on guaranteed sales to governments and tax incentives as a condition of entry (i.e., building barriers to adverse tax changes);
b. going slow on commitment, reducing activity, and thereby lessening the tax paid;
c. delaying projects until the situation clarifies.

To take these decisions rationally, the alternatives must be specified according to uniformly applied criteria and in language permitting easy comparisons. In such environments, the pressures for quantification are understandable and, if everyone concerned understands the "more or less" nature of risk assessment, then nothing essential is lost from the standpoint of decision-making.

PANEL PARADOX: RECONCILING THE EXPERTS

Applying formal methods when utilizing the services of expert panelists requires panelists to assign utilities to the consequences of actions, and then to reconsider the same actions and assign subjective probabilities to their occurrence. The results can mean that the experts agree on which action has the highest expected value (product of utility and probability) but for precisely opposite reasons.

For example, consider the case of a two-expert panel on England that recommends against investment, expert 1 on grounds that the pound will fall and the government be defeated and replaced by a militantly left-wing party, expert 2 on grounds that the pound will rise making exports uncompetitive and that the fiscally conservative government now in power will remain, making no tax concessions on exports. Consider further that their assignments of utility are identical and that their probability assignments also agree, except they are assigned to opposite cases, which constitutes the point at issue.

a) Assessment 1

	£ Rise	£ Fall	Prob
Stay	.06	.14	.20
Go	.24	.56	.80
	.30	.70	1.0

b) Assessment 2

	£ Rise	£ Fall	Prob
Stay	.56	.24	.80
Go	.14	.06	.20
	.70	.30	1.0

The tables above are constructed so that the experts' probability assessments for each event are displayed at the end of each row or column, and the combined scores inside the squares (e.g. rise/stay = .56) are the products of the respective row and column estimates (e.g., .70 × .80).

Why not simply average the experts' probability estimates? Paradoxically, the outcome may lead you to choose the opposite course recommended by your panel.

Averaging probabilities in this example would lead to .50 scores at each possibility, and a combined probability estimate of .25 for each row/column intersection. At the very least, this makes the "don't invest" alternative considerably less compelling than before in comparison with the "do invest" option; e.g. the "pound fall/government stay" possibility is now equally as likely as the gloomier alternatives forecast by the panel. Depending on the alternative uses available for the funds in question, a rational course might well be to invest in the U.K. despite the assessments of the experts.

On the other hand, if you average the combined assessments (i.e. the scores at the row/column intersections) you maintain the contradictory assessments of your panel members together with their combined negative conclusion, but in the process you destroy the independence of the probability estimates, making each alternative (rise, fall, stay, go) equally likely (.50 each).

In this example, we hold the utility assignments identical: if they also vary, there will always be one example such that each expert agrees on the choice of action, but the group procedure generates a different conclusion.

Handling a panel that agrees on its conclusions for opposite reasons thus confronts the decision maker with an unpalatable choice: accept the panel's verdict on probabilities but not necessarily on action, or go for consensus on action, but in the process undermine the panel's judgment on probabilities.

There is also a third possibility: override individual judgments and task someone to dictate the probability and utility assignments to the group.[12]

In practical terms, this paradox illustrates the usefulness of having a headquarters specialist who can recognize this dilemma and who can take the time to probe deeper into sources of agreement and disagreement among experts and thus dramatically enhance the quality of decision-making.

Political Risk Assessment Assessed

An important key to successful political risk analysis is the calibre of experts on the panel and how well they can be induced to perform sincerely. With that as given, the analytic techniques are helpful in insisting that complex judgments be broken down into discrete units, e.g., "the probability event A will occur as a result of factor B is C." Repeated trials using different factors in part answers objections that the factors so carefully delineated in the models will, in real life, occur together as a composite of mutually contributing and interfering circumstances. However, there are the issues (1) whether the company's questionnaire is adequate to capture all the factors and events that are important, and (2) whether the attempts at quantification will not mislead decision-makers into choosing among countries on political grounds when in reality there are no substantive grounds for making such a choice.

There remain two serious conceptual issues which, more than strict methodology, may account for the lukewarm enthusiasm senior management has for political risk analysis. First, the question of "objective" vs. "subjective" probability. Many executives, trained in the physical sciences, believe that probability only has meaning when events can be repeated over time (e.g., tossing a coin) so that a series of outcomes are possible. As for so-called subjective probability, in this view it is by no means apparent that even with fancy statistical manipulation one is dealing with anything more reliable than an expert's guess about the future. That guess may be worth something. But if statistically the weight that should be attached to it is 50 percent or less, then one would do as well or better tossing a coin. According to this line of reasoning, companies should watch out for and act prudently in the face of negative trends, but assigning judgments more refined than "maybe" to political risk forecasts is intellectually dishonest.

The other objection to "risk assessment" is passivity and emphasis upon threats to the possible neglect of opportunities. The likelihood of positive developments (e.g., corporate tax relief) might never be considered unless put forward in the questions to the panelists. Thus individual companies may miss out on the initial stages of an improving situation.

There is an additional set of consequences for the use of such methods by all companies. For the aggregate outcome may well be to generate the pessimistic outcomes individual companies seek to avoid.

Consider, for example, the list of "risk factors" above, starting with those governing host country capability of running the business. The significance of these factors can obviously be reduced by appropriate organizational strategies such as *fragmentation of production* so that end product outputs are geographically separated from raw materials or semi-processed imports; or by *limitations on technology transfer* and employment and training of host country personnel; or by *decreasing company commitments* in areas where barriers to host country participation may easily be overcome.

Other events, such as price controls and limitations on profit repatriation may be circumvented by using international financing (e.g., through the World Bank) and transfer pricing—methods that in effect may pose an added burden or risk premium on host country *foreign exchange reserves*. Such policies, carried out by an entire sector of a host country economy—i.e., the foreign-owned sector because all are using the same analytical methods—can in turn generate other political risk factors such as "*visibility of foreigners*" and "*economic performance*" difficulties that will create conditions for conflict and antagonism. In this way political risk analysis, as opposed to the more open-ended political issues analysis, can set up myopic and risky conditions for foreign operations.

So far management seems generally to be aware of the difficulties and is reluctant to place high confidence in advanced methods of political risk analysis. Rather, some managers appear to favor a "mini foreign office" approach in which desk officers are expected to develop enough familiarity with their respective operating theatres that they can make informed judgments on policy in those areas. Others avoid institutionalizing the specialty, using ad hoc staff groups with international experience to alert top management to overexposure in high risk countries.

Even so, unwelcome surprises occur. We shall now look at why this should be so and what can be done about it.

AVOIDING SURPRISES OR WHO SHOULD SCAN?

Should companies centralize or decentralize their scanning and issues assessment activities? Most American companies, concerned about issues, treat them as another staff function, centralized at corporate headquarters after some processing by operating divisions. Thus, corporate has mountains of data to digest and often relatively minor decisions must wait until openings occur in the busy schedules of top management.

Some other companies insist that their international operating heads make their own assessments, informing headquarters regularly on the main issue or issues of importance in their operating theatres. Thus, most data collection and assessment are performed in the field, and responses are developed mainly in the field, where they are to be implemented. Results are assessed centrally, with appropriate reaction to success or failure.[13]

Which system best protects against surprise? Is there any way to tell? An answer can be derived from examining the assessment process and the elements that can lead to unwelcome surprises.

There are perhaps five factors that can potentially lead to businesses being surprised by unwelcome events, even when paying attention to political and social trends.[14]

First, there is the decision of a host country to keep its impending moves secret until the government is ready to announce them formally; i.e., national budgetary measures in a Parliamentary country, or decisions to implement currency controls or wage and price controls, for example. While the actual date of decision may be surprising, however, the trends that cause such a measure to be considered are not. In such incidents, the actual surprise should be one of degree. Sufficient hedging should already have occurred in response to the unfavorable economic indicators to avoid unaffordable exposures. Yet there are legitimate surprises: Canada's National Energy Program shocked most people in the industry by its degree of radicalness; Canada's 1975 round of wage and price controls, coming after an election in which Prime Minister Trudeau had campaigned to victory by denigrating his opponent's electoral promises of controls, also surprised many companies. Determined Government secrecy is thus a legitimate cause of surprises.

Second, sheer government indecision can result in false alerts that undermine the credibility of valid alerts so that warnings will not receive due appreciation. This is a particular danger for analysts who are closely "plugged into" the government decision-making process and who are under pressure to give advance warning of "events." Restricting reports to "state of debate" can help, but cannot transcend sheer indecision of the policy makers themselves.

These two causes of surprise are mainly problems of data gathering. Other causes are traceable to problems of assessment—for instance, the breakdown of *deterrence*. Large companies may believe that no trading country would do such and such because, say, of the long-range effect on investor confidence. But the government goes ahead anyway.

Similarly, company analysts may believe mistakenly that a government lacks the means (legal or technical) to enforce a particularly unwelcome measure about which they have warning (e.g., Nasser's nationalization of the Suez Canal). Or company analysts may mistakenly believe that a country, hitherto noted for exemplary commercial policies, would *never* do a particular thing—only to find out that the country is more than ready to enact such measures after all. This is analogous to "doctrinal" surprise of military intelligence.

Finally, perhaps the most critical cause of company mistakes is simply the temptation to defer tough decisions. No one likes to receive negative indicators. The temptation is always there to send out for more reassuring data, to challenge the credibility of available data, to defer decision until more evidence is in, or to rationalize, using the ambivalence of available data as evidence supporting a contrary, more positive interpretation.

Organization and the structure of incentives for analysts can help counter these tendencies that lead to surprises. Data gathering on the spot with outside validation at headquarters can keep the effects of government secrecy (or outright deception) to a rock bottom minimum. Assessment problems can also be dealt with by a mix of centralization and decentralization. The tendency to defer decisions can be countered by holding host country division heads accountable for providing timely warnings—including questions of local technical ability—and for initiatives in minimizing exposures. However, for such matters as deterrence breakdowns (or host country readiness to assume greatly incurred risks) and of doctrinal surprise, distance may lend greater clarity than is available on the spot. Scanning activities at headquarters could better evaluate the broad patterns of change (increased nationalism, increasing local elite pressure on foreign business) than scanners more closely involved with day-to-day issues. The problem of false alerts can best be handled by frank exchanges between divisions and corporate scanners. In this connection, there is a case for corporate staff to devise an "Issue Filter" for assessing reports from the field and from internal validators.

Designing the Filter

Work done previously on predicting current outcomes and emerging issues can be used to set some basic themes against which to analyze trend lines.

Every operating area will have constant themes against which to analyze trends: host country performance requirements, stability/instability, public sector share of GNP, productivity and current account balances, potential changes of government. Filters flagging these choices can be provided by outside experts or by in-house specialists. It should be rough and ready, subject to correction—an open-ended checklist of the quasi-permanent issues in any jurisdiction for assessing reports both from the field and from validators.

Scanning Organization

The resulting mix of scanning activities is suggested by the diagram (opposite). As will readily be appreciated, it combines centralization and decentralization in such a way as to minimize the chance of unwelcome surprises. It also recognizes that some ambiguity is normal, and provides an arena for resolving these issues among headquarters and line division specialists before moving assessments forward to decision.

On the other hand, it also ensures that corporate is not overwhelmed with detail. Instead it matches regular assessments by division with outside opinion-resolving judgment and maintains continuous contact with the operating division. Line divisions are responsible for the quality of their inputs (measured against outside validation); corporate scanners are particularly accountable for surprises based on deterrence breakdown and doctrinal shifts in host countries. Decision-making in the host country is the primary responsibility of the division head. Corporate overrides could occur, but these would be minimized.

Using such an arrangement, the documents which top management sees on current issues can be a considerable distillation, showing (a) the top priority issue in each region, (b) action taken and results expected, and (c) items for decision, if necessary. Top priority emerging issues can be flagged in business plans if they pose a threat to corporate policy and can include action plans for dealing with the threat; strategic issues can remain a subject for tracking within planning/public affairs committees, appearing before top management only in settings appropriate to a systematic look at the long range environment.

The process of generating outside and in-house studies in support of the firm's strategic planning exercise will in all probability direct top management attention to critical possibilities before the final product is

Figure VIII.5. Typical Scanning Hierarchy

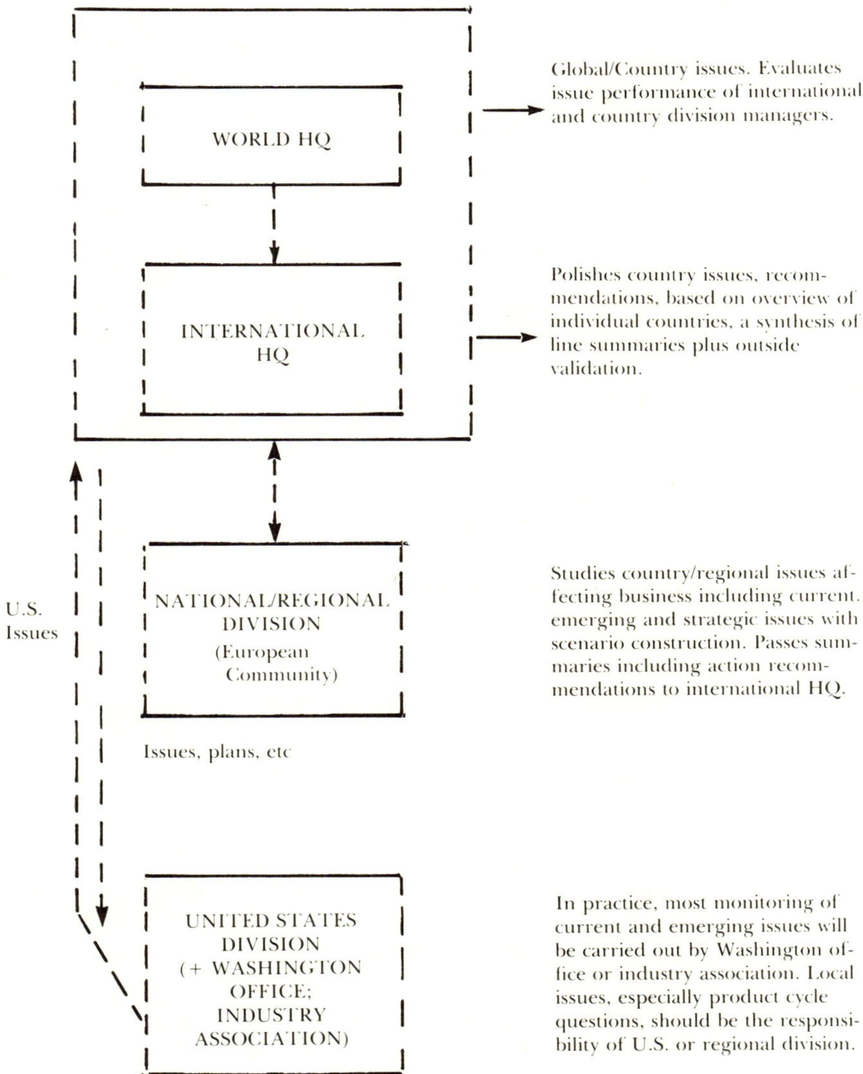

produced. That will in turn have an important effect on operating strategies, encouraging some developments and discouraging others.

SUMMARY

Recommendations include: methods of analyzing trends and predicting issues by compiling a political calendar, timetable of institutional meetings and other potential precipitates, and an analysis of company actions and policies in relation to issues (using the business cycle approach). The question of political risk analysis is discussed and political risk analysis compared with issues analysis. The question of surprises is also examined. In practice, the scanning process is as important as the scanning product and is likely to affect operational plans as much as strategic decisions. The process should mix centralization and decentralization in such a way as to minimize risk of surprises.

List of Terms and Concepts

Issues scanning
Resource allocation for issues scanning
Current issues
Emerging issues
Strategic issues
Observable trend categories
Data bases for each category
The GAMIS system
Structuring results
Predicting issue events
The product cycle approach
Charting cross impacts: Linked economies, GAIL
Political risk
Political risk method: Decompose risk into events
Identify political risk factors
Generate probabilities
Developing cross impacts
Using political risk
Political risk assessment assessed
Five sources of surprise
Who should scan: Headquarters vs. line

NOTES

1. See: Guidelines for Managing Corporate Issues Programs, The Conference Board, Report No. 795; Archie B. Carroll, *Business & Society*, Managing Corporate Social Performance, Little Brown, 1981, Chapter 12.

2. For a slightly different treatment see Bruce Lloyd, "Political Risk Management," Keith Shipton Development Special Study No. 7, 1976, pp. 10-11.
3. This example was suggested by Howard Chase.
4. See Talcott Parsons, Neil J. Smelser, *Economy and Society*, Free Press, New York, 1956.
5. Jeffrey D. Simon, "Political Risk Assessment: Past Trends and Future Prospects," *Columbia Journal of World Business*, Fall, 1982, 26-71.
6. Ghadar Fariborz, "Political Risk and the Erosion of Control: The Case of the Oil Industry," *Columbia Journal of World Business*, Fall 1982, p. 47.
7. Stephen Blank, Joseph LaPalombara, and Paul M. Sacks, "Political Analysis and Forecasting in the Private Sector: An Overview of the New Firm-Centric Analytical Formats," Forschungsinstitut der Friedrich-Ebert-Stiftung, *Vierteljahresberichte*, Nr 90, Dez 1982.
8. Stephen Blank, et al., op cit.; "Banks Revise Ways of Making Foreign Loans," *The Wall Street Journal*, 18 Feb, 1983, p. 31.
9. Described in Stephen Blank, op. cit., p. 376, and in considerably more detail in D.W. Bunn and M.M. Mustafouglu, "Forecasting Political Risk," *Management Science*, Vol. 24, No. 15, November 1978, pp. 1557-1567; Robert Schlaiffer, *Applied Statistical Decision Theory*, (1961) Harvard, esp. pp. 66-68.
10. Dick A. Leabo, *Basic Statistics*, 3rd Edition, (1968) Irwin, esp. chap. 17.
11. Leabo, op. cit., pp. 456-7.
12. Howard Raiffa, *Decision Analysis*, Addison-Wesley, 1968.
13. See Daniel Sharp, "Integrating External Business Environment Analysis into the Decision-Making Process," Presentation to Association of Political Risk Analysts, 13 April, 1982.
14. Richard K. Betts, "Surprise Despite Warning: Why Sudden Attacks Succeed," *Political Science Quarterly*, Winter 1980-81, pp. 551 ff.

Chapter IX

Conclusion

This work is about issues considered from the standpoint of an executive who wants to influence outcomes and who therefore wants to understand what strategies are likely to succeed and why.

Chapter One sketched the rise and decline of public relations as a management function and its succession by public affairs and issues management as approaches to navigating the hazards of the public policy process. Corporations today are more attuned to changes in public values and better able to make use of information about those changes in making policy decisions.

Chapter Two introduced the need for a theoretical framework against which to manage the relationship of company policy to public policy. To be satisfactory, such theory should (1) speak the language of management, that is, be expressable in primarily economic terms, and (2) provide guidance to managers about likely patterns of development and where optimal courses lie.

Chapter Three began laying the groundwork for such a theory. It opened by considering the relationship of individuals to each other and then to the state as game theoretic, then substituted the firm for the individual. A general issues framework was then developed, involving the generation of external costs and the problems of devising rules for internalizing them. With the state playing a role, strategic behavior and the creation of inducements for cooperation were essential to a democratic and minimally coercive resolution.

Chapter Four went further, discussing the concepts of public goods and private goods and the rational voter before developing an analytical model of government behavior. After looking at the factors determining the supply and demand for public goods, the relationship between tax prices and costs of political participation was found to explain political styles of business regulation. An appendix to the chapter outlined the problems involved in attaining committee agreement. The arguments in this chapter again testified to the importance of information in determining outcomes in the public policy process and the importance of taking positions that induce agreement by affecting the constituencies at the margins of political support for government leaders and legislators.

Chapter Five focused on the issues resolution process, i.e., how disputes come to be concluded, and introduced some new concepts of practical relevance to issues managers. The dynamics of collective action were examined, both for lobby groups and for sudden upwellings of political wrath, and optimal strategies developed for dealing with each of the "resolution modes": externality problems, critical mass and bargaining problems.

Chapter Six set out a complete procedural framework for coping with issues in a rational context, starting with issue origins and applying the models developed earlier to issues plans. A flow diagram at the end of the chapter set out the steps in the process.

Chapter Seven presented a series of cases to see whether the theoretical apparatus developed earlier could be helpful in explaining issues, actions and results. Cases included the different handling of pollution problems, product safety problems, marketing in different cultures, issues of gun control, of energy regulation and the preparation of strategic advice for a committee of inquiry into an environmental safety issue.

Chapter Eight examined the problems of anticipating issues, compared issues analysis and political risk analysis, and concluded by analyzing the sources of surprise and suggesting a form of organization to keep these to a minimum.

We are now in a position to make some more general statements about issues management as a business function. In particular, we can come to some interesting conclusions about (1) the relationship of issues management and profitability, (2) the problem of resource allocation to that function, and (3) evaluating productivity.

ISSUES MANAGEMENT AND THE FIRM

Issues Management and Profitability

It should be clear from the foregoing that a productive relationship to society is a scarce good commanding a price in the form of resources allocated to maintaining that relationship. A firm's profitability is the return on outputs produced from a combination of production factor inputs. But as we have demonstrated throughout the book, profitability is also dependent upon the reaction of the stakeholders of a business to the way in which the firm does business. Let us assume for simplicity a single product and perfect information so that the population is uniformly aware of the company and its activities.[1] We can write the firm's profitability as follows:

$$\pi = P_1Q_1 - (TC + R)$$

That is, profitability = total revenues from sales − total costs + costs of enhancing or maintaining the firm's reputation, (i.e., stakeholder approval of company activities).

Define R as inversely related to an endowed position, that is to the firm's goodwill or stock of social approval, "d," and directly related to any current hostility, "h":

$$R = 1/d.h$$

If a firm has a positive endowed social position and h = 0, then the break-even point for the firm is

$$P_1Q_1 = TC$$

Then,

$$P_1Q_1 - TC = 0$$

But this assumes an unrealistically benign environment. Although D may be substantial and positive, R can be expensive if "h" is given extreme negative value by the efforts of others in undermining the success of the firm. In such cases:

$$\frac{\partial\,(P_1Q_1 - TC)}{\partial R} \leq 0$$

That is, marginal increases in profits are offset by the declining support of the firm's stakeholders such that adverse tax and/or regulatory developments eliminate the gains. In the absence of coercion to render "h" ineffective (impossible in a democracy), only additional expenditures can influence "h". So the vanishing point.

Factors affecting "h" have already been examined in the case of government. They are no different for business, i.e.:

$$h = \int_{t1}^{t2} pt(ct)\,[r(c)t - r(f)t]\,.dt$$

except that r(f)t, the firm's political discount rate for policy, replaces r(p)t, the politician's discount rate. That is, hostility to the firm is a product of:

- hostile community memory (pt).
- critics' effort to expand pt (ct).
- the difference between social values and the firm's values; [r(c)t − r(f)t].
- over time (dt).

For governments, as we have seen, the maximum value "h" can have is zero, because at that point the difference between the community discount rate and the political discount rate is eliminated and the other factors affecting the supply of public goods will generate a positive return; similarly for a firm. If its policies are consonant with community values, "h" will no longer be an impediment to the achievement of success through normal business performance. By itself, however, that may be insufficient. If critics (ct) have pivotal power in the public policy process, then business must address them either (1) by plunging ahead, reckoning their power as insufficient to generate significant impediments; (2) by isolating them in that process using political techniques, or (3) going part way to address their concerns, depending on the cost, and the likely payoff in terms of "h" and R.

Another implication of our argument should also be noted: it is impossible to enhance business performance by spending solely on R goods, because the maximum value "h" can have is zero, after which point such spending lowers profits. It is true that "social spending" can in the real world enhance the reputation of the spending firm. But, ignoring information costs, this will be true only to the point of offsetting differences between the firm's policy discount rate and that of the community. Otherwise firms could improve their returns by holding $P_1Q_1 - TC$ constant and spend to increase stakeholder approval. Perhaps this would work for individuals known as "personalities," i.e., "famous for being famous"[2] but not for business firms past a certain point at which "h" reaches zero. Of course, when information is in imperfect supply, additional spending may be needed to ensure proper awareness and recognition of the firm's achievements. For this to offset "h" values, however, policies must be consonant with public values.

How Much Issues Management is Enough?

How much is enough? The answer based on our arguments so far is the amount required to ensure the firm realizes its full profitability—the amount required to bring "h" to zero and keep it there.

At the same time, the amount allotted to issues should show the same returns as other capital employed in the firm so that there are no opportunity losses.

Considering the amounts one could thus justifiably allocate to R, it would seem that companies expect to pay far too little for their "reputation goods." But let us try to apply this reasoning to a real world example.

Suppose Firm A learns that a Minister of Finance is contemplating a production tax the effect of which is to reduce A's profitability by 20 percent at current production levels. Suppose further that the firm's internal "hurdle rate" is such that the firm expects every dollar employed to double in four years, i.e., make 25 percent a year. Suppose, too, that Firm A's profit in the fiscal year just ended was declared at $100 million. What resources should be spent on combatting the tax?

The tax adds to the marginal cost of production so a cutback will be necessary to bring MC = AC, i.e., to re-optimize production in the new tax conditions. In effect, society has given up a portion of the firm's product in return for higher tax revenues from the firm. If the firm can, as a result of shorter supply, it will raise the price of the product, so that P_2Q_2 in the new tax conditions may equal P_1Q_1 in the old tax conditions. In this case, the loss of profitability would be virtually nil, at least in the short run. So the inclination of the firm to avoid risk of antagonizing a powerful government would outweigh the benefits of eliminating the tax.

Suppose, however, it was impossible for the firm to raise prices and that the tax would have to be absorbed in the form of 20 percent lower profits. Then, bearing in mind the hurdle rate, the firm would have a choice between two "gambles" or investments: (1) reduce investments in the business under tax and reallocate the funds to new fields with the 25 percent yields the company seeks, or (2) spend the equivalent percent of the potential profit loss to eliminate the tax. On the figures given, 20 percent profit loss = $20 million, therefore the amount to be spent on fighting the issue would equal $16 million. Considering that other firms in the industry would be making similar calculations, the government could look forward to an immensely rough ride and possible defeat in such an instance. In fact, however, most firms in this situation would be reluctant to spend much more than one percent of expected profit shortfalls, instead reallocating funds to new investment targets.

An argument in support of this is that the firm is thus responding to society's signals of what it expects from business, the confirmation of which is that corporate profitability is maintained despite the attack on a particular area of business. In practice, when business profitability in general is down, business representations to government increase dramatically, although the resources allocated are rarely proportional to the stakes.

To the extent business in general does try to maintain its reputation at satisfactory levels at considerably below market prices, it would not be surprising to find public values are ambivalent in support of production values and profit. Profit is the controlling variable, however, as are votes in the public sector. To the extent profits can be maximized without spending on issues, that spending will be minimized.

The sum of resources allocated to issues management should be such that the reputation of the firm permits it the maximum retention of profits. At the margin, therefore, poorly reputed companies with high profits would have to spend more to maintain R in the face of new issues than low profit companies in similar public regard. On the other hand, companies with high reputation endowments would spend less than companies in less happy public regard.

Similarly, societies that are chronically suspicious of business add to the costs of doing business in proportion to the difficulty of winning acceptance. This would be more expensive for more profitable companies than less profitable ones. If suspicion grows with corporate size, then some large, high value-added firms could find it impossible to do business in that society, although less efficient firms might be able to maintain themselves. Conversely, societies whose businesses are underperforming may improve profitability by changing public values and becoming more tolerant of company policies.

Issues Management and Productivity

On the face of the argument so far, measuring productivity ought to be easy. Just state how much input is required to generate optimum outputs, i.e., are the dollars allocated to "reputation goods" as profitable as the business as a whole, and are "h" values kept at zero?

Several problems arise from trying to apply such a definition, however. First, how to measure returns on "reputation goods"? Polling for the widespread recognition and favorable approval scores among key "publics" is one way to do this and is a standard public relations yardstick. For a company with no special issues problems and a small staff, such a yardstick might well be all that is required.

The problem with that definition is that it implies an identity between the propensity of a firm's customers to buy its product and citizens (including non-customers) to think well of the company. Truth may be just the opposite. A capital goods company, for example, may be extremely profitable ($P_1Q_1 - TC$) but the very reasons for its profitability may be increasing public hostility "h". This can arise as we have seen because TC does not include the costs being passed on to the community as externalities. Given that situation, profitability is actually at cross purposes with the efficiency of "reputation goods" generation. Only a change in company policy would bring the ratios of issues spending into line with profitability.

Another problem concerns the firm's ranking in the industry. To a large extent, the leading company in an industry will often be the chief spokesman not only for itself but for the industry as a whole. It will then spend more on "reputation goods" than the other companies, who will in turn "ride free." To that degree the issues departments of smaller companies might well appear more productive than those of the larger firm.

Having made these qualifications, one may now remember that profitability includes all R factors, so among firms of similar profitability and regard, issues management productivity will be inversely related to inputs. The difficulties intrinsic to evaluation therefore occur when the firm is performing below industry standard, either in terms of profitability or public regard or both. In those conditions, new policies may be necessary precursors of improvements, both in company and issues management efficiency.

Models

Many of those interested in public affairs will not have been sympathetic to the attempt to derive a consistent deductive framework for the management of public issues. Too elaborate, too "scientistic"! It is worth reminding ourselves that the case for such models is that they are necessary to provide a rational framework for explaining why some strategies will work and others will not. Accurate deductions based on carefully chosen assumptions produce hypotheses that when tested against experience should hold up rather better than the alternatives. The arguments in this book, properly used, should enable practitioners to stay on top of issues just as the more traditional management functions such as finance, and operations, manage in their respective fields.

It is particularly interesting to review how the models performed in explaining the variables of the various cases. On a general theoretical level, our arguments provide *inter alia* an explanation of why issues management and not simply PR is necessary for successful involvement in the public policy process. Our assumptions of maximizing behavior and of the role of the state as an interested party, we saw, were necessary to a rational explanation of how private desires are translated into public policies. But the same conditions also required that players be able to move strategically. Persuasion, while necessary, is not sufficient to provide inducements to public policy makers to take positions favorable (or unfavorable) to an enterprise. Instead, positive incentives must be created—either in terms of net public benefits (for which political leaders can take credit)—or in terms of stakeholder pressure, enough to warrant a legislator's response. Interestingly, this held true for economic issues and for purely political issues like gun control.

Our analysis also shed interesting light on the "issues-behavior" of large companies. It showed, for instance, that assumptions of maximizing behavior generate more possiblities for legitimate strategic action than appear to be utilized by well-managed corporations. These businesses, it appeared, were more concerned about preserving their good reputations than capturing relatively small advantages that theory showed might be available in certain circumstances. Ironically, in one example (Nestlé Alimenta), that concern for reputation resulted in a court case that had entirely counterproductive results. A second interesting discovery was that the existence or non-existence of formal "contract lines" in the form of explicit regulatory requirements did not always make much difference to corporate behavior. Rather, responses shown to be rational by the models formed the main lines of their issues strategies with or without actual legislative compulsion. In this connection, the laws setting standards for corporate behavior should be seen as a floor or framework to govern behavior in less well-managed companies. These rules then should be viewed as basic guidelines for minimum standards of management accountability and thus a set of formal reassurances for the public.

These conclusions emerged from the consideration of cases concerning the externalities model. Others emerged from our discussions of critical mass. Of these, the chief one was probably that the "system" or public policy process is generally more flexible and easier to move than theory predicts it needs to be.

Astute decision makers, including senior executives of large consumer-oriented companies, seem to employ a rational expectations model of public attitudes. If pressure is demonstrably building in a direction that affects them, they will move before waiting for it to peak. A similar lesson was demonstrated in business-government bargaining situations: opening moves that positioned a player squarely in the winning issues space with respect to public opinion tended to preclude serious resistance afterwards.

Good counter-strategy required that opponents seize upon mistakes in that initial positioning. Where, as in the case of the Firestone 500 Radial tires, the company failed to do this and instead helped its adversary correct its opening mistakes, the results were predictably bad for the company. Again, the system appears to be sensitive to areas of mature, i.e., solidly formed, stakeholder opinion. Further corroboration was provided by our example of a multinational company caught by Canada's National Energy Program. All things considered, its best approach was a Fabian strategy, letting others (together with market forces) carry the fight until public opinion changed in response to the failure of the policy. A corollary to this is that, when no political or policy movement takes place in response to public opinion, it is often because the political or other leaders have already discounted it. Alterations in their plans will only then follow if the explosion of outrage is sufficient to demonstrate clearly that new and different calculations are required, or else the passage of time changes the basic conditions.

Our discussions also examined the general question of the efficiency of the public policy process in allocating resources. Here our mainly deductive approach showed that, in terms of decision-making, the system is efficient: i.e., majority rule allocates benefits among stakeholders in such a way that the resulting majority is "dominant." These outcomes will leave the community perhaps slightly better off, but the result will not necessarily be Pareto optimal. On the contrary, where possible, it will make the issue losers pay the winners.

Clearly, however, to keep the system operating, there can be no permanent losers. Over time and over a range of issues, the total outcomes must be Pareto optimal. You win some and you lose some, with general betterment or at least broadly even results. Otherwise, over time, the permanent losers would rationally drop out or wreck the system. (Unless "the system" can successfully repress the losers, in which case its ability to function as a democracy may become impaired.)

The patterns of behavior described and analyzed by our issue models work as they do because of the information networks linking the stakeholders and providing feedback as positions are taken and changed. What we have been analyzing therefore amounts to a market solution of the problems in business and society.

Many commentators on business social responsibility suggest that firms themselves need to learn and acquire new norms of behavior to serve the public purpose.[3] Our argument on the contrary is that if the marketplace is conceived broadly enough as a political economy, then a well-managed business will respond in timely fashion to social as well as economic pressures. Moreover, given that most businessmen are managers, not philosopher-kings any more than are most contemporary politicians, it is extremely unlikely that a single, transcendental public purpose will emerge from most issues debates except perhaps for a narrow range of questions, such as global "commons" issues.[4] Even in some of these instances, there may be more scope for privatization as a complete or partial solution than is generally recognized at the moment.

The political-economic market is quirky. It aggregates supply and demand according to two different and not always interchangeable currencies: votes as well as money and other tangibles. It also provides goods for which all must pay without, however, requiring each of us to do so. Consequently, the political marketplace is replete with traps and paradoxes, rationality breakdowns and other behavioral patterns we have described. Understanding these patterns should permit executives to enter and play the process more effectively. Indeed, the growing capacity of executives to participate fully in this political marketplace is to be welcomed.

Some economists and other social scientists may deplore this latter development as a distortion of the main wealth-producing role of business or as an opening to the subversion of democracy by wealth and power. Yet the growing permeability of wealth-producing and political spheres (if they ever were distinct and impermeable) and the subjection of large business to scrutiny by the public policy process is arguably no bad thing. On the contrary, it provides a non or limited coercion solution to the problem of the large business corporation and its relationship to society. It makes management accountable, it brings corporate performance under the glare of all stakeholders, not just investors. It makes management power legitimate only insofar as it is able to win social approval. The result is not socialism, or state capitalism, or any other administrative arrangement to inhibit private entrepreneurial drive. It is simply democracy.

The discussions in this work are mainly about strategy, not the products of strategy. Our main objective was to demonstrate that the management of issues is a rational, coping activity, explicable in general economic terms just as are other management disciplines. Teaching the handling of issues, therefore, should be possible in terms of basic concepts—the why as well as the how.

To the extent that business can develop its political skills, it will succeed in having its long-term needs recognized and supported by the community out of a sense of justice. As technology increases the reach and consequences of business decision-making for the community, these political skills will become a necessary part of every manager's professional equipment.

Management's understanding of politics must, however, be grounded in the rational, utilitarian framework that governs other business decisions. Or else political issues and strategies will not be comprehensible and digestible within the framework of business. Without that alignment, the social and political responsiveness necessary to preserving management autonomy will be much more difficult to attain.

As well, the insights given by economic theory must be directly related to practice as much as possible. In academic life, practice may illuminate theory. But in the world of production, theory must improve practice to merit consideration, and it is to that world this work is directed.

NOTES

1. This discussion owes much to Gary Becker, *The Economic Approach to Human Behavior*, (1976) University of Chicago, esp. chap. 12, "A Theory of Social Interactions," pp. 213-281, with which it differs in certain regards.
2. See Daniel J. Boorstin, *The Image*, 1978, Atheneum, esp. Chapter 2.
3. For a recent excellent example, see Neil W. Chamberlain, *Social Strategy and Corporate Structure*, 1982, Columbia, MacMillan.
4. Such as Law of the Sea, Acid Rain, Population Control, depletion of natural resources, climate changes from "Greenhouse effect."

Chapter X

Epilogue: A Note on Commons Issues

Commons issues are a special type of externality problem in which individual pursuit of gain leads to a general reduction in welfare as external costs are absorbed by the same community that generates them. As countries and regions become increasingly interdependent, these issues may increasingly come to predominate in business-government relations. The purpose of this note is to outline the dynamics of the commons and indicate some special implications for future business-government relations, employing some of the concepts developed earlier in this book.

Commons problems arise from congestion.[1] Benefits arise from a business activity until a point is reached at which overcrowding sets in. Thereafter, each additional input reduces collective outputs, although incentives remain to encourage continued inputs.

The primary example from which the issue typology is derived is that of common land. Consider a New England village common, upon which a few grazing sheep will yield 100 pounds of wool each at the end of a year, but upon which 100 sheep grazing will yield nothing worth shearing. Assuming linear relationships, we can construct a table showing the effect of adding sheep to common land:

No. Sheep	Yield/Sheep *lbs.*	Total Yield *lbs.*
1	100	100
25	75	1,875
50	50	2,500
75	25	1,875
100	1	1

Note that output rises steadily up to 50 sheep. Thereafter, additional stock should be slaughtered. Yet private incentives remain to encourage grazing sheep in the 75–100 range. Although collective output declines, individual sheep owners still collect some excess return. The situation arises because the community mistakenly supplies land as a public good, although the common only exhibits jointness of supply and consumption up to 50 sheep. Thereafter each additional sheep adds costs that decrease the consumption available to others. Benefits, on the other hand, are treated as private, exclusive property of the sheepowners throughout.[2]

An obvious solution to this type of commons problem is to privatize costs, by allowing one group or individual to have exclusive grazing rights. This will internalize costs so that output will stabilize at the maximum, i.e., where marginal costs equal marginal returns.

However, privatization cannot work for commons problems where exclusive use, or property rights, are not readily enforceable, such as the effects of industrial production on climate, or on other life supporting capabilities of the planet, as forecast by the Club of Rome and other global modellers.[3] In the opinion of these experts, commons problems are emerging rapidly and we are already approaching the point at which more production will mean less welfare. For example, some National Council scientists now believe they have incontrovertible evidence that the continued burning of hydrocarbons is beginning to cause a "Greenhouse effect"—putting so much carbon dioxide into the atmosphere that the world's average temperature will rise, with attendant higher rainfall and increased risk to valuable coastal real estate. The full implications of the effect are not well understood, but the scientists counsel careful monitoring.[4] The warming, say the scientists, "would carry our planet into largely unknown territory."

Cases like these lend themselves to an alternative to privatization, namely a political solution based either on government action or on the rational interaction of business and government. Such approaches to the commons problem are akin to those of urban planners in dealing with traffic congestion: highway capacity (X) is managed such that the benefits (B) (in miles per hour to individual motorists) vary inversely with volume (N), i.e., the number of vehicles using the road simultaneously. In this model, benefits (B) increase with volume (N) up to a congestion point, beyond which the relationship turns negative (i.e., $dB/dN<0$). Highway scale X is optimized at the point where loss of benefits from congestion is equal to or slightly less than the willingness of motorists to pay an additional tax price for widening the road, as measured in votes (i.e., $dB/dN - dQ/dP \geq 0$)[5] (n.b. d = "change in").

Applied to commons questions involving business: considering B as the benefits (jobs, revenue, production) of a managed amount (X) of environmentally harmful production capacity, X should be such that for government the ratio of benefits (B) to volume of production (N) remained zero or greater (i.e., positive) as measured in votes, i.e., in terms of tax price/cost of political participation. That is $dB/dN - dQ/dP \geq 0$.

Companies, on the other hand, would have to ensure that in every jurisdiction in which they operate the public perception of dB is sufficient to outweigh costs of new public goods (in the form of restrictions on X) to politically significant taxpayers, i.e., that

$$\frac{dBi}{dNi} - \frac{dQ_1}{dPi} \geq 0$$

where B_i = benefits to the ith taxpayer of changes in the amount of production, N = the volume of production_i; Q_i = the tax price to the ith taxpayer, and Pi = costs of political participation to the ith taxpayer to generate new public goods.

Maximizing returns in this context will mean that companies must conduct business in a politically attractive as well as an economically attractive manner, while at the same time erecting barriers to precipitate government action by giving governments a case to answer. Companies will have three factors to optimize: perception of benefits from jobs (B), volume of production (N), and costs of political participation (P), and will be influential in the fourth, the ith taxpayer's perception of tax price (Q). Companies seeking to avoid regulation would thus control loss of benefits from volume of production so that it remains below tax prices for remedies, and keep political participation costs for their allies low enough that any attempt to reduce B by restricting N would elicit prompt opposition. Companies seeking regulation, say in the form of a national fund to assist in moving out of this kind of production, would not oppose perceptions of benefit loss outweighing tax prices of remedial programs, but would strive to keep political participation costs for allies less than the loss of benefits from restrictions on production volume.

On the government side, initiatives would concentrate on inducing companies operating with their jurisdiction to internalize excess costs being passed on such that the lost benefits from decreased production equalled the value of clean air to other voters, i.e., again dB = dQ/dP. Governments will be sensitive to lost benefits and also perhaps to lost tax revenue from decreased company profitability. To the extent countries A to M succeed, environmental pressure could be relieved on other countries N to Z, so progress initially may be confined to one or two major producing countries.

On the other hand, a drag on implementation will be international pollution spillovers. "Sending" countries will be less likely to impose costly environmental restrictions than "receiving" countries, especially if by doing so they would lose votes in pivotal constituencies.

In illustrating the difficult decisions that must be made, the commons model not only highlights the problems, but also points the way to the possibility of a decentralized solution. As outlined above, the model transforms the environmental problem of the commons into an issue of a series of exchanges—between businesses, between government and business and between governments.

Rather than determine the precise value of the trade-offis required in every instance, therefore, public policy need only supply the mechanisms by which decision-makers and stakeholders can weigh the costs and benefits of alternatives. In other words, instead of letting political pressure force the market, we can use the market to balance the pressures. For instance,

Within countries:

(a) pollution fines and taxes can be levied progressively more intensively as acceptable standards tighten. This could encourage companies to shed worn-out, polluting facilities;
(b) revenues from fines and taxes could go into a fund to accelerate movement towards new, cleaner technology or tasks. (Alternatively, tax credits could be created.) Similar payments might be used to "bribe" some communities into accepting toxic waste disposal sites.

Between countries:

(c) pollution receiving countries could establish tax credits within their jurisdictions for branch plants of firms in sending countries. The credits would enable the branches to acquire anti-pollution technology for lease back to firms in the sending country. With the credit equal to the cost of the anti-pollution equipment, the result should encourage a shift away from polluting plant in the sending country. Costs of the shift would be absorbed in loss of tax revenue by the sending jurisdiction.

An optimal corporate strategy would include some or all of these elements:

1. *Consciously transfering manufacturing technology* such that X is reduced according to national issues sensitivities as well as more usual economic data. Like a snake sheds its old skin, companies will regularly pass along older technologies to locations where their benefits will be regarded as positive, replacing them as that perception declines. (This process will be constrained by pressure for uniform, state-of-the-art international standards.)
2. *Emphasizing the contribution private market solutions* can make to commons problems, especially regarding (a) resource depletion, (b) inducements to curb population expansion (through private affluence and public health), and (c) improved agricultural productivity.
3. *Urging an important but restricted role for government,* limited to the provision of real lighthouse effects, such as the establishment of international greenbelts, ensuring the free flow of international commerce, improved public education, and international databases.
4. *Supporting these with research institutes* to ensure policy-makers and the public can see top-notch research reflecting private sector economic reality.

The epilogue suggests some new implications in relationships of interdependence for a class of issues likely to grow in importance. The commons model represents an extension of the externalities situation that dominated business-government relations during the 1970s. The main difference is that it is international in scope. The strategic problems discussed in the note suggest that, as the issue develops, governments and companies will compete to balance different public tolerances for production technologies, allocating volume according to the willingness of citizens to trade off costs and benefits. Decentralized, market-driven solutions could be possible. The specific suggestions given go beyond the compromise strategies discussed in the section on externalities to illustrate how private producers and governments can get ahead of this class of issues as it develops. The broad question facing all companies, especially multinational companies, and some governments, is whether they are prepared to recognize a unique responsibility in assisting in the solution of commons problems, or whether they prefer to adopt a defensive, resistant approach, thereby leaving all serious initiatives to stakeholder groups.

NOTES

1. Garrett Hardin, "The Tragedy of the Commons," *Science* (1968) Vol. 162, No. 3859, pp. 1243-48.
2. Thomas Schelling, *Micromotives and Macrobehavior*, 1978, Norton, pp. 115.
3. A sampling of such studies: Donnella H. Meadows, Dennis L. Meadows, Jorgen Randers, and William Behrens III, *The Limits of Growth*, 1972, New American Library; Mihajlo D. Mesarovic and Eduard Pestel, *Mankind at the Turning Point*, 1974, Dutton and New American Library; Jan Tinbergen, (Coordinator), *Reshaping the International Order*, 1976, New American Library; Ervin Laszlo, *Goals for Mankind*, 1978, New American Library; Bohdan Hawrylyshyn, *Road Maps to the Future*, 1980, Pergamon; Gerald O. Barney, Study Director, *The Global 2000 Report to the President: Entering the 21st Century*, 3 vols., U.S. Government Printing Office. For countervailing optimism, see Herman Kahn et. al., *The Next 200 Years*, 1976, Morrow. More specific studies include the reports of The Brandt Commission: *North, South* (1980) and *The Common Crisis* (1983), MIT Paperbacks. For a business viewpoint, see *Toward an Unlimited Future, A Report of the Global One Hundred*, Business International, August 1983.
4. Richard A. Kerr, Carbon Dioxide and a Changing Climate, *Science*, 4 Nov. 1983, vol. 222, No. 4623, p. 491.
5. For a discussion of the urban planners' approach, Inman, "A Generalized Congestion Function for Highway Travel," 5 *Journal of Urban Economics*, (1978) 21-34, summarized in Barnes, (1982-3), p. 588, n. 16. The relationship of tax price (Q) to political participation costs (P) is discussed in the chapter on government, above. The statement $dB/dN - dQ/dP \geq 0$ simply shows that taxes and political participation costs are still higher than the loss of motoring convenience from congestion (at the optimum highway capacity X).

Appendix: Review of Formulae Used in the Text

The mathematical expressions in this book amount to little more than compact notation to express ideas already set forth in words. The formulae are in reality little more than check lists which group the elements to be considered by managers and indicate the relationship each element has to the other. The purpose of this review is to ensure that readers understand the formulae and the notation. It should be remembered that the formulae are not meant as ends in themselves, but rather as shorthand descriptions of human activity in a form convenient for managers.

(1) *The Rational Voter* (p. 42)

$$R = p.b. + c - d$$

"R" is the utility or satisfaction from taking part in elections. At 0, the voter is indifferent between participating and not participating; at positive values, the voter wants to participate, and at negative values, the voter will not participate. The variables:

p = probability of affecting the outcome;
b = satisfaction from the outcome preferred;
c = private satisfaction from participation;
d = private costs of participation

In most areas, given the likelihood that p is practically zero for most electoral situations, the decision whether to participate will depend upon the difference between private benefits and costs.

The equation can also be written in "integrated" form (p. 63). This shows how voter utility would fluctuate between time 1 and time 2 and, as a diagram,

$$R = \int_{t1}^{t2} pb + (c - d) \cdot dt$$

could look like (a), (b) or (c), depending upon subjectively estimated costs and benefits and sense of personal effectiveness.

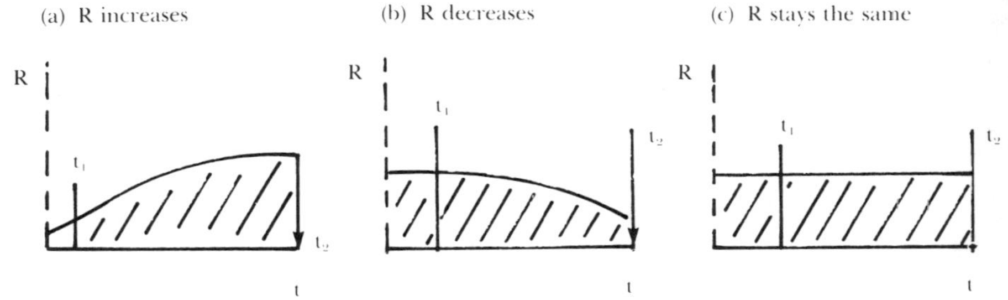

The total utility between t_1 and t_2 is the area under the curve between those points. The formula for finding those values at point t is

$$\frac{p.b.t.}{2} + \frac{(c - d)\ t,}{2}$$

with the area under the curve being the difference between the values t_1 and t_2 respectively: i.e.,

$$(\frac{P.b.t_1}{2} - \frac{(c-d)_1}{2}) - (\frac{p.b.t._2}{2} + \frac{(c-d)\ t_2}{2})$$

Clearly, as t_1 increases, the natural tendency for R is to increase, other factors staying the same. This makes sense, as paying attention to issues or elections becomes more useful as the day of decision arrives. But if news coverage is weak, polls are difficult to get to, or the more one learns of the choices the more indifferent one becomes (that is, b falls off to zero), then R will decrease over time. R will stay the same if utility from the approaching deadline is offset by fuzziness between the competing choices, growing indifference towards any of the possible candidates or other factors increase private costs of participation. Note, therefore, a short campaign that makes participation easy may attract a higher turnout than a long campaign in which following issues is costly in effort and time, and a contest can develop over the best time to maximize R for one's own supporters vs. the R for one's adversaries.

(2) *Government Output* (p. 45)

$$E_t = kE_{t-1} + e^*$$

How much will government or a department of the government spend this year? That amount, E_t, is predicted by last year's expenditure (E_{t-1}) multiplied by the priority government assigns that alternative this year. The variables:

E_t = tax expenditure this year;
k = priority weighting;
E_{t-1} = tax expenditure the previous year
e^* = error estimate (could be zero) for the forecast

(3) *Public Support for Government* (p. 46)

$$N_p - N_r = 0$$

Public support (N_p) and the support for relection (N_r) are equal, so that if an election were held today, the government would be returned. At this point, the power of the bureaucracy (B_t) is maximized.

(4) *Bureaucratic Power and Public Goods Supply* (p. 46)

$$E_t = k(B_t)E_{t-1} + e^*$$

Tax expenditure (E_t) is determined by last year's expenditures (E_{t-1}) times this year's priority (k), which in turn reflects the power of the bureaucracy to impose policies on its political overseers (B_t).

(5) *Demand for Public Goods* (p. 47)

$$D = f(Q,I,P)$$

Demand (D) for public goods is a function (f) of tax price (Q), personal income (I), and the costs of political participation (P).

(6) *Public Hostility* (p. 49)

$$h = \int_{t1}^{t2} pt(ct)[r(c)t - r(p)t]$$

Community hostility depends upon memory (pt), how well it is kept alive by critics (ct), and the difference between community values or preferences and those of political leaders ($r(c)t - r(p)t$).

Note the relationship to the rational voter calculation (No. 1) except that the maximum value of h = zero, i.e., the absence of hostility. Note, too, the importance of critics (ct) and values (r(p)t − r(p)), for memory can only vary between 0 ("sorry, don't remember") and 1 ("oh, yes, I remember: I have total recall—I thought you knew"). As with the rational voter calculation, this too gains from being written in integrated form, to show how h would fluctuate in time;

$$h = \int_{t1}^{t2} pt(ct)\,[r(c)t - r(p)t\ t]$$

As a diagram:

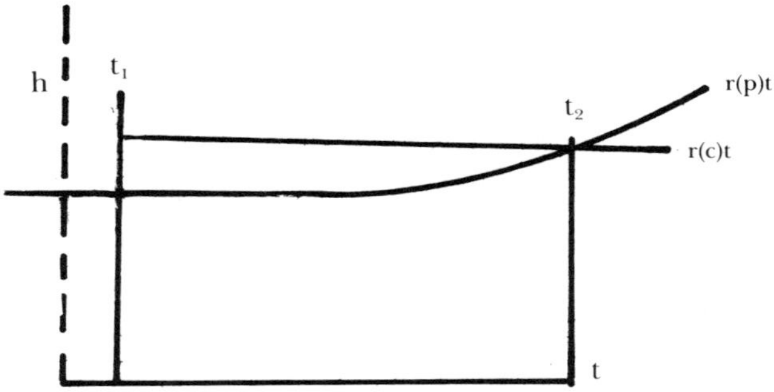

At t_1 community values r(c)t and those of the political leaders r(p)t diverge widely, at t_2, the date of the election, these values have been made consonant, and "h" vanishes.

(7) *Government Output* (p. 50)

$$E_t = k[(B_t)\ h\ f(Q,I,P)]E_{t-1} + e^*$$

This statement combines the previous ones to say that policy output in the form of tax expenditures (E_t) is determined by the priority weighing of last year's policy, where the priority weighting (k) is determined by that bargaining power of officials (B_t), public hostility (h), and the relationship of tax price, income and costs of political participation to the voter (f(Q,I,P)).

(8) *Choice of Policy Instrument* (p. 56)

$$Q - P \leq 0$$

Tax price (Q) is equal to or less than the cost of political participation, in choosing a measure. Otherwise, those negatively affected by Q will have an inducement to resist the policy and oppose the government (<

less than, > more than. When written above an equal sign bar, then the symbols mean equal to or less/more than respectively.)

(9) *Political Majority* (p. 57)

$$\Sigma Q_1 \ldots k = \frac{\Sigma P_1 \ldots j}{2} + P_i$$

Σ = sum of. The sum of tax prices for programs 1 to K is equivalent to the sum of costs of political participation for a majority of taxpayers, P_1 to j, where P_i is the cost/reward to taxpayer i whose vote makes the majority.

(10) *Critical Mass* (p. 85)

(a)

$$R = \int_{t1}^{t2} p.b^e + (c - d)dt$$

This is our rational voter Eq. (1) written in integrated form, with "e" an index of conversion greater than 1, which shows the number of other people each rational voter discusses the issue with and wins over.

(b)

$$dR/dT = ep.b^{e-1}$$

This states that the change in R, i.e., value to voters of political participation, and therefore, by implication, participation itself, changes with respect to time such that the increase in participation is determined by the conversion index (e) times the probability of making a difference (p) times the benefits of change raised to the conversion index minus one. As explained in the text, issues can be decided by a burst of outrage that unites the public against an offending organization. To achieve that union, there must be emotional content and an expectation of being effective. The key question then is how rapidly those feelings can be welded together. The rate of increase is determined by how many others a critic wins over, their belief in their own effectiveness, their evaluation of the benefits of victory, and repetitions to other potential converts by each new convert. This process accounts for the amount of upward rise in supporters over each unit of time in which it occurs, and also the fall off in support once discussion of the issue becomes boring and "e" a zero or negative value.

(11) *Critical Mass and Iron Triangles* (p. 89)

(a) *In-Group Relations*: $Wx \cap Sx = 0$

The x-beating set of solutions (Wx) as part of a favored set of solutions

(Sx) is a "null set," i.e., does not exist. There is no set of favored solutions that beats x.

(b) *Post-Critical Mass*: $W_x \cap S_x \neq 0$

x-beating solutions belonging to the favored set of solutions are not a null set, i.e., there now exists a set of x-beating solutions that is part of the favored set.

Symbols: $\cap$ belongs to: 0 null or empty set, Σ sum of, iϵs = those belonging to set S, iϵ - S, those belonging to non-S.

(12) *Probability of Two Independent Events* (p. 67)

$$p.A \times p.B = p(A.B)$$

The probability of independent events A and B occurring at the same time is the product of the individual probabilities; p.A + p.B − (pA.pB) = (p.A or p.B) The probability of *either* event A or B occurring is the sum of individual probabilities minus the probability of their occurring together.

An example of the application of this logic to politics is the equation for the probability of a coalition forming in which a particular member of a committee of n-members is pivotal: $Pn_s = (s-1)!(N-S)!/n!$

In words: the probability is the ratio of the number of ways the coalition minus the pivotal member can form times the number of ways the opposing group can form to the number of possible alignments.

(13) *Issues and Profitability* (p. 223)

$$\pi = P_1Q_1 - (TC + R)$$

states that a firm's profitability depends on its revenues from sales of product Q_1 at price P_1 minus its total costs of producing or selling Q_1 plus the costs of maintaining the right of the firm to its profits, i.e., the resources expended on preserving or enhancing the firm's reputation and legitimacy.

(14) *Reputation* (p. 223)

$$R = 1/d \cdot h$$

The magnitude of reputation spending is inversely related to the firm's endowed position (akin to goodwill) "d" times the costs of preventing public hostility. Ideally h will be zero. The factors influencing h for the firm are the same as those for politicians, as set out in (6), above.

(15) *Optimality* (p. 223)

Given that a firm is encountering public hostility, how much should it cost to reduce it? The expression

$$\frac{\partial\ (P_iQ_1 - TC)}{\partial R} < 0$$

states the plight of the firm, namely that the costs of correcting R outweigh each unit increase in revenue from sales. An optimum would be that the same expression equalled 1, i.e., that:

$$\frac{\partial\ (P_1Q_1 - TC)}{\partial R} = 1$$

Thus, every new dollar spent on changing R matches the effectiveness of a new dollar spent on increasing sales, and no reallocation of spending will result in inprovement.

By the same reasoning, we can say that spending to reduce hostility should produce results at the same rate as spending to increase revenue from sales.

A Note on the Commons (p. 235)

$$\left|\frac{\Delta B}{\Delta n}\right| - \left|\frac{\Delta Q}{\Delta P}\right| = 0$$

The statement describes the arena of decision shared by producers and governments, that is, marginal loss of benefits from congestion vs. marginal costs of new public goods to rectify matters. The expression dB/dn is negative to taxpayers, but positive to stakeholders of n. From the standpoint of government, intervention will be rational up to the point that Q confers dB/dn − P benefits on taxpayers (assuming P represents a majority). For companies, the trade-off is dB/dn − Q, i.e., how to minimize the burden of interventions. In practice, the most effective strategies should reduce dB/dn so the level of benefit loss equals or is less than costs of political participation, especially for pivotal constituencies (d = Δ = "change in").

Bibliography

The following books and articles provide excellent treatments of political and economic behavior from the standpoint of collective choice or business practice. Mueller (1978) contains a comprehensive bibliography and surveys the main themes and ideas. For less formal, more politically and historically-oriented discussions, see especially Hirschman (1970, 1979), Rude (1980), and Schultze (1977).

Aranson, Peter H. (1981), *American Government: Strategy and Choice*. Winthrop.

Arrow, Kenneth J. (1951), *Social Choice and Individual Values*. New York: John Wiley & Sons (rev. ed. 1963).

Barnes, David W. (1982-3), "Enforcing Property Rights: Extending Property Rights Theory to Congestible and Environmental Goods." *Environmental Affairs* (10):583-639.

Bator, Frances M. (1958), "The Anatomy of Market Failure." *Quarterly Journal of Economics* 72:351-359.

Baumol, William J. (1965), *Welfare Economics and the Theory of the State*, 2nd rev. ed. Cambridge, MA: Harvard University Press.

Becker, G.C. (1976), *The Economic Approach to Human Behavior*. Chicago: University of Chicago Press.

Bergstrom, T.C. and Goodman, Robert P. (1973), "Private Demand for Public Goods." *American Economic Review* 63(3):280-296.

Berle, Adolf (1963), *The American Economic Republic*. London: Jackson Ltd.

Betts, Richard K. (1980-81), "Surprise Despite Warning: Why Sudden Attacks Succeed." *Political Science Quarterly* (Winter):551.

Bishop, Robert I. (1977), "Game Theoretic Analyses of Bargaining." *Quarterly Journal of Economics*, 559-602.

Black, Duncan (1958), *The Theory of Committees and Elections*. Cambridge: Cambridge University Press.

Blank, Stephen, LaPalombara, Joseph, and Sacks, Paul M. (1982), "Political Analysis and Forecasting in the Private Sector: An Overview of the New Firm-Centric Analytical

Formats." Forschungsinstitute der Friedrich Ebert Stiftung, *Vierteljahresberichte* Nr. 90, Dez.

Bjork, Gordon C. (1968), *Private Enterprise and Public Interest.* Engelwood Cliffs, NJ: Prentice-Hall.

Brams, Steven J. (1976), *Paradoxes in Politics: Introduction to the Non-observers in Political Science.* New York: The Free Press.

Breton, Albert (1974), *The Economic Theory of Representative Government.* Chicago: Aldine.

Buchanan, James M. (1967), *Public Finance in the Democratic Process.* Chapel Hill: C. Lynch Hill, University of North Carolina Press.

Buchanan, James M. and Tullock, G. (1962), *The Calculus of Consent.* Ann Arbor: University of Michigan Press.

Buchholz, Rogene A. (1985), *Essentials of Public Policy for Managers.* Engelwood Cliffs, NJ: Prentice-Hall.

Bunn, D.W. and Mustafaogli, M.M. (1978), "Forecasting Political Risk." *Management Survey* 24(15 November):1557-1567.

Carneiro, Robert L. (1970), "A Theory of the Origins of the State." *Science* 169:

Carroll, Archie B. (1982), *Business and Society.* Boston: Little Brown.

Chase, W. Howard (1984), *Issue Management, Origins of the Future.* Stamford, CT: Issue Action Publications.

Coase, R.H. (1960), "The Problem of Social Cost." *Journal of Law and Economics* 3:1-44.

Coleman, James M. (1964), *Introduction to Mathematical Sociology.* New York: Free Press.

Coleman, James M., et al. (1974), "Social Processes in Physicians Adoption of a New Drug." In A. Etzioni and E. Etzioni-Halevy, *Social Change: Sources, Patterns and Consequences.* New York: Basic Books.

Conference Board Reports: No. 679, Managing Corporate External Relations; No. 701, Business Credibility: The Critical Factors; No. 733, Action Plans for Government Relations; No. 758, This Business of Issues; No. 794, Assessing the Political Environment; No. 795, Guidelines for Managing Corporate Issues Programs.

Dahl, Robert A., and Lindblom, Charles E. (1957), *Politics, Economics and Welfare.* New York: Harper & Row.

Davis, Otto A., Hinich, M.J., and Ordeshook, P.C. (1970), "An Expository Development of a Mathematical Model of the Electoral Process." *American Political Science Review* 64(June):426-428.

Dempster, M.A.M. and Wildavsky, Aaron (1966), "A Theory of the Budgetary Process." *American Political Science Review* 40:529-547.

Denzau, Arthur, et al. (1979), "Spending Limitations, Agenda Control and Voters' Expectations." *National Tax Journal* 32(2, Supplement):189–200.

Dominguez, George S. (1982), *Government Relations: A Handbook.* New York: Wiley.

Downs, A. (1957), *An Economic Theory of Democracy.* New York: Harper & Row.

Etzioni, A. and Etzioni-Halevy, E. (1974), *Social Change: Sources, Patterns and Consequences.* New York: Basic Books.

Farquaharson, R. (1969), *A Theory of Voting.* New Haven, CT: Yale University Press.

Fox, J. Ronald (1982), *Managing Business-Government Relations.* Irwin.

Friedman, Milton (1962), *Capitalism and Freedom.* Chicago: Univesity of Chicago Press.

Friedman, Milton (1980), *Free to Choose: A Personal Strategy.* New York.

Furniss, Norman A. (1972), "The Political Implications of the Public Choice-Property Rights School." *American Political Science Review* 72:399-410.

Furobotyn, Eirik G., and Pejovich, Svetozar (1972), "Property Rights and Economic Theory: A Survey of Recent Literature." *Journal of Economic Literature* 10(Dec.):1137-62.

Ghadar, Fariborz (1982), "Political Risk and the Erosion of Control: The Case of the Oil Industry." *Columbia Journal of World Business* (Fall):47-51.

Gollner, Andrew B. (1983), *Social Change and Corporate Strategy.* Stamford, CT: Issue Action Publications.

Gordon, Wendell (1983), "Welfare Maxima in Economics." *Journal of Economic Issues* 17(March):1-16.

Greenwood, W.J. (1977), *Issues in Business and Society* (3rd ed.). Boston: Houghton Mifflin.

Grefe, Edward A. (1981), *Fighting to Win.* New York: Harcourt Brace, Jovanovich.

Hardin, G. (1968), "The Tragedy of the Commons." *Science* 162:1243-48.

Hargreaves, John and Jan Daurman (1975), *Business Survival and Social Change.* New York: Halsted-Wiley.

Hirschman, Albert (1979), *Shifting Involvements.* Princeton, NJ: Princeton University Press.

Hirschman, Albert (1977), *The Passions and the Interests.* Princeton, NJ: Princeton University Press.

Hirschman, Albert (1970), *Exit, Voice and Loyalty.* Cambridge, MA: Harvard University Press.

Howard, Nigel (1971), *Paradoxes of Rationality: Theory of Metagames and Political Behavior.* Cambridge, MA: MIT Press.

Kirkland, Richard L. (1982), "Taxing the Business Lobby." *Fortune*, Oct. 18.

Krueger, A.O. (1974), "The Political Economy of the Rent Seeking Society." *American Economic Review* 64(June 3):291-303.

Laver, Michael (1980), *The Politics of Private Desires.* Penguin.

Liebhafsky, H.H. (1971), *American Government and Business.* New York: Wiley.

Lindblom, Charles E. (1977), *Politics and Markets.* New York: Basic Books.

Lindsay, C.M. (1976), "A Theory of Government Enterprise." *Journal of Political Economy* 84(Oct.):1061-77.

Lloyd, Bruce (1976), *Political Risk Management.* Keith Shepton, Developments Special Study, No. 7.

Luce, R.D. and Raiffa, H. (1957), *Games and Decisions.* New York: Wiley.

Mahon, John F. (1982), "Public Affairs Structures and Activities in Large American Corporations." *Academy of Management Proceedings*, pp. 336-370.

Mishan, E.J. (1971), "The Postwar Literature on Externalities, An Interpretative Essay." *Journal of Economic Literature* 9(March):1-28.

Mitnick, Barry M. (1980), *The Political Economy of Regulation.* New York: Columbia Univesity Press.

Mueller, Dennis C. (1979), *Public Choice.* Cambridge: Cambridge University Press.

Niemi, Richard G. (1983), "An Exegesis of Farquaharson's Theory of Voting." *Public Choice* 40(3):293ff.

Niskanen, W.A., Jr. (1971), *Bureaucracy and Representative Government.* Chicago: Aldine-Atherton.

North, Douglass C. and Thomas, Robert P. (1973), *The Rise of the Western World.* Cambridge: Cambridge University Press.

Nozick, Robert (1974), *Anarchy, State and Utopia.* New York: Basic Books.

Olson, Mancur H. (1982), *The Rise and Fall of Nations.* New Haven, CT: Yale University Press.

Olson, Mancur H. (1965/1971), *The Logic of Collective Action.* Cambridge, MA: Harvard University Press.

Parsons, Talcott and Smelser, Neil J. (1956), *Economy and Society.* Glencoe, IL: Free Press.

Plott, Charles R. (1969), "The Notion of Equilibrium and Its Possibility Under Majority Rule." *American Economic Review* 57:787-806.

Plott, Charles R. (1976), "Axiomatic Social Choice Theory: An Overview and Interpretation." *American Journal of Political Science* 20:511-596.

Plott, Charles R. and Levine, M.A. (1979), "A Model of Agenda Influence in Committee Decisions." *American Economic Review* 68:140-160.

Preston, Maurice (1982), *Public Goods and the Public Sector.* New York: Macmillan.

Quirk, Paul J. (1981), *Industry Influence in Federal Regulatory Agencies.* Princeton, NJ: Princeton University Press.

Raiffa, H. (1983), *The Art and Science of Negotiation*. Cambridge, MA: Harvard/Belknap.
Raiffa, H. (1968), *Decision Analysis: Introductory Lectures on Choices Under Uncertainty*. Reading, MA: Addison-Wesley.
Raiffa, H. and Schlaifer, R. (1961), *Applied Statistical Decision Theory*. Cambridge, MA: Harvard University Press.
Rawls, John (1971), *A Theory of Justice*. Cambridge, MA: Harvard University Press.
Riker, W.H. and Ordeshook, P.C. (1973), *An Introduction to Positive Political Theory*. Engelwood Cliffs, NJ: Prentice-Hall.
Rude, George (1980), *Ideology and Popular Protest*. Pantheon.
Samuelson, Paul A. (1954), "The Pure Theory of Public Expenditure," *The Review of Economics and Statistics* 36:387-389.
Schelling, Thomas (1978), *Micromotives and Macrobehavior*. New York: Norton.
Schelling, Thomas (1960), *The Strategy of Conflict*. Cambridge, MA: Harvard University Press.
Schramm, Percy (1962), *Hitler als Militärischer Führer*. Frankfurt a, Main.
Schultze, Charles L. (1977), *The Public Use of Private Interest*. Washington, DC: The Brookings Institution.
Schumpeter, Joseph A. (1950), *Capitalism, Socialism, and Democracy*. New York: Harper & Row.
Sen, Amartya (1977), "Social Choice Theory: A Re-Examination." *Econometrica* 45.
Sen, Amartya (1970), "The Impossibility of a Paretian Liberal." *Journal of Political Economy* 77:152-157.
Shepsle, K.A. (1982), "Political Solutions to Market Problems." Working Paper No. 74, Center for the Study of American Business, Washington University, St. Louis, MO, June.
Simm, Jeffrey D. (1982), "Political Risk Assessment: Past Trends and Future Prospects." *Columbia Journal of World Business* (Fall); 477ff.
Snyder, G.H. and Diesing, P. (1977), *Conflict Among Nations*. Princeton, NJ: Princeton University Press.
Stigler, George J. (1982), "The Theory of Economic Regulation." *Bell Journal of Economics and Management Science*, 2.
Stigler, George J. (1975), *The Citizen and the State*. Chicago: University of Chicago Press.
Tilly, Charles, et al. (1975), *The Rebellious Century, 1830-1930*. Cambridge, MA: Harvard University Press.
Trebilcock, M.J., et al. (1982), *The Choice of Governing Instrument*. Ottawa: Economic Council for Canada.
Van Den Doel, H. (1979), *Democracy and Welfare Economics*. Cambridge: Cambridge University Press.
Wagner, R. Harrison (1979), "On the Unification of Two Person Bargaining Theory." *Journal of Conflict Resolutions* 23:71-101.
Walters, Ingo and Gladwyn T. (1980), *Multinationals Under Fire*. New York: Wiley.
Weidenbaum, Murray (1977), *Business, Government and the Public*. Engelwood Cliffs, NJ: Prentice-Hall.
Weingast, Barry (1981), "Regulation, Reregulation and Deregulation: The Political Foundations of Agency-Clientele Relationships." *Law and Contemporary Problems* 44(1):147-177.
Wilson, James Q. (1980), *The Politics of Regulation*. New York: Basic Books.
Winkler, Robert L. (1980), "The Consensus of Subjective Probability Distribution." *Management Science* 15(Oct.):1361-1375.

Index

ABOUT THE AUTHOR

Guy Stanley is a consultant to business and government in the field of issues management. His clients include some of North America's largest companies, industry associations, and public sector organizations. He also teaches courses in business and public policy in the M.B.A. program at the University of Connecticut, Stamford, and regularly leads workshops on managing external issues for private and public sector executives.

Born in Canada, he holds a Ph.D. in contemporary international history from the London School of Economics and Political Science, and is a graduate of the University of Victoria in British Columbia, and Upper Canada College in Toronto. He currently divides his time among New York, Ottawa, and his farm in Connecticut.